The Gen X Series

MATHS OLYMPIAD 8

Useful for Maths Olympiads Conducted at School, National & International Levels

Author
Prasoon Kumar

Peer Reviewer
Jyotsna Gopikrishnan

Strictly According to the Latest Syllabus of Maths Olympiad

Published by:

F-2/16, Ansari road, Daryaganj, New Delhi-110002
☎ 23240026, 23240027 • *Fax:* 011-23240028
✉ info@vspublishers.com • 🌐 www.vspublishers.com

 Online Brandstore: amazon.in/vspublishers

Regional Office : Hyderabad
5-1-707/1, Brij Bhawan (Beside Central Bank of India Lane)
Bank Street, Koti, Hyderabad - 500 095
☎ 040-24737290
✉ vspublishershyd@gmail.com

Follow us on:

BUY OUR BOOKS FROM: AMAZON FLIPKART

© Copyright: *V&S PUBLISHERS*
ISBN 978-93-579405-7-3
New Edition

DISCLAIMER

While every attempt has been made to provide accurate and timely information in this book, neither the author nor the publisher assumes any responsibility for errors, unintended omissions or commissions detected therein. The author and publisher makes no representation or warranty with respect to the comprehensiveness or completeness of the contents provided.

All matters included have been simplified under professional guidance for general information only, without any warranty for applicability on an individual. Any mention of an organization or a website in the book, by way of citation or as a source of additional information, doesn't imply the endorsement of the content either by the author or the publisher. It is possible that websites cited may have changed or removed between the time of editing and publishing the book.

Results from using the expert opinion in this book will be totally dependent on individual circumstances and factors beyond the control of the author and the publisher.

It makes sense to elicit advice from well informed sources before implementing the ideas given in the book. The reader assumes full responsibility for the consequences arising out from reading this book.

For proper guidance, it is advisable to read the book under the watchful eyes of parents/guardian. The buyer of this book assumes all responsibility for the use of given materials and information.

The copyright of the entire content of this book rests with the author/publisher. Any infringement/transmission of the cover design, text or illustrations, in any form, by any means, by any entity will invite legal action and be responsible for consequences thereon.

Publisher's Note

General Trade and Mass Appeal books across various genres have helped **V&S Publishers** to gain widespread popularity. In a short span of 10 years, we have successfully published more than 1000 titles across 9 languages in our 50 subject categories. Being into the publishing business for about 40 years, we have always been a dynamic publishing house, with a massive distribution network, across India; including E-commerce platforms.

Understanding the need of inculcating knowledge and developing a spirit of healthy competition amongst students to make them ready for the world outside schools and colleges; we created Olympiad Series under the **GEN X SERIES Imprint** which, owning to its rich content and unique representation became popular amongst students, in no time. The motivation is not to improve marks in terms of numbers, but is to make sure that the students are already prepared to face competitive environment with respect to college admissions and cracking various entrance examinations, while ensuring their conceptual clarity.

Published for classes 1-10 across subjects English, Mathematics, Science, Computers, General Knowledge, the books are unlike any other in the market and are written in a guidebook pattern and exhaustively include examples and Multiple-Choice Questions.

Here, we present the latest Edition of **MATHS OLYMPIAD CLASS 8.**

Unique Features of the book are as follows:

- Authored by Subject Matter Experts' and Peer reviewed by School Principals and HOD's for the respective subjects
- Books based on principles of Applied Psychology and Bloom's Taxonomy
- Suited for Olympiad Examinations held at School level, National level & International Level irrespective of organizing body.
- The only Olympiad Book in India written in Guidebook Pattern with Concise Theory, images and illustrations.
- Exhaustively include Examples, MCQs, Subjective Questions, and HOTS with Answer Keys & Solutions.
- Multiple Model Papers for thorough practice also given inside the book with solutions.
- OMR sheets appended at the end of the book for simulating exam environment.

Besides, we are also planning to launch an App very soon for the Olympiad preparation which further testifies our constant endeavor to keep up with student demands. We have made sure to closely follow syllabus patterns of not only Olympiad conducting bodies but also education boards & organizations like CBSE and NCERT, to make sure that our books prove useful to students; helping them to boost their academic performance in schools as well.

P.S. While every care has been taken to ensure the correctness of the content, if you come across any error, howsoever minor, do not hesitate to discuss with teachers while pointing that out to us in no uncertain terms.

We wish you All the Best!

DISTINCTIVE

WHY OLYMPIADS?

Olympiads are just like competitive exams; conducted by various bodies at national and international levels. The aim is to experience a competitive examination at the school level and also to help students to discover their interest acrss subjects like English, Mathematics, Science and General Knowledge.

WHY V&S OLYMPIADS?

We at V&S Publishers aim to build an avid-reading student audience. Hence, our resolve is to follow an innovative pedagogic pattern which would help students to navigate through the book with utmost ease and comfort. Crisp theory practical examples and illustrations keep our book interactive and comprehensive.

01 LEARNING OBJECTIVES
They list the whole chapter as subtopics, helping the teachers to guide children in a step-by-step manner.

02 DID YOU KNOW
Enhance your knowledge by getting acquainted with some amazing facts across various subjects like science, Mathematics and English.

03 MULTIPLE CHOICE QUESTIONS
MCQs act as an excellent learning aid, helping you to understand and work on your mistakes.

04 THINGS TO REMEMBER
A quick recap of the chapter in a summarized format helps in faster revision along with conceptual clarity.

05 HOTS
The High Order Thinking Questions aim to help the student to solve Application-based questions and gain practical understanding of the subject.

FEATURES

06 SUBJECTIVE QUESTIONS
Help to place the knowledge gained in orderly fashion by using **"WH"** questions, mostly in the form of bullet points.

07 ACHIEVER'S SECTION
Offers a quick revision of the book along with some new facts for the students to discover.

08 A SET OF OMR SHEETS
To allow the student to practice question in an exam-like format which would help them to get the "feel" of how Olympiad exams take place.

09 MODEL TEST PAPERS
Two model test papers are provided at the end of each book, which help the student to test the knowledge which they have gained after thorough reading of all chapters.

10 ANSWER KEY & SOLUTIONS
Detailed Answer Key along with explanations aid the pupil to indentify, understand the mistakes they make during the course of Olympiad preparation.

COMPLEMENT SCHOOL SYLLABI
The syllabi across all Olympiad examination closely follow the pattern of academic books. Hence, they not only provide a competitive examination experience, but also help to revise topics for school examinations as well, while strengthening conceptual precision.

ENHANCEMENT OF ANALYTICAL & LOGICAL REASONING
Practicing analytical ability questions, not only helps in developing intellectual ability but also plays a vital role in building critical thinking ability which helps an individual to think about a question or a crisis like situation in day to day life; from all aspects and directions.

Note to Parents

Dear Parents,

Olympiad examinations come with a plethora of advantages. First and foremost among such advantages is the application of knowledge studied, in the form of multiple-choice questions. It helps the child not only to step away from rote learning, but also helps them to exhibit their competencies across various subjects.

In addition to this, Olympiads help the student to understand the importance of revision and practice, and to imbibe upon these practices; which also prove useful in academic performance of the child.

The Olympiads are conducted across multiple subjects, and help the child to recognize their field of interest, thereby encouraging the students to make a career in the field where they can excel the most.

However, cognitive development of a child is not just limited to the four walls of classroom. Following steps can be encouraged by you, to ensure their ward is able to grasp various concepts with ease or lesser difficulty:

- **Eat a balanced diet:** Ensure intake of vitamins and minerals to keep you active. Include fruits and super foods like millet in your diet to ensure healthy functioning of organs. Huge intake of junk food should be avoided.
- **Indulge in outdoor activities:** Outdoor games break the monotony of life. Play your heart out in greenery to keep yourself alert, active and fit.
- **Sleep well:** A sound sleep of 7-8 hours refreshes the brain and makes it ready to understand new topics with more clarity. A sleep derived person faces difficulty in doing even the simplest tasks of day to day life.
- **Reduce your Screen time:** More screen time leads to not only weakening of eyesight but decreases concentration span. Regulated Screen time should be encouraged
- **Do not hesitate to raise a hand:** Having a doubt in class? Do not hesitate to ask your parents or teachers. This ensures more Conceptual Clarity and hence leads to Application based understanding of various subjects and topics.
- **Teach and Learn:** No need to do rote-learning. Once you understand a topic teach or explain it to your friends, siblings and parents. It brings clarity and ensures the child does his revision this way.
- **Keep smiling:** A positive attitude promotes a growth mindset and encourages the child to be more inquisitive and try to learn something new, everyday!

HAPPY LEARNING!

Contents

SECTION 1: MATHEMATICAL REASONING

1. Playing with Numbers — 9
2. Rational Numbers — 17
3. Squares and Square Roots — 26
4. Cubes and Cube Roots — 32
5. Exponents and Powers — 38
6. Profit and Loss — 44
7. Algebraic Expressions and Their Identities — 51
8. Linear Equations in One Variable — 59
9. Quadrilaterals — 65
10. Mensuration — 72
11. Visualising Solid Shapes — 78
12. Data Handling — 85
13. Direct and Inverse Variations — 92
14. Factorisation — 100
15. Introduction to Graphs — 105

SECTION 2: LOGICAL REASONING

1. Alphabet Test — 114
2. Odd One Out — 118
3. Coding Decoding — 120
4. Direction Sense Test — 124
5. Series Completion — 128
6. Pattern — 131
7. Number Ranking — 135
8. Analytical Reasoning — 138
9. Venn Diagram — 142
10. Embedded Figure — 146
11. Completion of Incomplete Pattern — 153
12. Water Images — 162
13. Figure Matrix — 166

SECTION 3: ACHIEVER'S SECTION

Some Thoughtful Questions — 177
Model Test Paper–1 — 179
Model Test Paper–2 — 185

ANSWER KEYS (Access Content Online on Dropbox) — 192
APPENDIX — 200

SECTION 1
MATHEMATICAL REASONING

Playing with Numbers

Learning Objectives : In this chapter, students will learn about:
- ✓ Numbers in general form
- ✓ Letters for Digit
- ✓ Tests of Divisibility

CHAPTER SUMMARY

Numbers in General Form

In general, any two digit number *pq* made of digits *p* and *q* can be written as,

$$pq = 10 \times p + q = 10p + q$$
$$qp = 10 \times q + p = 10q + p$$

Similarly,

A 3-digit number *pqr* made of digits *p*, *q* and *r* can be written as,

$$pqr = 100\,p + 10q + r$$

Example 1: Ravi took a number *pq*. He reversed the digits of the number and then when he added the original number he got 187. If $p > q$, then find the values of *p* and *q*.

Solution: $pq \Rightarrow 10p + q$

After reversing the digits, $qp \Rightarrow 10q + p$

$\therefore \quad pq + qp \Rightarrow (10p + q) + (10q + p)$
$\qquad = 11p + 11q = 11(p+q)$

$\Rightarrow 11(p+q) = 187$
$\Rightarrow p + q = 17$

[17 can be obtained by adding 9 and 8 only].

$\because p > q, \therefore p = 9, q = 8.$

Example 2: Sangam takes a number '*ab*' and reversed its digits. Afterwards, he subtracted the new number from the original number to obtain 27 as a result. Find *a* and *b*, if, $ab > ba$.

Solution: $ab \Rightarrow 10a + b$

After reversing the digits, $ba \Rightarrow 10b + a$

$\therefore \quad ab - ba \Rightarrow (10a + b) - (10b + a)$

$\Rightarrow 9(a - b) = 72$
$\Rightarrow a - b = 8$ ...(i)

$\therefore a = 9, b = 1$ only satisfies the above equation (i).

Example 3: If we take a number '*abc*' and interchange the first and last digits to obtains '*cba*', then,

$$abc - cba = 198$$
$$abc + cba = 88p$$

are obtained. Find *p*, *a*, *b* and *c*.

Solution: $abc = 100\,a + 10\,b + c$
$cba = 100\,c + 10\,b + a$

$\therefore \quad abc - cba = 99\,(a - c) = 198$
$\Rightarrow (a - c) = 2$ ...(i)
$abc + cba = 88p \Rightarrow 101\,(a + c) + 2ab = 800 + 80 + p$
$\Rightarrow 20b = 80$
$\Rightarrow b = 4, \ a + c = \dfrac{800 + p}{101}$ ...(ii)

p, a, c are natural numbers.

Therefore, $p = 8, a + c = \dfrac{808}{101} = 8$ ...(iii)

$a = 5, c = 3, b = 4$ [From (i), (ii), (iii)].

$\therefore a = 5, b = 4, c = 3, p = 8.$

Letters For Digits

Here, some mathematical puzzles are solved using general techniques.

Example 4: Determine a, b, c, if,

$$\begin{array}{r} 4\,a \\ +9\,8 \\ \hline c\,b\,3 \end{array}$$

Solution: $4a = 40 + a$

$98 = 90 + 8$

$\therefore \quad 4a + 98 = 138 + a$

$a + 8$ gives 3 on addition, if, $a = 5$

On addition, 1 is left as a carry which is added to $(4 + 9)$.

$\therefore \quad cb = 4 + 9 + 1 = 14$

$\therefore \quad c = 1, b = 4, a = 5$

Example 5: $\begin{array}{r} 7\,a \\ \times 6 \\ \hline a\,a\,a \end{array}$, Find a.

Solution: $7a = 70 + a$.

$\therefore \quad (70 + a) \times 6 = 420 + 6a$

$\because \; a$ is a natural number, and, $(420 + 6a)$ give $(a\,a\,a)$ as a result.

$\therefore \; a = 4$

Example 6: Find a, b, c, if,

$$\begin{array}{r} a\,8\,3 \\ \times c\,9 \\ \hline a\,0\,4\,a \\ +1\,5\,b\,b\,0 \\ \hline c\,c\,a\,0\,a \end{array}$$

Solution: $3 \times 9 = 27$

$\therefore \quad a = 7$

$\therefore \quad \begin{array}{r} 7\,8\,3 \\ \times c\,9 \\ \hline 7\,0\,4\,7 \\ +1\,5\,b\,b\,0 \\ \hline c\,c\,7\,0\,7 \end{array}$

$\because \; 4 + b$ gives such a number whose unit's place digit is zero.

$\therefore \; b = 6$. Now, $\begin{array}{r} 7\,0\,4\,7 \\ +1\,5\,6\,6\,0 \\ \hline 2\,2\,1\,0\,7 \end{array}$

$\therefore \; c = 2$

TRIVIA

King's Cross station in London has a platform zero! It is the longest platform at the station.

Tests of Divisibility

1. **Divisibility by 10:** Numbers whose digit in one's place is zero are divisible by 10, otherwise, not.
2. **Divisibility by 2:** If the one's digit of a number is 0,2,4,6,8 then the number is divisible by 2.
3. **Divisibility by 3 and 9:**

    (i) A number N is divisible by 9, if, the sum of its digits is divisible by 9.

    (ii) A number N is divisibility by 3, if, the sum of its digits is divisible by 3.
4. **Divisibility by 5:** If the one's digit of a number is 0 or 5, then the number is divisible by 5.
5. **Divisibility by 11:** A number $abcdefg$ is divisible by 11, if,

    $(a + c + e + g) - (b + d + f) = 0$

MUST REMEMBER

- Numbers whose digit in one's place is zero are divisible by 10, otherwise, not.
- If the one's digit of a number is 0,2,4,6,8 then the number is divisible by 2.
- A number N is divisible by 9, if, the sum of its digits is divisible by 9.
- A number N is divisibility by 3, if, the sum of its digits is divisible by 3.

MULTIPLE CHOICE QUESTIONS

1. What is the next number in the series 5, 10, 26, 50, 122, ...
   (a) 129
   (b) 170
   (b) 204
   (d) 138

2. A number is divisible by 63 if it is divisible by:
   (a) 7
   (b) 9
   (c) both 7 and 9
   (d) both 3 and 7

3. What is the sum of first 15 natural numbers?
   (a) 122
   (b) 106
   (c) 105
   (d) 120

4. 7835 + 2b1 = 8126, then the value of b will be:
   (a) 9
   (b) 8
   (c) 7
   (d) 3

5. What is the sum of first 20 odd numbers?
   (a) 350
   (b) 400
   (c) 355
   (d) 420

6. $\begin{array}{r} 1\,8\,2 \\ \times\,2\,2 \\ \hline a\,0\,0\,a \end{array}$, the value of '$a$' will be:
   (a) 2
   (b) 3
   (c) 4
   (d) 8

7. What will be the last digit of 7^{333}?
   (a) 1
   (b) 7
   (c) 3
   (d) 9

8. Which of the following numbers is divisible by 11?
   (a) 1221
   (b) 1223
   (c) 1332
   (d) 1343

9. $\begin{array}{r} 7\,3\,x\,5 \\ -\,2\,y\,7\,7 \\ \hline 4\,5\,1\,8 \end{array}$, the value of $(x + y)$ will be:
   (a) 16
   (b) 17
   (c) 18
   (d) 15

10. $\begin{array}{r} a\,a \\ \times\,a\,a \\ \hline b\,8\,b \end{array}$, Given $1 \le a, b \le 9$ then the value of (ab) will be:
    (a) 32
    (b) 16
    (c) 8
    (d) 4

11. 763*312, which number should the * be replaced with to make the number divisible by 9?
    (a) 7
    (b) 5
    (c) 8
    (d) 6

12. 76215*, if the replacement of * by a number gives a number which is divisible by 11, the number will be:
    (a) 8
    (b) 7
    (c) 6
    (d) 9

13. $\begin{array}{r} A\,B\,C \\ A\,B\,C \\ +\,A\,B\,C \\ \hline B\,B\,B \end{array}$, the values of A, B, C are digits from 1 to 9. What will be value of B?
    (a) 8
    (b) 4
    (c) 1
    (d) 3

14. What will be the sum of first 22 even natural numbers?
    (a) 506
    (b) 406
    (c) 484
    (d) 253

15. One candle was guaranteed to burn for 6 hours, the other for 2 hours. They were both lit at same time. After some time one candle was twice as long as the other. For how long had they been burning?
    (a) 3 hours
    (b) $\frac{6}{5}$ hours
    (c) $\frac{4}{3}$ hours
    (d) $\frac{3}{2}$ hours

16. Find a 3-digit number, such that all its digits are prime and the 3 digits are the factors of the number?
    (a) 735
    (b) 537
    (c) 435 9
    (d) 245

17. Complete the square given below and find the value of the sum of missing numbers. The sum of the magic square is 34.

5	x	e	d
16	y	7	c
a	13	b	6
2	z	9	f

(a) 68   (b) 39
(c) 78   (d) 84

18. Three numbers are such that their sum is 10 and their product is maximum. The product will be:
   (a) 32   (b) 36
   (c) 45   (d) 42

19. What will be the one's place digit of 6^{222}?
   (a) 4   (b) 8
   (c) 1   (d) 6

20. Find the smallest number which can be expressed as the sum of two cubes of natural numbers.
   (a) 1729   (b) 1001
   (c) 1728   (d) 1332

21. $$\begin{array}{r} P\ A\ T \\ +\ E\ A\ T \\ \hline F\ E\ E\ A \end{array}$$, where, P, A, T, E, F are digits from 1 to 9 what will be the value of F?
   (a) 4   (b) 3
   (c) 2   (d) 1

22. Sum of 3 numbers = product of these 3 numbers. If the numbers are consecutive and natural, find the triplet having least value for their sum.
   (a) 2, 3, 4   (b) 1, 2, 3
   (c) 3, 4, 6   (d) 1, – 1, 0

23. The square of a number is having 5 at its units place and 2 at its tenths place, then the least natural number having these properties are:
   (a) 5   (b) 15
   (c) 25   (d) 4

24. The product 135 × 135 will be equal to:
   (a) 19625   (b) 16925
   (c) 18225   (d) 16235

25. Which of the following number is not a perfect square?
   (a) 1024   (b) 441
   (c) 1681   (d) 1282

26. 26 + 34 × 17 ÷ 4 = 34, which of the two signs should be interchanged to get the desired result?
   (a) No change   (b) ÷, +
   (c) ×, ÷   (d) +, ×

27. Which is the least number divisible by 2, 3, 5 and 55 ?
   (a) 110   (b) 550
   (c) 660   (d) 330

28. What is the square number just greater than 60, which can be expressed as a sum of two successive triangular numbers?
   (a) 72   (b) 64
   (c) 81   (d) 100

29. What will be one's place digit for 9^{201}?
   (a) 9   (b) 1
   (c) 3   (d) 7

30. What is the value of P if P, Q, R are replaced by any digits from 1 to 9 such that $PQ \times QP = RQPR$.
   (a) 6   (b) 8
   (c) 7   (d) 5

31. The general form of abc is:
   (a) $100a + 10b + c$
   (b) $100b + 10c + a$
   (c) $100c + 10a + b$
   (d) None of the above

32. The generalised form of 129 is:
   (a) 100 + 90 + 2
   (b) 100 + 20 + 9
   (c) 100 + 2 + 9
   (d) None of the above

33. The usual form of 100 × 7 + 10 × 1 + 8 is:
   (a) 108   (b) 708
   (c) 718   (d) 170
   Explanation: 100 × 7 + 10 × 1 + 8
   = 700 + 10 + 8 = 718

34. Which of the following numbers are not divisible by 5?
    (a) 20 (b) 125
    (c) 122 (d) 200

35. Which of the following numbers are divisible by 10?
    (a) 99 (b) 45
    (c) 110 (d) 75

36. Which of the following are divisible by 2?
    (a) 98 (b) 99
    (c) 101 (d) 121

37. If a number is divisible 9, then it is divisible by:
    (a) 6 (b) 7
    (c) 3 (d) 11

38. If the three digit number 24x is divisible by 9, the value of x is:
    (a) 3 (b) 7
    (c) 1 (d) None of the above

39. The number 2146587 is divisible by:
    (a) 7 (b) 3
    (c) 11 (d) None of the above

40. The number 15287 is divisible by:
    (a) 3 (b) 7
    (c) 9 (d) None of the above

41. The general form of 1809 is:
    (a) $1 \times 1000 + 8 \times 100 + 9$
    (b) $1800 + 9$
    (c) $1000 + 809$
    (d) None of the above

42. Which of the following numbers is divisible by 2?
    (a) 29 (b) 19
    (c) 22 (c) 47

43. Find the value of Q.
    Q 1
    +2 3
    ─────
    4 4
    ─────
    (a) 1 (b) 2
    (c) 3 (d) 4

44. Suppose A is a digit. Find the value of A if 31A + 1A3 = 501.
    (a) 1 (b) 2
    (c) 3 (d) 4

45. Which value is divisible by 5?
    (a) 36 (b) 90
    (c) 26 (d) 81

46. Which of the following is divisible by 9?
    (a) 108 (b) 107
    (c) 109 (d) 105

47. Which of the following is divisible by 3?
    (a) 160 (b) 170
    (c) 180 (d) 190

48. If the three-digit number 80x is divisible by 9, what is the value of x?
    (a) 1 (b) 9
    (c) 7 (d) 4

49. If the three-digit number 6 × 8 is divisible by 9, then what is the value of x?
    (a) 1 (b) 2
    (c) 3 (d) 4

50. Which number is divisible by 10?
    (a) 89 (b) 70
    (c) 75 (d) 15

HOTS

1. Umesh tossed a coin three times. What is the probability that Umesh gets more heads than tails?
   (a) 0.5 (b) 0.125
   (c) 0.375 (d) None of these

2. If 28 men can do a piece of work in 65 days, how many men can do it in 35 days?
   (a) 48 men (b) 52 men
   (c) 56 men (d) 62 men

3. The sum of digits of a two-digit number is 9. If 9 is subtracted from the number, its digits are interchanged. What is the half of that number?
   (a) 26 (b) 27
   (c) 28 (d) 29

4. The product of two numbers is 1575 and their quotient is $\frac{9}{7}$. What is the difference between the numbers?
   (a) 5 (b) 10
   (c) 15 (d) 20

5. Suppose A is a digit. Find the value of A if 31A + 1A3 = 501.
   (a) 1 (b) 2
   (c) 3 (d) 4

SUBJECTIVE QUESTIONS

1. What are the factors of $7y^2 - 19y - 6$?
   Answer:
   $7y^2 - 19y - 6$
   $= 7y^2 - 21y + 2y - 6$
   $= 7y(y-3) + 2(y-3)$
   $= (y-3)(7y+2)$

2. The distance between two stations is 300 km. Two trains start simultaneously from these stations and move towards each other. The speed of one of them is 7 km/h more than that of the other. If the distance between them after 2 hours of their start is 34 km, what is the speed of each train?

   Answer:
   Speed of one train = x km/hr.

   A — C — D — B

   Speed of 2nd train = $(x+7)$ km/hr.
   $x \cdot 2 + 34 + (x+7)2 = 300$
   $\Rightarrow 2x + 34 + 2x + 14 = 300$
   $\Rightarrow 4x + 48 = 300$
   $\Rightarrow 4x = 252$
   $\Rightarrow x = 63$ km/hr
   Speed of the two trains is 63 km/hr, 70 km/hr.

3. Four-fifth of a number is 10 more than two-thirds of the number. What is that number?
   Answer:
   Let the number be x.
   $$\frac{4}{5} \text{ of } x = \frac{2}{3} \text{ of } x + 10$$
   $\Rightarrow \frac{4x}{5} = \frac{2x}{3} + 10$
   $\Rightarrow \frac{4x}{5} - \frac{2x}{3} = 10$
   $\Rightarrow \frac{12x - 10x}{15} = 10 \Rightarrow 2x = 10 \times 15$
   $\Rightarrow x = \frac{10 \times 15}{2} = 75$

4. The denominator of a rational number is greater than the numerator by 3. If 3 is subtracted from the numerator and 2 is added to its denominator, the new number becomes $\frac{1}{5}$. What is the original number?

Answer:

Let the numerator be x.

Denominator $= x + 3$.

Fraction $= \dfrac{x}{x+3}$

If, $\dfrac{x-3}{x+3+2} = \dfrac{1}{5}$

$\Rightarrow \quad 5x - 15 = x + 5$

$\Rightarrow \quad 4x = 20 \Rightarrow x = 5$

Fraction $= \dfrac{5}{5+3} = \dfrac{5}{8}$

5. Find the remainder when 51439786 is divided by 3. Do that without performing actual division.

Answer:

We know that if a number is divided by 3, then the remainder is obtained by dividing the sum of digits by 3.

Here, the sum of digits (5+1+4+3+9+7+8+6) is 43.

i.e., 43 ÷ 3 gives 1 as a remainder.

∴ The remainder will be 1 when 51439786 is divided by 3.

Rational Numbers   2

Learning Objectives : In this chapter, students will learn about:
- ✓ Rational Numbers
- ✓ Terminating and Non-terminating decimals
- ✓ Properties of rational numbers
- ✓ Rational numbers between two rational numbers

CHAPTER SUMMARY

Rational Numbers

A number in the form of $\frac{a}{b}$, where, 'a' and 'b' are integers, and $b \neq 0$, is called a rational number.

Example: $\frac{-1}{2}, \frac{3}{5}, \frac{4}{90}$, etc.

Equivalent Rational Numbers

Two rational numbers $\frac{m}{n}$ and $\frac{p}{q}$ are equivalent, if $m \times q = n \times p$.

Infinite number of rational numbers, each of which is equivalent to a given rational number, can be formed. The equivalent rational numbers can be obtained by multiplying the numerator and denominator of the given rational number by the same non-zero integer.

$$\therefore \frac{a}{b} = \frac{a \times p}{b \times p} = \frac{a \times q}{b \times q} \text{ (where, } p \neq 0 \text{ and } q \neq 0).$$

A rational number, whose numerator and denominator has only one common factor equal to 1 is said to be standard form of a rational number.

> **TRIVIA**
> There are 385072 ways of arranging the numbers 1 - 18 in a circle so that the sum of each pair of adjacent numbers is prime.

Terminating and Non-Terminating Decimals

If the denominator of a rational number has no factors other than 2 or 5 or both it is called terminating decimal, otherwise, the decimal will be non-terminating decimal.

Example: $\frac{1}{5}, \frac{1}{25}, \frac{1}{50}, \frac{1}{100}$ are terminating decimals and $\frac{1}{70}, \frac{70}{85}, \frac{14}{75}, \frac{17}{55}$ are non-terminating decimals.

While checking for terminating or non-terminating decimal first reduce the rational number into its standard form.

Example 1: Which of the following rational numbers is the smallest ?

(a) $\frac{-15}{7}$, (b) $\frac{-5}{28}$,

(c) $\frac{-25}{49}$, (d) $\frac{-35}{42}$.

Solution: LCM of denominators, *i.e.,* 7,28,49,42 is 588.

Now, $\frac{-15}{7} = \frac{-15 \times 84}{7 \times 84} = \frac{-1260}{588}$

$\frac{-5}{28} = \frac{-5 \times 21}{28 \times 21} = \frac{-105}{588}$

Rational Numbers   17

$$\frac{-25}{49} = \frac{-25 \times 12}{49 \times 12} = \frac{-300}{588}$$

$$\frac{-35}{42} = \frac{-35 \times 14}{42 \times 14} = \frac{-490}{588}$$

∵ $\frac{-1260}{588}$ is the smallest of the four rational numbers.

∴ $\frac{-15}{7}$ is the smallest rational number among the given rational numbers.

Example 2: The sum of two rational numbers is $\frac{7}{8}$. If one of them is $\frac{1}{4}$, find the other number.

Solution: Let the other rational number be x.

∴ $\frac{1}{4} + x = \frac{7}{8}$

⇒ $x = \frac{7}{8} - \frac{1}{4} = \frac{7}{8} - \frac{2}{8} = \frac{5}{8}$

∴ Required rational number = 5/8.

Example 3: With what rational number should $\frac{-25}{343}$ be multiplied to get $\frac{5}{14}$ as quotient?

Solution: Let required number be x,

∴ $\frac{-25}{343} \times x = \frac{5}{14}$

⇒ $x = \frac{5}{14} \times \frac{-343}{25} = \frac{-49}{10}$

∴ Required number = $\frac{-49}{10}$

Example 4: Simplify:

$$\frac{7}{12} \times \frac{28}{3} - \frac{7}{10} \times \frac{5}{13} + \frac{2}{13} \times 169$$

Solution: We have

$$\frac{7}{12} \times \frac{28}{3} - \frac{7}{10} \times \frac{5}{13} + \frac{2}{13} \times 169$$

$$= \frac{7}{12} \times \frac{28}{13} - \frac{7 \times 5}{10 \times 13} + 26$$

$$= \frac{7 \times 14}{6 \times 13} - \frac{7}{26} + 26 = \frac{7}{26}\left(\frac{14}{3} - 1\right) + 26$$

$$= \frac{7}{26} \times \frac{11}{3} + 26 = \frac{77}{78} + 26 = \frac{77 + 2028}{78} = \frac{2105}{78}$$

Properties of Rational Numbers

1. **Commutative Property of Addition:** If x and y are two rational numbers, then $x + y = y + x$.

2. **Associative Property of Addition:** Let x, y and z be any three rational numbers, then $(x + y) + z = x + (y + z)$.

3. **Property of Zero:** Let x be any rational number, then,

   $0 + x = x + 0 = x$, and,

   $0 \times x = x \times 0 = 0$.

4. **Additive/Multiplicative Inverse Property:** Let x be any rational number then, $(-x)$ is called the additive inverse of x, as.

   $x + (-x) = (-x) + x = 0$.

   Let x $(x \neq 0)$ be any rational number, then, $\left(\frac{1}{x}\right)$ is called the multiplicative inverse of x, as.

   $x \times \frac{1}{x} = \frac{1}{x} \times x = 1$.

5. **Associative Property of Multiplication:** Let x, y and z be three rational numbers then, $x \times (y \times z) = (x \times y) \times z$.

6. **Distributive Property:** Let x, y and z be any three rational numbers, then,

   $x \times (y + z) = xy + xz$, or, $x \times (y - z) = xy - xz$.

7. **Property of 1:** Let x be any rational number, then $x \times 1 = 1 \times x = x$.

Example 5: Let x, y, z be any three rational numbers, then which of the following alternatives is not true?
(a) $(x + y) + z = (x + y) + (y + z) - y$
(b) $x \div (y \div z) = (x \div y) \div (y \div z)$
(c) $(x + y) \times z = (x - y) z + 2 (y \times z)$
(d) $(x + y) \div z = (x \div z) + (y \div z)$

Solution:

∴ Option (b) is not true.

Example 6: $x \times 0 = 0 \times x$, is true, but $x \div 0 = 0 \div x$, is true or false? Justify.

Solution: $x \times 0 = 0 \times x = 0$ is satisfied by property of zero, but, if, $x \div 0 = 0 \div x$, then, in L.H.S., 0 comes in denominator, which violates the condition of rational number. So, that statement is false.

Rational Numbers between Two Rational Numbers

- Between any two rational numbers, there exists infinitely many rational numbers.
- Let 'a' and 'b' be two rational numbers, such that, $a < b$, then,
$$a < \frac{a+b}{2} < b.$$
- Unlike natural numbers and integers, rational numbers do not have successors and predecessors.

Example 7: Find two rational numbers between $\frac{2}{13}$ and $\frac{5}{3}$.

Solution: LCM of 3 and 13 = 3 × 13 = 39.

∴ $\frac{2}{13} = \frac{2 \times 3}{13 \times 3} = \frac{6}{39}$

$\frac{5}{13} = \frac{5 \times 13}{3 \times 13} = \frac{65}{39}$

Between the two integers 6 and 65, there are, 65 −6 −1 = 58 integers,

∴ We choose any two integers, say, 8, and 23, then,

$$\frac{6}{39} < \frac{8}{39} < \frac{23}{39} < \frac{65}{39}$$

∴ Two integers between $\frac{2}{13}$ and $\frac{5}{3}$ are $\frac{8}{39}$ and $\frac{23}{39}$.

Example 8: Find ten rational numbers between $\frac{2}{3}$ and 3.

Solution: LCM of 3 and 1 = 3 × 1 = 3.

$\frac{2}{3} = \frac{2}{3}$, and $\frac{3}{1} = \frac{3 \times 3}{1 \times 3} = \frac{9}{3}$

Between the two integers 2 and 9, there are, 9 − 2 −1 = 6 integers, but, we require 10 rational numbers.

∴ we multiply the common denominator by any natural number, which is greater than 1, say 2, then,

$\frac{2}{3} = \frac{2 \times 2}{3 \times 2} = \frac{4}{6}$ and $\frac{3}{1} = \frac{9 \times 2}{3 \times 2} = \frac{18}{6}$

∴ Ten rational numbers between $\frac{2}{3}$ and 3 are

$$\frac{5}{6}, \frac{6}{6}, \frac{7}{6}, \frac{8}{6}, \frac{9}{6}, \frac{10}{6}, \frac{11}{6}, \frac{12}{6}, \frac{13}{6}, \frac{14}{6} \text{ or}$$

$$\frac{5}{6}, 1, \frac{7}{6}, \frac{4}{3}, \frac{3}{2}, \frac{5}{3}, \frac{11}{6}, 2, \frac{13}{6} \text{ and } \frac{7}{3}$$

MUST REMEMBER

- A rational number, whose numerator and denominator has only one common factor equal to 1 is said to be standard form of a rational number.
- If the denominator of a rational number has no factors other than 2 or 5 or both it is called terminating decimal, otherwise, the decimal will be non-terminating decimal.
- Between any two rational numbers, there exists infinitely many rational numbers.
- Unlike natural numbers and integers, rational numbers do not have successors and predecessors.

MULTIPLE CHOICE QUESTIONS

1. If $\frac{3}{5}$ of a number exceeds its $\frac{2}{7}$ by 44, then what is the number?
   (a) 144
   (b) 148
   (c) 140
   (d) 160

2. A bus is moving at an average speed of $60\frac{2}{5}$ km/hr. How much distance will it cover in $7\frac{1}{2}$ hours?
   (a) 423 km
   (b) 453 km
   (c) 443 km
   (d) 463 km.

3. The sum of two numbers is $\frac{-4}{3}$. If one of them is –5 then what is the other number?
   (a) $\frac{11}{3}$
   (b) $\frac{-11}{3}$
   (c) $\frac{16}{3}$
   (d) $\frac{19}{3}$

4. In a school $\frac{5}{8}$ of the students are boys. If the number of girls are 270, what is the number of boys in the school?
   (a) 440
   (b) 450
   (c) 420
   (d) 400

5. A cord of length $58\frac{1}{2}$ m has been cut into 26 pieces of equal length. What is the length of each piece?
   (a) $2\frac{1}{4}$ m
   (b) $\frac{32}{75}$ m
   (c) $\frac{64}{75}$ m
   (d) $\frac{8}{15}$ m

6. The product of two numbers is $\frac{-16}{35}$. If one of the number is $\frac{-15}{14}$ what is the other number?
   (a) $\frac{16}{75}$
   (b) $\frac{32}{75}$
   (c) $\frac{64}{75}$
   (d) $\frac{8}{15}$

7. What should be subtracted from $\frac{-5}{3}$ to get $\frac{5}{6}$?
   (a) $\frac{-5}{2}$
   (b) $\frac{-3}{2}$
   (c) $\frac{3}{2}$
   (d) $\frac{-5}{4}$

8. What is additive inverse of $\frac{-7}{9}$?
   (a) $\frac{7}{9}$
   (b) $\frac{-9}{7}$
   (c) $\frac{9}{7}$
   (d) 1

9. The sum of two rational numbers is – 3. If one of the number is $\frac{-10}{3}$ what is the other number?
   (a) $\frac{1}{3}$
   (b) $\frac{13}{3}$
   (c) $\frac{19}{3}$
   (d) $\frac{-19}{3}$

10. The cost of $7\frac{1}{2}$ metres of cloth is ₹ $78\frac{3}{4}$. What is the cost of one metre of cloth?
    (a) ₹ $13\frac{1}{2}$
    (b) ₹ $10\frac{1}{2}$
    (c) ₹ $16\frac{1}{2}$
    (d) ₹ $12\frac{1}{2}$

11. By what number should $\frac{-33}{8}$ be divided to get $\frac{-11}{2}$?
    (a) $\frac{1}{4}$
    (b) $\frac{1}{2}$
    (c) $\frac{3}{4}$
    (d) $\frac{1}{3}$

Rational Numbers

12. By what rational number should we multiply $\dfrac{-16}{63}$ to get $\dfrac{-4}{7}$.

    (a) $\dfrac{7}{4}$ (b) $\dfrac{9}{4}$
    (c) $\dfrac{3}{4}$ (d) $\dfrac{13}{4}$

13. What number should be added to $\dfrac{-7}{8}$ to get $\dfrac{4}{9}$?

    (a) $\dfrac{75}{72}$ (b) $\dfrac{85}{72}$
    (c) $\dfrac{83}{72}$ (d) $\dfrac{95}{72}$

14. What is reciprocal of $\left(\dfrac{1}{2}+\dfrac{1}{5}\right)$?

    (a) $\dfrac{7}{10}$ (b) $\dfrac{10}{7}$
    (c) $\dfrac{-7}{10}$ (d) $\dfrac{-10}{7}$

15. Which rational number is in between $\dfrac{-2}{3}$ and $\dfrac{-1}{4}$?

    (a) $\dfrac{-5}{24}$ (b) $\dfrac{-5}{12}$
    (c) $\dfrac{5}{12}$ (d) None of these

16. What is the reciprocal of $\left(\dfrac{1}{5}\times\dfrac{2}{5}\div\dfrac{4}{5}\right)$?

    (a) $\dfrac{1}{10}$ (b) $\dfrac{1}{5}$
    (c) 10 (d) 5

17. What should be added to $\dfrac{-3}{5}$ to get $\dfrac{-1}{3}$?

    (a) $\dfrac{4}{5}$ (b) $\dfrac{2}{5}$
    (c) $\dfrac{4}{15}$ (d) $\dfrac{8}{15}$

18. What is the additive inverse of $\left(\dfrac{3}{4}-\dfrac{2}{3}+\dfrac{1}{5}\right)$?

    (a) $\dfrac{17}{60}$ (b) $\dfrac{-17}{60}$
    (c) $\dfrac{60}{17}$ (d) $\dfrac{-60}{17}$

19. What is the value of $\dfrac{3}{4}\div\dfrac{5}{8}\times\dfrac{3}{7}+\dfrac{2}{9}-\dfrac{1}{3}$?

    (a) $\dfrac{127}{315}$ (b) $\dfrac{117}{315}$
    (c) $\dfrac{107}{315}$ (d) None of these

20. What is the value of

    $2-\left[5-\left\{4-\dfrac{3}{2}\left(2-\dfrac{2}{3}\right)\right\}\right]$?

    (a) 1 (b) –1
    (c) 2 (d) –2

21. How many rational numbers lie between $\dfrac{1}{5}$ and $\dfrac{1}{3}$?

    (a) One (b) Two
    (c) Three (d) Infinite

22. If x is a non-zero rational number, then what is the value of x^0?

    (a) 1 (b) 0
    (c) –1 (d) Not defined

23. Which number is the largest among the following numbers?

    $\dfrac{4}{-9}, \dfrac{-5}{12}, \dfrac{7}{-18}, \dfrac{-2}{3}$

    (a) $\dfrac{7}{-18}$ (b) $\dfrac{4}{-9}$
    (c) $\dfrac{-5}{12}$ (d) $\dfrac{-2}{3}$

24. Which number is the smallest among the following numbers?

    $\dfrac{-7}{12}, \dfrac{-5}{6}, \dfrac{13}{-18}, \dfrac{23}{-24}$

    (a) $\dfrac{-5}{6}$ (b) $\dfrac{-7}{12}$
    (c) $\dfrac{-5}{6}$ (d) $\dfrac{23}{-24}$

25. Closure property of rational number will be valid for _____.
    (a) Addition (b) Subtraction
    (c) Multiplication (d) All of these.

26. The difference between two numbers is 22 and their product is 240, what is the difference between their reciprocals?
    (a) $\dfrac{11}{120}$ (b) $\dfrac{-11}{120}$
    (c) $\dfrac{11}{109}$ (d) $\dfrac{-11}{109}$

27. If $a : b = 2 : 3$, then what will be the value of $\dfrac{a+b}{a-b}$?
    (a) $\dfrac{-3}{2}$ (b) $\dfrac{3}{2}$
    (c) -5 (d) $\dfrac{-1}{5}$

28. If $a : b = 1 : 2$, then $\dfrac{(a+b)^2}{ab} =$
    (a) $\dfrac{9}{2}$ (b) $\dfrac{9}{8}$
    (c) $\dfrac{9}{4}$ (d) $\dfrac{1}{4}$

29. The sum of two numbers 'p' and 'q' is 16 and their product is 48, then, $\left(\dfrac{1}{p^2}\right)^2 + \left(\dfrac{1}{q^2}\right)^2 =$
    (a) 2.06×10^{-4} (b) $\dfrac{3}{16}$
    (c) 4.12×10^{-5} (d) 3.9545×10^{-3}

30. The sum of two numbers is 24 and their difference is 10, then, value of $\dfrac{x}{y} =$ [where $x > y$].
    (a) $\dfrac{27}{18}$ (b) $\dfrac{17}{7}$
    (c) $\dfrac{118}{16}$ (d) $\dfrac{14}{34}$

HOTS

1. Two octagonal perfect dice with numbers 1 to 8 are thrown together. What is the probability that both the numbers are even?
   (a) $\dfrac{1}{4}$ (b) $\dfrac{1}{32}$
   (c) $\dfrac{7}{64}$ (d) $\dfrac{1}{2}$

2. One of the letters from the word SOCIOLOGY is chosen at random. What is the probability that this letter is O?
   (a) $\dfrac{1}{3}$ (b) $\dfrac{1}{6}$
   (c) $\dfrac{1}{9}$ (d) None of these

3. What is the simplified value of
   $\dfrac{1}{3} + \left[\dfrac{4}{9} + \left(\dfrac{-8}{13}\right)\right] \times \dfrac{169}{2}$?
   (a) $\dfrac{-26}{9}$ (b) -2
   (c) $\dfrac{-127}{9}$ (d) $\dfrac{-126}{3}$

4. How many rational numbers are there in between $\dfrac{3}{4}$ and 1?
   (a) 0 (b) 1
   (c) 2 (d) Countless

5. What should be subtracted from $-\dfrac{2}{3}$ to get -1?
   (a) $\dfrac{1}{3}$ (b) $-\dfrac{1}{3}$
   (c) $\dfrac{2}{3}$ (d) $-\dfrac{2}{3}$

SUBJECTIVE QUESTIONS

1. The sum of two rational numbers is $-\dfrac{1}{2}$. If one of the number is $\dfrac{5}{6}$, what is the other number?

   Answer:
   Let the other number be x.
   $$x + \dfrac{5}{6} = -\dfrac{1}{2}$$
   $$x = -\dfrac{1}{2} - \dfrac{5}{6} = \dfrac{-3-5}{6} = -\dfrac{8}{6} = -\dfrac{4}{3}$$

2. By what rational number should $\dfrac{-8}{39}$ be multiplied to obtain $\dfrac{1}{26}$?

   Answer:
   Let the rational number be x.
   $$x \times \dfrac{-8}{39} = \dfrac{1}{26}$$
   $$x = \dfrac{1}{26} \times \dfrac{-39}{8} = \dfrac{-3}{16}$$

3. Ankit earns ₹ 32000 per month. He spends $\dfrac{1}{4}$ of his income on food. $\dfrac{3}{10}$ of the remainder on house rent and $\dfrac{5}{21}$ of the remainder on education of children. How much money is still left with him?

   Answer:
   Food $= \dfrac{1}{4}$ of $32000 = 8000$

   House rent $= \dfrac{3}{10}$ of $(32000 - 8000)$
   $= \dfrac{3}{10} \times 24000 = 7200$

   Education $= \dfrac{5}{21}$ of $(24000 - 7200)$
   $= \dfrac{5}{21} \times 16800 = 4000$

   Money left with him
   $= 32000 - (8000 + 7200 + 4000)$
   $= 32000 - 19200 = ₹ 12800$

4. By what number should $\left(\dfrac{-2}{3}\right)^{-3}$ be divided so that the quotient may be $\left(\dfrac{4}{27}\right)^{-2}$?

   Answer:
   $$\left(-\dfrac{2}{3}\right)^{-3} \div x = \left(\dfrac{4}{27}\right)^{-3}$$
   $$\left(-\dfrac{2}{3}\right)^{-3} \times \dfrac{1}{x} = \left(\dfrac{4}{27}\right)^{-3}$$
   $$x = \dfrac{\left(-\dfrac{2}{3}\right)^{-3}}{\left(\dfrac{4}{27}\right)^{-3}} = \dfrac{\left(\dfrac{4}{27}\right)^{3}}{\left(-\dfrac{2}{3}\right)^{3}}$$
   $$= \dfrac{4}{27} \times \dfrac{4}{27} \times \dfrac{4}{27} \times \dfrac{3}{-2} \times \dfrac{3}{-2} \times \dfrac{3}{-2} = \dfrac{-8}{729}$$

5. Using commutativity and associativity of addition of rational numbers, express following as a rational number:
   $$\dfrac{2}{5} + \dfrac{7}{3} + -\dfrac{4}{5} + -\dfrac{1}{3}$$

   Answer:
   Firstly, group the rational numbers with same denominators
   $$\dfrac{2}{5} + -\dfrac{4}{5} + \dfrac{7}{3} + -\dfrac{1}{3}$$
   Now the denominators which are same can be added directly.
   $$\dfrac{(2+(-4))}{5} + \dfrac{(7+(-1))}{3}$$
   $$\dfrac{(2-4)}{5} + \dfrac{(7-1)}{3}$$

$$\frac{-2}{5}+\frac{6}{3}$$

By taking LCM for 5 and 3 we get, 15

$$\frac{(-2\times 3)}{(5\times 3)}+\frac{(6\times 5)}{(3\times 5)}$$

$$\frac{-6}{15}+\frac{30}{15}$$

Since the denominators are same can be added directly

$$\frac{(-6+30)}{15}=\frac{25}{15}$$

Further can be divided by 3 we get,

$$\frac{24}{15}=\frac{8}{5}$$

Squares and Square Roots   3

Learning Objectives : In this chapter, students will learn about:
- Basics of Square and Square root

CHAPTER SUMMARY

Square means product of the number with the number itself.
Example: $x^2 = x \times x$
$5^2 = 5 \times 5 = 25$

Perfect Square
A natural number is called a perfect square, if it is the square of some natural number.

Example 1: Find the number whose square is 1764.
Solution:

2	1764
2	882
3	441
3	147
7	49
7	7
	1

$1764 = 2 \times 2 \times 3 \times 3 \times 7 \times 7$
$= 2^2 \times 3^2 \times 7^2 = (42)^2$

Example 2: By what least number should 6300 be divided to get a perfect square number.
Solution: $6300 = 2 \times 2 \times 3 \times 3 \times 5 \times 5 \times 7$
To make 6300 a perfect square, it should be divided by 7. As 7 is alone in above prime factors.

Some Properties of Perfect Squares
I. A number ending in 2, 3, 7, 8, is never a perfect square.

Example: 22, 113, 257, 218 are not perfect squares.

II. The squares of an even number is always even.
Example: $8^2 = 64$, $12^2 = 144$, $18^2 = 324$

III. The squares of an odd number is always odd.
Example: $7^2 = 49$, $11^2 = 121$, $27^2 = 729$

IV. For every natural member n, sum of first n odd natural numbers $= n^2$
Example: $1 + 3 + 5 = 3^2 = 9 =$ Sum of first 3 odd numbers

V. Pythagorean Triplet
Three natural numbers a, b, c are said to form a Pythagorean Triplet (a, b, c) if
$a^2 + b^2 = c^2$

Example: $(8, 15, 17)$ is a Pythagorean triplet as $8^2 + 15^2 = 17^2$.
$64 + 225 = 289$

Example 3: Find the Pythagorean triplet whose smallest number is 12.
Solution: For every natural number, $m > 1$.
$(2m, m^2 - 1, m^2 + 1)$
$2m = 12 \Rightarrow m = \dfrac{12}{2} = 6$

So, the numbers are $2m = 2 \times 6 = 12$
$m^2 - 1 = 6^2 - 1 = 35$
$m^2 + 1 = 6^2 + 1 = 37$
So, required Pythagorean triplet is $(12, 35, 37)$

Square Root of a Perfect Square by Prime Factorisation Method

1. Resolve the given number into prime factors.
2. Make pairs of similar factors.
3. In product of prime factors, we have to choose one factor out of every pair.

Example 4: Find the square root of 11025.

Solution: $\sqrt{11025}$
$= \sqrt{5 \times 5 \times 3 \times 3 \times 7 \times 7}$
$= 5 \times 3 \times 7$
$= 105$

Example 5: Find the least number that should be multiplied to 360 to make it a perfect square.

Solution: $360 = 2 \times 2 \times 2 \times 3 \times 3 \times 5$.

To make 360 a perfect square, we must multiply it by $2 \times 5 = 10$

Example 6: Evaluate $\sqrt{6241}$ using long division method.

Solution:

```
   7 | 62 41  | 79.
   7 | 49
 149 | 1341
   9 | 1341
 158 | ××××
```

$\sqrt{6241} = 79$

Example 7: By what least number should 7623 be multiplied to get a perfect square.

Solution: $7623 = 3 \times 3 \times 7 \times 11 \times 11$

To make it a perfect square, it must be multiplied by 7.

TRIVIA

153, 370, 371 and 407 are the only three-digit numbers equal to the sum of the cubes of their digits.

MUST REMEMBER

➡ Square means product of the number with the number itself.
➡ A natural number is called a perfect square, if it is the square of some natural number.

MULTIPLE CHOICE QUESTIONS

1. What is the value of x if $\sqrt{\dfrac{2x-1}{3}} = 5$?
   (a) 26 (b) 28
   (c) 36 (d) 38

2. What is the greatest number of five digits which is a perfect square?
   (a) 99586 (b) 99856
   (c) 99568 (d) 99865

3. What is the least number which must be subtracted from 6459 to make it a perfect square?
   (a) 56 (b) 58
   (c) 59 (d) None of these

4. By what least number should 384 be multiplied so that the product may be a perfect square?
   (a) 2 (b) 58
   (c) 4 (d) 6

5. What is the smallest number of four digits which is a perfect square?
   (a) 1016 (b) 1024
   (c) 1036 (d) 1048

6. What is the greatest number of four digits which is a perfect square?
   (a) 9801 (b) 9816
   (c) 9824 (d) 9864

7. Find the least number which must be added to 2292 to make it a perfect square.
   (a) 10 (b) 11
   (c) 12 (d) 14

8. Find the smallest number by which 557568 must be divided so that it become a perfect square.
   (a) 2 (b) 3
   (c) 4 (d) 6

9. Find the smallest number by which 396 must be multiplied so that the product becomes a perfect square.
   (a) 3 (b)
   (c) 9 (d) 11

10. What is the least number which must be added to 6203 to obtain a perfect square?
    (a) 32 (b) 34
    (c) 36 (d) 38

11. Find the smallest square number that is divisible by each of the number 8, 15 and 20.
    (a) 900 (b) 1600
    (c) 2500 (d) 3600

12. What is the least number that must be added to 1300 so as to get a perfect square?
    (a) 36 (b) 39
    (c) 49 (d) 69

13. What is the length of the diagonal of a square whose perimeter is equal to the perimeter of an equilateral triangle of side 4 cm?
    (a) 4.24 cm (b) 4.04 cm
    (c) 4.14 cm (d) 4.64

14. The product of two positive numbers is $29\dfrac{31}{49}$ and one of them is three times the other. Find the larger number.
    (a) $\dfrac{22}{7}$ (b) $\dfrac{66}{7}$
    (c) $\dfrac{37}{7}$ (d) $\dfrac{68}{7}$

15. The area of a rectangular field whose length is three times its breadth is 348 m². What is the perimeter of the field?
    (a) 82.16 m (b) 84.16 m
    (c) 86.16 m (d) None of these

16. Which of the following is not a Pythagorean triplet?
    (a) (3, 4, 5) (b) (6, 8, 10)
    (c) (2, 3, 4) (d) (12, 35, 37)

17. The area of a square field is 60025 m². A man cycles along its boundary at 18 km/hour. In how much time will he return to the starting point?
    (a) 166 seconds (b) 176 seconds
    (c) 196 Seconds (d) None of these

18. What is the length of each side of a square whose area is equal to the area of a rectangle of length 13.6 m and breadth 3.4 meters?
    (a) 4.8 m (b) 5.8 m
    (c) 6.8 m (d) 7.8 cm

19. The perimeter of a square field is 76m. What is its area?
    (a) 324 m^2 (b) 289 m^2
    (c) 361 m^2 (d) 329 m^2

20. Which of the following is the square of an even number?
    (a) 729 (b) 324
    (c) 441 (d) 625

21. Which of the following is the square of an odd number?
    (a) 2209 (b) 1444
    (c) 2704 (d) 4096

22. Which of the following is not a perfect square?
    (a) 1156 (b) 1764
    (c) 1849 (d) 1349

23. What is the cost of erecting a fence around a square field whose area is 9 hectares if fencing costs ₹ 35 per meter?
    (a) ₹ 28000 (b) ₹ 32000
    (c) ₹ 36000 (d) ₹ 42000

24. In a cinema hall, the number of rows is equal to number of seats in each row. If the capacity of the hall is 2025 what is the number of seats in each row?
    (a) 35 (b) 45
    (c) 55 (d) 65

25. Which of the following is a Pythagorean triplet?
    (a) (2,3,5) (b) (5,7,9)
    (c) (6,9,11) (d) (8,15,17).

HOTS

1. One of the factors of $x^2 + 6\sqrt{3}\, x - 48$ is $(x - 2\sqrt{3})$. What is the other factor?
   (a) $x + 8\sqrt{3}$ (b) $x - 8\sqrt{3}$
   (c) $x + 6\sqrt{3}$ (d) $x - 6\sqrt{3}$

2. The square root of 0.0004 is
   (a) 0.2 (b) 0.02
   (c) 0.002 (d) None of these

3. What is the value of $\sqrt{\dfrac{1.21 \times 0.9}{1.1 \times 0.11}}$?
   (a) 2 (b) 3
   (c) 9 (d) 11

4. What is the value of $\dfrac{\sqrt{0.2401} - \sqrt{0.1681}}{\sqrt{0.2401} + \sqrt{0.1681}}$?
   (a) $\dfrac{2}{45}$ (b) $\dfrac{4}{45}$
   (c) $\dfrac{8}{45}$ (d) $\dfrac{16}{45}$

5. The diagonal of a square is $4\sqrt{2}$ m. What is its perimeter?
   (a) 12 m (b) 16 m
   (c) 24 m (d) None of these

Squares and Square Roots

SUBJECTIVE QUESTIONS

1. Find the greatest number of four digits which is a perfect square.

   Answer:

   Greatest four digit number = 9999

   ```
     9 | 9999   | 9
       |   81   |
    ---+--------+
   189 | 1899   |
       | 1701   |
    ---+--------+
   198 | × 198  |
   ```

   Required number = 9999 – 198 = 9801

2. Find the least number which must be added to 6203 to obtain a perfect square.

   Answer:

   $78^2 = 6084$

   $79^2 = 6241$

   So, 6241 – 6203 = 38

   38 is added to 6203 to make it a perfect square.

3. Which of the following numbers are perfect squares?

   (i) 484   (ii) 625
   (iii) 576   (iv) 941
   (v) 961   (vi) 2500

   Answer:

   (i) 484

   First find the prime factors for 484

   $484 = 2 \times 2 \times 11 \times 11$

   By grouping the prime factors in equal pairs we get,

   $= (2 \times 2) \times (11 \times 11)$

   By observation, none of the prime factors are left out.

   $\therefore$ 484 is a perfect square.

   (ii) 625

   First find the prime factors for 625

   $625 = 5 \times 5 \times 5 \times 5$

   By grouping the prime factors in equal pairs we get,

   $= (5 \times 5) \times (5 \times 5)$

   By observation, none of the prime factors are left out.

   $\therefore$ 625 is a perfect square.

   (iii) 576

   First find the prime factors for 576

   $576 = 2 \times 2 \times 2 \times 2 \times 2 \times 2 \times 3 \times 3$

   By grouping the prime factors in equal pairs we get,

   $= (2 \times 2) \times (2 \times 2) \times (2 \times 2) \times (3 \times 3)$

   By observation, none of the prime factors are left out.

   $\therefore$ 576 is a perfect square.

   (iv) 941

   First find the prime factors for 941

   $941 = 941 \times 1$

   We know that 941 itself is a prime factor.

   $\therefore$ 941 is not a perfect square.

   (v) 961

   First find the prime factors for 961

   $961 = 31 \times 31$

   By grouping the prime factors in equal pairs we get,

   $= (31 \times 31)$

   By observation, none of the prime factors are left out.

   $\therefore$ 961 is a perfect square.

   (vi) 2500

   First find the prime factors for 2500

   $2500 = 2 \times 2 \times 5 \times 5 \times 5 \times 5$

   By grouping the prime factors in equal pairs we get,

   $= (2 \times 2) \times (5 \times 5) \times (5 \times 5)$

   By observation, none of the prime factors are left out.

   $\therefore$ 2500 is a perfect square.

4. Find the smallest number by which the given number must be multiplied so that the product is a perfect square:

   (i) 23805   (ii) 12150

Answer:

(i) 23805

First find the prime factors for 23805

$23805 = 3 \times 3 \times 23 \times 23 \times 5$

By grouping the prime factors in equal pairs we get,

$= (3 \times 3) \times (23 \times 23) \times 5$

By observation, prime factor 5 is left out.

So, multiply by 5 we get,

$23805 \times 5 = (3 \times 3) \times (23 \times 23) \times (5 \times 5)$

$= (3 \times 5 \times 23) \times (3 \times 5 \times 23)$

$= 345 \times 345$

$= (345)^2$

∴ Product is the square of 345.

(ii) 12150

First find the prime factors for 12150

$12150 = 2 \times 3 \times 3 \times 3 \times 3 \times 3 \times 5 \times 5$

By grouping the prime factors in equal pairs we get,

$= 2 \times 3 \times (3 \times 3) \times (3 \times 3) \times (5 \times 5)$

By observation, prime factor 2 and 3 are left out.

So, multiply by $2 \times 3 = 6$ we get,

$12150 \times 6 = 2 \times 3 \times (3 \times 3) \times (3 \times 3) \times (5 \times 5) \times 2 \times 3$

$= (2 \times 3 \times 3 \times 3 \times 5) \times (2 \times 3 \times 3 \times 3 \times 5)$

$= 270 \times 270$

$= (270)^2$

∴ Product is the square of 270.

Squares and Square Roots

Cubes and Cube Roots | 4

Learning Objectives: In this chapter, students will learn about:
- ✓ Basics of Cube and Cube roots

CHAPTER SUMMARY

When a number is multiplied by its square, then the number is said to be cubed, and the product is called the cube of that number.

In general, cube of a natural number 'a' will be $a \times a \times a = a^3$.

A natural number is said to be a perfect cube if it is obtained by multiplying a natural number twice by itself, i.e., a natural number 'η' is a perfect cube if there exists a natural number m such that
$$\eta = m \times m \times m = m^3.$$

Example 1: Is 1728, a perfect cube?

Solution: Here
$$1782 = \underline{2 \times 2 \times 2} \times \underline{2 \times 2 \times 2} \times \underline{3 \times 3 \times 3}$$

In the prime factorisation of 1728, the prime factors can be grouped into triplets of equal factors and no prime factor is left over. Thus, 1728 is a perfect cube.

Example 2: Find the number of cubes of side 5 cm which can be generated by a cuboid of volume 500 cm³.

Solution: Volume of cube = $5 \times 5 \times 5 = 5^3 = 125$ cm³.

Let the number of cubes be x.

∴ $\quad x \times 125 = 500$

⇒ $\quad x = 4$

∴ Number of cubes that can be generated by a cuboid of volume 500 cm³ = 4.

Cubes of Negative Integers and Rational Numbers

The cube of a negative integer will be negative. If 'p' is a natural number, then,
$$(-p)^3 = -p^3$$

Example 3: Find the cube of $\left(\dfrac{-11}{12}\right)$.

Solution: $\left(\dfrac{-11}{12}\right)^3 = \dfrac{-1331}{1728}$

Example 4: Evaluate: $\left(\dfrac{64}{125}\right)^{2/3}$

Solution: Since $\left(\dfrac{64}{125}\right)^{1/3} = \dfrac{4}{5}$

∴ $\left(\dfrac{64}{125}\right)^{2/3} = \left(\dfrac{4}{5}\right)^2 = \dfrac{16}{25}$

Cube Roots

A natural number m is the cube root of a natural number n, if, $m^3 = n$.

The cube root of a number n is denoted by the symbol $\sqrt[3]{n}$.

Cube Root Using Ones Digit

Observing the unit digits of the number and their cubes, we find that these units digits are either the same or ten's complements. (Remember, complement of 2 in 10 is 8 and vice versa, complement of 3 in 10 is 7 and vice versa, etc.,)

The numbers ending with 0 or 1 or 4 or 5 or 6 or 9 have their respective cubes ending with the same digit.

Example 5: Find the cube root of 9261.

Solution: Since the perfect cube 9261 ends in 1, the cube root must end in 1. Further, it is a 4-digit number. So, its cube root must be a 2-digit number. Also, $20^3 = 8000$, $30^3 = 27000$

∴ The cube root of 9261 must be equal to 21.

TRIVIA

One 18 inch pizza has more 'pizza' than two 12 inch pizzas. Area of 18" pizza is $\pi \times 9^2 = 254$ square inches. Area of two 12" pizzas is $2\pi \times 6^2 = 226$ square inches.

Cube Root By Prime Factorisation

Example 6: What is the smallest number by which 20577 should be divided so that the quotient is a perfect cube? Find the cube root of the quotient.

Solution: $20577 = 3 \times 19 \times 19 \times 19$

∴ the quotient should be equal to $19 \times 19 \times 19$

∴ Required number = 3

Hence, 3 is the cube root of quotient

$= \sqrt[3]{\dfrac{19 \times 19 \times 19 \times 3}{3}} = 19$

Example 7: Evaluate:

$\sqrt[3]{-16} \times \sqrt[3]{363} \times \sqrt[3]{\dfrac{1}{2662}} \times \sqrt[3]{99}$

Solution: Here

$\sqrt[3]{a} \times \sqrt[3]{b} \times \sqrt[3]{c} \times \sqrt[3]{d} = \sqrt[3]{abcd}$.

$\sqrt[3]{-16} \times \sqrt[3]{363} \times \sqrt[3]{\dfrac{1}{2662}} \times \sqrt[3]{99}$

$= \sqrt[3]{\left(\dfrac{-16 \times 363 \times 99}{2662}\right)}$

$= \sqrt[3]{\dfrac{(2 \times 2 \times 2 \times 2) \times (3 \times 11 \times 11) \times (3 \times 3 \times 11)}{(2 \times 11 \times 11 \times 11)}}$

$= \sqrt[3]{\dfrac{2 \times 2 \times 2 \times 3 \times 3 \times 3 \times 11 \times 11 \times 11}{11 \times 11 \times 11}}$

$= 6$

Example 8: Two numbers are in the ratio 5 : 6. The sum of their cube is 21824. Find the number.

Solution: Let the numbers be $5a$ and $6a$.

∴ $(5a)^3 + (6a)^3 = 21824$

⇒ $341 a^3 = 21824$

⇒ $a^3 = \dfrac{21824}{341} = 64$

⇒ $a = 4$

∴ Numbers are 5×4 and 6×4

⇒ Numbers are 20 and 24.

MUST REMEMBER

➡ When a number is multiplied by its square, then the number is said to be cubed, and the product is called the cube of that number.

➡ A natural number is said to be a perfect cube if it is obtained by multiplying a natural number twice by itself, i.e., a natural number 'η' is a perfect cube if there exists a natural number m such that $η = m \times m \times m = m^3$.

➡ The cube of a negative integer will be negative.

➡ The numbers ending with 0 or 1 or 4 or 5 or 6 or 9 have their respective cubes ending with the same digit.

Cubes and Cube Roots

MULTIPLE CHOICE QUESTIONS

1. Which of the following numbers is a perfect cube?
   (a) 256 (b) 243
   (c) 1331 (d) 250

2. What will be the volume of a cube having edge length 12m? (in m^3)
   (a) 1728 (b) 1628
   (c) 2248 (d) 1848

3. What is the smallest number by which 576 is divided so that the quotient is a perfect cube?
   (a) 8 (b) 9
   (c) 4 (d) 72

4. If, $1^3 + 2^3 + 3^3 = (1 + 2 + 3)^2$, $1^3 + 2^3 + 3^3 + 4^3 = (1 + 2 + 3 + 4)^2$, then, $1^3 + 2^3 + 3^3 + 4^3 + 5^3 + 6^3 + 7^3$
   (a) 900 (b) 441
   (c) 784 (d) 484

5. Observing the pattern in Q. 4, Find the sum of $1^3 + 3^3 + 5^3 + 7^3 + 9^3$
   (a) 1225 (b) 2025
   (c) 825 (d) 1625

6. Simplify: $[\sqrt{12^2 + 16^2}]^3$
   (a) 400 (b) 8000
   (c) 64000 (d) 512000

7. Simplify: $\left(\dfrac{64}{125}\right)^{2/3}$
   (a) $\dfrac{4}{5}$ (b) $\dfrac{8}{25}$
   (c) $\dfrac{16}{25}$ (d) $\dfrac{4}{25}$

8. A natural number is of the form $(3n + 2)$. Its cube will be of the form:
   (a) $3n$ (b) $3n + 1$
   (c) $3n + 2$ (d) None of these

9. A rational number p is such that $p < 1$, then,
   (a) $p^3 > 1$ (b) $p^3 < 0$
   (c) $p^3 < p$ (d) $p^3 > p$

10. A real number 'p' is such that $p > 1$, then
    (a) $p^3 < 1$ (b) $p^3 > p$
    (c) $p^3 < p$ (d) $p^3 < 0$

11. Three numbers are in ratio 2 : 3 : 4 and sum of their cubes is 2673. The sum of these numbers are.
    (a) 27 (b) 26
    (c) 28 (d) 29

12. $\left(\dfrac{4913}{343}\right)^{\frac{1}{3}} = ?$
    (a) $\dfrac{25}{7}$ (b) $\dfrac{17}{7}$
    (c) $\dfrac{27}{7}$ (d) $\dfrac{37}{7}$

13. Simplify: $\sqrt[3]{0.008} + \sqrt[3]{0.343} - \sqrt{0.25}$
    (a) 0.4 (b) 0.5
    (c) 0.8 (d) 0.7

14. Which of the following is not a perfect cube?
    (a) 2744 (b) 704969
    (c) 513 (d) 343

15. The length of edge of a cube whose volume is 74.088 m^3 will be
    (a) 4.52 m (b) 4.62 m
    (c) 4.22 m (d) 4.2 m

16. What is the smallest number by which 3087 may be multiplied so that the product is a perfect cube?
    (a) 2 (b) 3
    (c) 7 (d) None of these

17. What is the smallest number by which 8788 must be divided so that the quotient is a perfect cube?
    (a) 2 (b) 3
    (c) 4 (d) 6

18. What is the smallest number by which 392 may be divided so that the quotient is a perfect cube?
    (a) 7 (b) 8
    (c) 49 (d) None of these

19. Which of the following is a cube of odd numbers ?
    (a) 2197 (b) 5129
    (c) 215 (d) 1278

20. Which of the following is a cube of even numbers?
    (a) 343 (b) 2197
    (c) 1728 (d) 4913

21. Which of the following is a perfect cube?
    (a) 441 (b) 514
    (c) 412 (d) 343

22. What is the value of $\sqrt[3]{\dfrac{216}{2197}}$?
    (a) $\dfrac{3}{13}$ (b) $\dfrac{6}{13}$
    (c) $\dfrac{7}{13}$ (d) $\dfrac{8}{13}$

23. The value of $x^3 y^2$, if $x = 3$, $y = -3$ will be:
    (a) 729 (b) 81
    (c) 343 (d) 243

24. Find the least number which should be added to 500, to make it a perfect cube.
    (a) 128 (b) 63
    (c) 12 (d) 229

25. What is the least number which should be subtracted from 1370 to make the resultant, a perfect square?
    (a) 29 (b) 39
    (c) 49 (d) 370

26. $\sqrt[3]{0.000000064} =$
    (a) 0.004 (b) 0.002
    (c) 0.0004 (d) 0.00004

27. $19^3 - 9^3$ will have _____ as one of its factors
    (a) 19 (b) 9
    (c) 10 (d) None of these.

28. $21^3 + 27^3$ will have ——— as one of its factors
    (a) 21 (b) 27
    (c) 48 (d) None of these

29. Which is the least number which should be added to 1720 to make it a perfect cube?
    (a) 269 (b) 8
    (c) 469 (d) 58

30. $1^3 + 2^3 + 3^3 + 4^3 + \ldots n^3 = \left[n\left(\dfrac{n+1}{2}\right) \right]^2$, where '$n$' is a natural number, then
    $1^3 - 2^3 + 3^3 - 4^3 + 5^3 - 6^3 + 7^3 - 8^3 + 9^3 - 10^3 =$
    (a) 3025 (b) –575
    (c) –1800 (d) 2425

Cubes and Cube Roots

HOTS

1. By what number should we divide 135 to get a perfect cube?
   (a) 3 (b) 5
   (c) 7 (d) 9
2. What should be divided by 53240 to make it a perfect cube?
   (a) 5 (b) 10
   (c) 15 (d) 20
3. Which of the following is a perfect cube?
   (a) 125 (b) 36
   (c) 75 (d) 100
4. Which of these numbers is not a cube number?
   (a) 10000 (b) 343
   (c) 64 (d) 729
5. When the square of a number is subtracted from the cube of the same number, it becomes 100. Find the number.
   (a) 1 (b) 2
   (c) 4 (d) 5

SUBJECTIVE QUESTIONS

1. What is the smallest number by which 8788 must be divided so that the quotient is a perfect cube?

   Answer:

   $8788 = 2 \times 2 \times 13 \times 13 \times 13$

   For quotient to be a perfect cube, it must be divided by $2 \times 2 = 4$

2. Write the cubes of 5 natural numbers, which are multiples of 3 and verify the followings:

   "The cube of a natural number which is a multiple of 3 is a multiple of 27"

   Answer:

   We know that the first 5 natural numbers, which are multiple of 3, are 3, 6, 9, 12 and 15
   So now, let us find the cube of 3, 6, 9, 12 and 15
   $3^3 = 3 \times 3 \times 3 = 27$
   $6^3 = 6 \times 6 \times 6 = 216$
   $9^3 = 9 \times 9 \times 9 = 729$
   $12^3 = 12 \times 12 \times 12 = 1728$
   $15^3 = 15 \times 15 \times 15 = 3375$

   We found that all the cubes are divisible by 27

   ∴ "The cube of a natural number which is a multiple of 3 is a multiple of 27"

3. Write the cubes of 5 natural numbers which are of the form 3n + 1 (e.g. 4, 7, 10, ...) and verify the following:

   "The cube of a natural number of the form $3n + 1$ is a natural number of the same from i.e. when divided by 3 it leaves the remainder 1"

   Answer:

   We know that the first 5 natural numbers in the form of $(3n + 1)$ are 4, 7, 10, 13 and 16
   So now, let us find the cube of 4, 7, 10, 13 and 16
   $4^3 = 4 \times 4 \times 4 = 64$
   $7^3 = 7 \times 7 \times 7 = 343$
   $10^3 = 10 \times 10 \times 10 = 1000$
   $13^3 = 13 \times 13 \times 13 = 2197$
   $16^3 = 16 \times 16 \times 16 = 4096$

   We found that all these cubes, when divided by '3', leave the remainder 1.

   ∴ the statement "The cube of a natural number of the form $3n + 1$ is a natural number of the same from i.e. when divided by 3 it leaves the remainder 1" is true.

4. Write the cubes 5 natural numbers of the form $3n + 2$ (i.e. 5, 8, 11….) and verify the following:

"The cube of a natural number of the form 3n+2 is a natural number of the same form i.e. when it is divided by 3, the remainder is 2'

Answer:

We know that the first 5 natural numbers in the form $(3n + 2)$ are 5, 8, 11, 14 and 17

So now, let us find the cubes of 5, 8, 11, 14 and 17

$5^3 = 5 \times 5 \times 5 = 125$

$8^3 = 8 \times 8 \times 8 = 512$

$11^3 = 11 \times 11 \times 11 = 1331$

$14^3 = 14 \times 14 \times 14 = 2744$

$17^3 = 17 \times 17 \times 17 = 4913$

We found that all these cubes, when divided by '3', leave the remainder 2.

∴ the statement "The cube of a natural number of the form $3n + 2$ is a natural number of the same form, i.e. when it is divided by 3, the remainder is 2' is true.

5. Write the cubes of 5 natural numbers of which are multiples of 7 and verify the following:

"The cube of a multiple of 7 is a multiple of 7^3.

Answer:

The first 5 natural numbers, which are multiple of 7, are 7, 14, 21, 28 and 35

So, the Cube of 7, 14, 21, 28 and 35

$7^3 = 7 \times 7 \times 7 = 343$

$14^3 = 14 \times 14 \times 14 = 2744$

$21^3 = 21 \times 21 \times 21 = 9261$

$28^3 = 28 \times 28 \times 28 = 21952$

$35^3 = 35 \times 35 \times 35 = 42875$

We found that all these cubes are multiples of 7^3 (343) as well.

∴ The statement "The cube of a multiple of 7 is a multiple of 7^3 is true.

Exponents and Powers 5

Learning Objectives : In this chapter, students will learn about:
- ✓ Powers and exponents

CHAPTER SUMMARY

Powers

The power of a number tells how many times to use the number in a multiplication.

It is written as a small number to the right and above the base number.

Example: $8^2 = 8 \times 8 = 64$

- $a^n = a \times a \times a \times a \times \ldots \times a$
  [n times]
- It is read as 'a raised to the power n'.
- $a^0 = 1$, where, a is any real number ($a \neq 0$).

Exponent

An exponent refers to the number of times a number is multiplied by itself.

Example: 2^3 means $2 \times 2 \times 2 = 8$
2^3 is not equal to $2 \times 3 = 6$

- If a is a non-zero rational number and m and n are natural numbers, then

1. $a^m \times a^n = a^{m+n}$ [product law of exponents]
2. $(a^m)^n = a^{mn}$ [power law of exponents]
3. $a^m \div a^n = a^{m-n}$ [quotient law of exponents]
4. $(a \times b)^m = a^m \times b^m$
5. $\left(\dfrac{a}{b}\right)^m = \dfrac{a^m}{b^m}$ ($b \neq 0$)

- If 'a' is a non-zero rational number and m is a positive integer, then,

$$a^{-m} = \dfrac{1}{a^m}, \text{ or, } (a^{-m})^{-1} = a^m$$

- a^{-m} is the reciprocal of a^m.

Example 1: Simplify: $\left(\dfrac{-2}{3}\right)^{-1} \div \left(\dfrac{2}{3}\right)^3 \times \left(\dfrac{3}{2}\right)^{-2}$

Solution: $\left(\dfrac{-2}{3}\right)^{-1} = -\left(\dfrac{2}{3}\right)^{-1}, \left(\dfrac{3}{2}\right)^{-2} = \left(\dfrac{2}{3}\right)^2$

$\therefore -\left(\dfrac{2}{3}\right)^{-1} \div \left(\dfrac{2}{3}\right)^3 \times \left(\dfrac{2}{3}\right)^2 = -\left(\dfrac{2}{3}\right)^{-1-3+2}$

$= -\left(\dfrac{2}{3}\right)^{-2} = -\left(\dfrac{4}{9}\right)^{-1} = -\left(\dfrac{9}{4}\right)$

Example 2: Simplify: $(5^{-1} + 3^{-1}) \times \left(\dfrac{1}{8}\right)^{+1} - (6^{-1} + 2^{-1}) \times (4)^{-1}$

Solution: $(5^{-1} + 3^{-1}) \times \dfrac{1}{8} - (6^{-1} + 2^{-1}) \times (4)^{-1}$

$= \left(\dfrac{1}{5} + \dfrac{1}{3}\right) \times \dfrac{1}{8} - \left(\dfrac{1}{6} + \dfrac{1}{2}\right) \times \dfrac{1}{4} = \dfrac{8}{15} \times \dfrac{1}{8} - \dfrac{2}{3} \times \dfrac{1}{4} = \dfrac{1}{15} - \dfrac{1}{6} = \dfrac{2-5}{30} = \dfrac{-1}{10}$

Example 3: Find the value of $\left[\left\{\left(\dfrac{-1}{3}\right)^2\right\}^{-2}\right]^{-1}$.

Solution: We have $\left(\dfrac{-1}{3}\right)^2 = \dfrac{1}{9}, \left(\dfrac{1}{9}\right)^{-2} = \left(\dfrac{1}{81}\right)^{-1} = 81$

$$(81)^{-1} = \dfrac{1}{81}$$

$\therefore \quad \left[\left\{\left(\dfrac{-1}{3}\right)^{+2}\right\}^{-2}\right]^{-1} = \dfrac{1}{81}$

TRIVIA

The volume of a deep-pan pizza with radius Z and depth A is Pi × Z × Z × A

Example 4: Express 0.0006542 in the standard form.

Solution: Here, the number is less than 1.
Thus, $0.0006542 = 6.542 \times 10^{-4}$.

Example 5: Express the number of seconds in 5 years in standard form. (Do Not consider leap year).

Solution: Number of seconds in one hour = 60 × 60
∴ Number of seconds in one day
= (60 × 60) × 24
∴ Number of seconds in one year
= {(60 × 60) × 24} × 365
∴ Number of seconds in 5 years
= 60 × 60 × 24 × 365 × 5
= 157680000
= 1.5768×10^8 seconds

Example 6: Simplify :

$(7.3)^{-3} \times \left(\dfrac{29.2}{4}\right)^{-1} \div (7.3)^7 + (14.6)^2 \div (14.6)^{-3}$

Solution:

$(7.3)^{-3} \times \left(\dfrac{29.2}{4}\right)^{-1} \div (7.3)^7 + (14.6)^{2+3}$

$= (7.3)^{-3} \times (7.3)^{-1} \div (7.3)^7 + (14.6)^5$

$= (7.3)^{-4-7} + (14.6)^5$

$= (7.3)^{-11} + (14.6)^5$

$= \left(\dfrac{1}{7.3}\right)^{11} + (14.6)^5$

Example 7: Find the value of $\dfrac{x}{y}$, if, $x = 4.9 \times 10^{-5}$, $y = 7 \times 10^{-8}$

Solution: Here $x = 4.9 \times 10^{-5}, y = 7 \times 10^{-8}$

$\dfrac{x}{y} = \dfrac{4.9 \times 10^{-5}}{7 \times 10^{-8}} = 0.7 \times (10)^{-5-(-8)}$

$= 0.7 \times (10)^3$
$= 700$

Example 8: If x is a rational number and a, b, c are any integers, then prove
$$x^{a-b} \div x^{c-b} \times x^{c-a} = 1$$

Solution:

$x^{(a-b)-(c-b)} \times x^{c-a} = (x)^{a-c} \times (x)^{c-a}$

$= (x)^{(a-c)+(c-a)}$

$= x^0 = 1$

Exponents and Powers

- The power of a number tells how many times to use the number in a multiplication.
- An exponent refers to the number of times a number is multiplied by itself.

MULTIPLE CHOICE QUESTIONS

1. What is the value of $[(5^{-1} \times 3^{-1})^{-1} \div 6^{-1}]$?
   - (a) 60
   - (b) 80
   - (c) 90
   - (d) 110

2. What is the value of $\left(\frac{1}{2}\right)^{-2} + \left(\frac{1}{3}\right)^{-2} + \left(\frac{1}{4}\right)^{-2}$?
   - (a) 26
   - (b) 27
   - (c) 28
   - (d) 29

3. What is the value of p for which $\left(\frac{4}{9}\right)^4 \times \left(\frac{4}{9}\right)^{-7} = \left(\frac{4}{9}\right)^{2p-1}$?
   - (a) 1
   - (b) 0
   - (c) –1
   - (d) –2

4. If $5^{2x+1} \div 25 = 125$, what is the value of x?
   - (a) 1
   - (b) 2
   - (c) 3
   - (d) 4

5. By what number should $\left(\frac{-3}{2}\right)^{-3}$ be divided so that the quotient is $\left(\frac{9}{4}\right)^{-2}$?
   - (a) $\frac{3}{2}$
   - (b) $\frac{-3}{2}$
   - (c) $\frac{-1}{3}$
   - (d) $\frac{1}{2}$

6. What is the value of $(4^{-1} + 8^{-1}) \div \left(\frac{2}{3}\right)^{-1}$?
   - (a) $\frac{3}{2}$
   - (b) $\frac{1}{4}$
   - (c) $\frac{1}{8}$
   - (d) $\frac{1}{16}$

7. What is the value of $\left(\frac{1}{2}\right)^{-3} + \left(\frac{1}{3}\right)^{-3} + \left(\frac{1}{4}\right)^{-3}$?
   - (a) 27
   - (b) 25
   - (c) 99
   - (d) 87

8. By what number should $\left(\frac{1}{2}\right)^{-1}$ be multiplied so that the product is $\left(\frac{-5}{4}\right)^{-1}$?
   - (a) $\frac{2}{5}$
   - (b) $\frac{-2}{5}$
   - (c) $\frac{1}{5}$
   - (d) $\frac{-1}{5}$

9. By what number should $(-6)^{-1}$ be multiplied so that the product becomes 9^{-1}?
   - (a) $\frac{-1}{3}$
   - (b) $\frac{2}{3}$
   - (c) $\frac{-2}{3}$
   - (d) $\frac{1}{3}$

10. What is the standard form of 0.00000000837?
    - (a) 8.37×10^9
    - (b) 8.37×10^{-9}
    - (c) 83.7×10^{-8}
    - (d) 837×10^{-7}

11. What is the value of x for which $\left(\frac{7}{12}\right)^{-4} \times \left(\frac{7}{12}\right)^{3x} = \left(\frac{7}{12}\right)^5$?
    - (a) –1
    - (b) 1
    - (c) 2
    - (d) 3

12. The value of $(3^{-1} + 4^{-1})^{-1} \div 5^{-1} = $?
    - (a) $\frac{7}{10}$
    - (b) $\frac{7}{15}$
    - (c) $\frac{7}{5}$
    - (d) $\frac{60}{7}$

13. If $(2^{3x-1} + 10) \div 7 = 6$ then what is the value of x?
    - (a) 0
    - (b) 1
    - (c) –2
    - (d) 2

14. What is the usual form of 0.000467×10^4?
    - (a) 4.67
    - (b) 46.7
    - (c) 0.467
    - (d) 0.0467

Exponents and Powers

15. If $\left(\dfrac{5}{4}\right)^{-2} \div \left(\dfrac{-5}{4}\right)^{-3} = \left(\dfrac{-4}{5}\right)^{x}$, find x?
    (a) –1 (b) 1
    (c) 2 (d) –2

16. What will be the value of $\left[(2)^{\frac{1}{2}}\right]^{4x}$, where $x = -0.5$?
    (a) 2 (b) $\dfrac{1}{4}$
    (c) $\dfrac{1}{2}$ (d) 4

17. Express 1 micron in standard form.
    (a) $\dfrac{1}{100000}$ m (b) 1×10^{-6} m
    (c) $\dfrac{1}{10000}$ m (d) 1×10^{-5} m

18. The value of $(5^{-3} + 5^{-2} + 5^{-1} + 5^{0})$ is :
    (a) 5^{-4} (b) 2.248
    (c) 1.248 (d) 3.248

19. If $5^{2p} + 5^{p} + 5^{0} = 651$, then $p =$
    (a) 2 (b) 3
    (c) 4 (d) 5

20. If $\dfrac{5^{3}}{5^{2}} \div \dfrac{3^{5}}{2^{5}} \times \dfrac{2^{x}}{3^{x}} = 0.0578$, then $x =$
    (a) 2 (b) 3
    (c) 4 (d) 6

21. $(32)^{2x+1} = (8)^{-x}(4)^{-4}$, the value of x will be:
    (a) 1 (b) –1
    (c) 2 (d) –2

22. By what number should $(23)^{-3}$ be multiplied with so that the product becomes $(69)^{-1}$?
    (a) $\dfrac{529}{4}$ (c) $\dfrac{529}{7}$
    (c) $\dfrac{529}{3}$ (d) $\dfrac{529}{6}$

23. $(5^{-1} + 6^{-1}) \div 22 = k^{-1}$, then k will be equal to:
    (a) 20 (b) 30
    (c) 40 (d) 60

24. The distance between earth and the sun is 15×10^{7} km. Express this distance in metres.
    (a) 15×10^{11} m (b) 1.5×10^{9} m
    (c) 1.5×10^{11} m (d) 1.5×10^{8} m

25. Simplify :
    $\left(\dfrac{25}{16}\right)^{4} \div \left(\dfrac{225}{144}\right)^{-3}$
    (a) $\left(\dfrac{5}{4}\right)^{2}$ (b) $\left(\dfrac{5}{4}\right)^{14}$
    (c) $\left(\dfrac{5}{4}\right)^{12}$ (d) $\left(\dfrac{5}{4}\right)^{3}$

26. $(6+3) \times 9^{-1} \div 3^{-1} + 2^{-2} =$
    (a) $\dfrac{5}{4}$ (b) $\dfrac{7}{4}$
    (c) $\dfrac{13}{4}$ (d) $\dfrac{7}{8}$

27. Find the value of $\dfrac{p^{m}}{p^{n}} \times \dfrac{n^{p}}{m^{p}} \div \dfrac{m^{p+n}}{p^{n+m}}$ if $m \neq 0$, $p \neq 0$ and $m = n = p$.
    (a) 1 (b) p^{2p}
    (c) $p^{2p} + 1$ (d) p^{3p}

28. The size of a plant cell is 0.00001275 m. Express this measure in standard form.
    (a) 1275×10^{-6} (b) 1275×10^{-5} m
    (c) 1.275×10^{-5} (d) 1.275×10^{-6} m

29. $\left[\left(\dfrac{1}{3}\right)^{-2} - \left(\dfrac{1}{4}\right)^{-2}\right]^{-2} \times 7^{2} =$
    (a) 49 (b) 0
    (c) 7 (d) 1

30. $2^{3x+5} \times 3^{2x+5} = (6)^{3x+2}$, then $3^{x} =$
    (a) 6 (b) 52
    (c) 144 (d) 216

HOTS

1. In 10 days earth picks up 2.6×10^8 kg of dust from the atmosphere. How much dust will it pick up in 45 days?
   (a) 1.17×10^9 kg (b) 1.17×10^7 kg
   (c) 1.17×10^5 kg (d) 1.17×10^4 kg

2. What is the value of $\dfrac{x^0 - y^0}{x^0 + y^0}$?
   (a) 0   (b) 1
   (c) 2   (d) –1

3. If $(-3)^{m+1} \times (-3)^5 = (-3)^7$, then the value of m is:
   (a) 5   (b) 7
   (c) 1   (d) 3

4. 1.8×1011 is equal to:
   (a) 180000000000
   (b) 18000000000
   (c) 1800000000
   (d) 1800000000000

5. 0.09×10^{10} is equal to:
   (a) 900000000   (b) 9000000
   (c) 9000   (d) 9

SUBJECTIVE QUESTIONS

Simplify:
(i) $(4^{-1} \times 3^{-1})^2$
(ii) $(5^{-1} \div 6^{-1})^3$
(iii) $(2^{-1} + 3^{-1})^{-1}$
(iv) $(3^{-1} \times 4^{-1})^{-1} \times 5^{-1}$
(v) $(4^{-1} - 5^{-1}) \div 3^{-1}$

Answer:
(i) $(4^{-1} \times 3^{-1})^2$

$\left(\dfrac{1}{4} \times \dfrac{1}{3}\right)^2$ (we know that $a^{-n} = \dfrac{1}{an}$)

$\left(\dfrac{1}{12}\right)^2 = \dfrac{1}{144}$

(ii) $(5^{-1} \div 6^{-1})^3$

$\left(\dfrac{1}{5} \div \dfrac{1}{6}\right)^3$ (we know that $a^{-n} = \dfrac{1}{an}$)

$\left(\dfrac{1}{5} \times 6\right)^3$ (we know that $\dfrac{1}{a} \div \dfrac{1}{b} = \dfrac{1}{a} \times \dfrac{b}{1}$)

$\left(\dfrac{6}{5}\right)^3 = \dfrac{216}{125}$

(iii) $(2^{-1} + 3^{-1})^{-1}$

$\left(\dfrac{1}{2} + \dfrac{1}{3}\right)^{-1}$ (we know that $a^{-n} = \dfrac{1}{an}$)

LCM of 2 and 3 is 6

$\left(\dfrac{3+2}{6}\right)^{-1}$

$\left(\dfrac{5}{6}\right)^{-1}$ (we know that $\dfrac{1}{a^{-n}} = an$)

$\dfrac{6}{5}$

(iv) $(3^{-1} \times 4^{-1})^{-1} \times 5^{-1}$

$\left(\dfrac{1}{3} \times \dfrac{1}{4}\right)^{-1} \times \dfrac{1}{5}$ (we know that $a^{-n} = \dfrac{1}{an}$)

$\left(\dfrac{1}{12}\right)^{-1} \times \dfrac{1}{5}$ (we know that $\dfrac{1}{a^{-n}} = an$)

$12 \times \dfrac{1}{5} = \dfrac{12}{5}$

(v) $(4^{-1} - 5^{-1}) \div 3^{-1}$

$\left(\dfrac{1}{4} - \dfrac{1}{5}\right) \div \dfrac{1}{3}$ (we know that $a^{-n} = \dfrac{1}{an}$)

LCM of 4 and 5 is 20

$\dfrac{(5-4)}{20} \times \dfrac{3}{1}$ (we know that $\dfrac{1}{a} \div \dfrac{1}{b} = \dfrac{1}{a} \times \dfrac{b}{1}$)

$\dfrac{1}{20} \times 3 = \dfrac{3}{20}$

Exponents and Powers

Profit and Loss   6

Learning Objectives : In this chapter, students will learn about:
- ✓ Concept of Profit and Loss
- ✓ Discount
- ✓ Compound Interest

CHAPTER SUMMARY

Profit and Loss

Profit or gain = Selling price − cost price

Profit percent = $\dfrac{\text{profit}}{\text{cost price}} \times 100$

Loss = Cost Price − Selling Price

Loss percent = $\dfrac{\text{loss}}{\text{cost price}} \times 100$

Example 1: Rajesh sold a scooter for ₹ 23000 and earned a profit of 15%. What is the cost price of scooter?

Solution: S.P. = ₹ 23000

Profit = 15%

Cost Price = $\dfrac{23000 \times 100}{(100+15)} = \dfrac{100 \times 23000}{115}$

$= 100 \times 200 = ₹\ 20000$

Example 2: Mohan buys a mobile for ₹ 3680 and sell it at a gain of $7\dfrac{1}{2}\%$. What is its selling price?

Solution: Here C.P. = ₹ 3680, Gain = $\dfrac{15}{2}\%$.

S.P. = $\dfrac{215}{200} \times 3680$ = Rs. 3956.

Example 3: On selling a shoe for ₹ 987 a shopkeeper loses 6%. What is the cost price of the shoe?

Solution: S.P. = ₹ 987.

Loss = 6%

C.P. of the shoe = $\dfrac{100}{94} \times 987 = ₹1050$

Example 4: Raju bought apples at 10 for ₹ 25 and sold them at ₹ 25 per dozen. What is the gain or loss percent?

Solution: C.P. of one apple = ₹ $\dfrac{25}{10}$

and S.P. of one apple = ₹ $\dfrac{25}{12}$

∴ Loss = $\dfrac{25}{10} - \dfrac{25}{12} = \dfrac{150-125}{60} = \dfrac{25}{60}$

Loss percent = $\dfrac{\text{Loss}}{\text{C.P.}} \times 100 = \dfrac{\frac{25}{60}}{\frac{25}{10}} \times 100$

$= \dfrac{25}{60} \times \dfrac{10}{25} \times 100 = \dfrac{100}{6} = \dfrac{50}{3} = 16\dfrac{2}{3}\%$

TRIVIA

142857 is a circular number
142857 × 2 = 285714
142857 × 3 = 428571
142857 × 4 = 571428
142857 × 5 = 714285

Discount

In order to increase the sale, sometimes the shopkeepers offer a certain percentage of rebate on the market price. This rebate is called as discount.

Marked Price : In departmental store, every article is tagged with a card and its price is written on it. It is called marked price of that article.

Example 5: The marked price of a shirt is ₹ 1250 and a shopkeeper allows a discount of 7% on it. What is the selling price of the shirt?

Solution: M.P. = ₹ 1250

Discount = 7%

Discount = 7% of 1250

$= \dfrac{7 \times 1250}{100} = 87.50$

S.P. = 1250 – 87.50 = ₹ 1162.50

Example 6: Find the single discount equivalent to two successive discounts of 25% and 10%.

Solution: Let the M.P. be ₹ 100.

First discount = ₹ 25

Price after first discount = 100 – 25 = 75

Second discount = 10% of 75

$= \dfrac{10 \times 75}{100} = ₹ 7.50$

Price after second discount
= ₹ (75 – 7.50) = ₹ 67.50

Net selling price = ₹ 67.50

Single discount equivalent to given successive discounts = 100 – 67.50 = 32.5%

Compound Interest

When interest is compounded annually

Then $A = P\left(1 + \dfrac{R}{100}\right)^n$

where, A = Amount

P = Principal value

R = Rate percent

N = time in years

C.I. = A – P

Example 7: Find the amount and compound interest of ₹ 8000 for 3 years compounded annually at 10% per annum.

Solution: Here P = ₹ 8000, R = 10%, n = 3 years.

Now $A = P\left(1 + \dfrac{R}{100}\right)^n$

$\Rightarrow A = 8000\left(1 + \dfrac{10}{100}\right)^3 = 8000\left(\dfrac{11}{10}\right)^3$

$\Rightarrow A = 8000 \times \dfrac{11}{10} \times \dfrac{11}{10} \times \dfrac{11}{10}$

$= 8 \times 1331 = 10648$

$\therefore$ C.I. = 10648 – 8000 = ₹ 2648

Example 8: At what percent per annum will ₹ 4000 amount to ₹ 4410 in 2 years when compounded annually?

Solution: Here P = ₹ 4000

A = ₹ 4410

n = 2 years

R = ?

Now $A = P\left(1 + \dfrac{R}{100}\right)^n$

$\Rightarrow 4410 = 4000\left(1 + \dfrac{R}{100}\right)^2$

$\Rightarrow \dfrac{4410}{4000} = \left(1 + \dfrac{R}{100}\right)^2 \Rightarrow \left(\dfrac{21}{20}\right)^2$

$= \left(1 + \dfrac{R}{100}\right)^2$

$\Rightarrow 1 + \dfrac{R}{100} = \dfrac{21}{20} \Rightarrow \dfrac{R}{100} = \dfrac{21}{20} - 1$

$\Rightarrow \dfrac{R}{100} = \dfrac{1}{20}$

$\Rightarrow R = \dfrac{100}{20} = 5\%$

Example 9: In how many years will ₹ 1800 amount to ₹ 2178 at 10% per annum when compounded annually?

Solution: Here P = ₹ 1800; A = ₹ 2178; R = 10%; n = ?

∴ $A = P\left(1 + \dfrac{R}{100}\right)^n$

⇒ $2178 = 1800\left(1 + \dfrac{10}{100}\right)^n$

⇒ $\dfrac{2178}{1800} = \left(1 + \dfrac{10}{100}\right)^n$

⇒ $\dfrac{1089}{900} = \left(\dfrac{11}{10}\right)^n$

⇒ $\left(\dfrac{11}{10}\right)^2 = \left(\dfrac{11}{10}\right)^n$

⇒ $n = 2$ yeras.

MUST REMEMBER

➤ In order to increase the sale, sometimes the shopkeepers offer a certain percentage of rebate on the market price. This rebate is called as discount.

➤ In departmental store, every article is tagged with a card and its price is written on it. It is called marked price of that article.

MULTIPLE CHOICE QUESTIONS

1. By selling an umbrella at a profit of ₹ 60 a shopkeeper made a profit of 20%. What is the cost price of umbrella?
   (a) ₹ 300 (b) ₹ 320
   (c) ₹ 400 (d) ₹ 420

2. 72% of 250 students are good in science. How many students are not good in science?
   (a) 180 (b) 70
   (c) 120 (d) 130

3. An item marked at ₹ 840 was sold for ₹ 714. What is the discount percent?
   (a) 15% (b) 25%
   (c) 30% (d) None of these

4. What is the selling price if a profit of 5% is made on a fan bought for ₹ 560 and expenses of ₹ 40 made on its repair?
   (a) ₹ 600 (b) ₹ 630
   (c) ₹ 650 (d) ₹ 680

5. A shopkeeper buys 80 articles for ₹ 4800 and sells them for a profit of 16%. What is the selling price of one article?
   (a) ₹ 66.90 (b) ₹ 69.60
   (c) ₹ 63.60 (d) ₹ 68.90

6. If 8% VAT is included in the prices, then what is the original price of a bucket bought for ₹180?
   (a) ₹ 166.66 (b) ₹ 162.66
   (c) ₹ 163.66 (d) ₹ 164.66

7. A milkman sold two of his cows for ₹ 20000 each. On one he made a gain of 5% and on the other a loss of 10%. What is his overall gain or loss?
   (a) 1269.84 Loss (b) 1269.84 Profit
   (c) 1169.84 Loss (d) 1169.84 Profit

8. Rahman bought a mobile for ₹ 3300 including a tax of 10%. What is the price of mobile before VAT was added?
   (a) ₹ 2500 (b) ₹ 3000
   (c) ₹ 2800 (d) ₹ 400

9. An article is sold at ₹ 5225 after allowing discount of 5%. What is its marked price?
   (a) ₹ 5500 (b) ₹ 5400
   (c) ₹ 5600 (d) ₹ 5450

10. What is the compound interest on ₹ 62500 for $1\frac{1}{2}$ years at 8% per annum compounded half yearly?
    (a) ₹ 7804 (b) ₹ 7004
    (c) ₹ 7204 (d) ₹ 7624

11. A scooter was bought for ₹ 42,000. Its value depreciated at the rate of 8% per annum. What is its value after one year?
    (a) ₹ 40640 (b) ₹ 38,640
    (c) ₹ 39,640 (d) None of these

12. By selling 20 pens a shopkeeper gains equal to the selling price of 4 pens. What is his gain percent?
    (a) 15% (b) 20%
    (c) 25% (d) 30%

13. If the S.P. of 10 articles is equal to the C.P. of 11 articles, what is the gain percent?f
    (a) 5% (b) 10%
    (c) 15% (d) 20%

14. Mohan purchased a tape recorder and spent ₹ 66 on its repair. He sold the tape recorder for ₹ 7130 and made a profit of 24%. At what price did he buy the tape recorder?
    (a) ₹ 5684 (b) ₹ 5284
    (c) ₹ 5784 (d) ₹ 5648

15. A publisher offers a discount of 10% on his books and still makes a profit of 20%. What is the actual cost of a book if it is marked at ₹ 320?
    (a) ₹ 220 (b) ₹ 240
    (c) ₹ 210 (d) ₹ 260

16. What is a single discount equivalent to two successive discounts of 20% and 10%?
    (a) 28% (b) 38%
    (c) 22% (d) 32%

Profit and Loss

17. In what time will ₹ 800 amount to Rs 882 at 5% per annum compounded annually?
    (a) 2 years (b) 2.5 years
    (c) 3 years (d) 4 years

18. What sum will become ₹ 9724.05 in 2 years if the rate of interest is 10% compounded half yearly?
    (a) ₹ 6000 (b) ₹ 6800
    (c) ₹ 7200 (d) ₹ 8000

19. What is the rate percent per annum if ₹ 2000 amount to ₹ 2662 in $1\frac{1}{2}$ years, if interest is compounded half yearly?
    (a) 20% (b) 10%
    (c) 25% (d) 16%

20. A dealer offers a discount of 20%, 10% and 5%. What is the single equivalent rate of discount?
    (a) 32.6% (b) 31.6%
    (c) 28.6% (d) 33.6%

21. The cost of a mobile phone is ₹ 3000. A gain of 10% should be made after a discount of 20%. What is the marked price of the mobile phone?
    (a) ₹ 4000 (b) ₹ 4125
    (c) ₹ 4025 (d) ₹ 4100

22. Rajesh has to pay 6% sales tax in addition to the price of a certain article. What is the price if he pays ₹ 53 to buy the article?
    (a) ₹ 45 (b) ₹ 50
    (c) Rs 48 (d) None of these

23. Bunti buys a leather coat costing ₹ 900 at ₹ 999, after paying the sales tax. What is rate of sales tax charged on the coat?
    (a) 10% (b) 9%
    (c) 11% (d) None of these

24. A shopkeeper increases the price of an item by 10% and then allows a discount of 15%. How much does the customer pay if the item was initially priced at ₹ 1200?
    (a) ₹ 1120 (b) ₹ 1140
    (c) ₹ 1122 (d) 1124

25. What amount will Jay receive if he deposits ₹ 8000 for 3 years at 10% per annum compounded annually?
    (a) ₹ 10228 (b) ₹ 10348
    (c) ₹ 10548 (d) ₹ 10648

26. A businessman marks his goods at 40% above the cost price and allows a discount of 25%. What is his gain percent?
    (a) 5% (b) 10%
    (c) 15% (d) 20%

27. The cost price of 12 books is equal to selling price of 15 books. What is the loss percent?
    (a) 10% (b) 20%
    (c) 15% (d) 25%

28. Calculate the compound interest on ₹ 10000 at 10% per annum for 3 years, if interest is compounded annually?
    (a) ₹ 3130 (b) ₹ 1331
    (c) ₹ 3310 (d) ₹ 13310

29. The value of a machine depreciates at the rate of 20% per annum. It was purchased 2 years ago if its present value is ₹ 4000, for how much was it purchased?
    (a) ₹ 6250 (b) ₹ 6280
    (c) ₹ 6520 (d) ₹ 5650

30. If the simple interest on a sum of money at 5% per annum for 3 years is ₹ 1200, then what is the compound interest on the same sum for the same period at the same rate?
    (a) ₹ 1261 (b) ₹ 1225
    (c) ₹ 1241 (d) ₹ 1251

HOTS

1. The difference between the S.I. and C.I. on ₹ 2500 for 2 years at 20% when the compound interest is payable annually is
   (a) ₹ 50   (b) ₹ 70
   (c) ₹ 100   (d) ₹ 200

2. In what time will ₹ 64,000 amount to ₹ 68921 at 5% per annum if interest payable is compounded half yearly?
   (a) 1.5 years   (b) 2.5 years
   (c) 2 years   (d) 3.5 years

3. A mobile set is sold for ₹ 1498 and the seller gains 7% on it. What is its cost price?
   (a) 1200   (b) 1400
   (c) 1440   (d) 1460

4. The cost of the article was ₹ 15500 and ₹ 500 was spent on its repairing. If it is sold for a profit of 15%. The selling price of the article is:
   (a) ₹16400   (b) ₹17400
   (c) ₹18400   (d) ₹19400

5. Two bicycles were sold for Rs. 3990 each, gaining 5% on one and losing 5% on the other. The gain or loss percent on the whole transaction is
   (a) Neither gain nor loss
   (b) 2.5% gain
   (c) 2.5% loss
   (d) 0.25% loss

SUBJECTIVE QUESTIONS

1. A number is increased by 20% and then decreased by 30%. What is the net increase or decrease percent?

   Answer:
   Let the number be 100.
   $$= 100 + 20 = 120$$
   $$\therefore 30\% \text{ of } 120 = \frac{30 \times 120}{100} = 36$$
   and $120 - 36 = 84$
   Decrease percent $= 100 - 84 = 16\%$

2. Raja's income is 60% more than that of Peter. By what percent is Peter's income less than Raja's?

   Answer:
   Let Peter's income $= 100$
   Raja's income $= 100 + 60 = 160$
   % of Peter's income less than Raja's income
   $$= \frac{60}{160} \times 100 = 37.5\%$$

3. What is the percentage of pure gold in 22-carat gold if 24-carat gold is 100% pure?

   Answer:
   Percentage of pure gold $= \frac{22}{24} \times 100$
   $$= \frac{22 \times 25}{6} = \frac{11 \times 25}{3}$$
   $$= 91.66\%$$

4. By selling 33 m of cloth, a draper loses an amount equal to the selling price of 3 m of cloth. What is the gain or loss percent?

   Answer:
   Loss percent $= \frac{3}{33} \times 100 = \frac{100}{11} = 11\frac{1}{9}\%$

5. A table was sold at a gain of 10%. Had it been sold for ₹ 65 more the gain would have been 14%. What is the cost price of the table?

   Answer:
   Let the C.P. be ₹ x.
   S.P. $= x + 10\%$ of $x = x + \frac{10x}{100} = \frac{110x}{100}$
   In 2nd case,

Profit and Loss

$$S.P. = x + 14\% \text{ of } x = x + \frac{14x}{100} = \frac{114x}{100}$$

$$\Rightarrow \quad \frac{114x}{100} - \frac{110x}{100} = 65$$

$$\Rightarrow \quad 114x - 110x = 6500$$

$$\Rightarrow \quad x = \frac{6500}{4} = ₹\,1625$$

6. What is the rate of discount being given on a shirt whose selling price is ₹ 546 after deducing a discount of ₹ 104 on its marked price?

Answer:

Selling Price = ₹ 546

Discount = ₹ 104

Marked price = ₹ (546 + 104) = ₹ 650

Let Rate of discount = $x\%$

$x\%$ of 650 = 104

$$\Rightarrow \frac{x \times 650}{100} = 104 \Rightarrow x = \frac{104 \times 100}{650} = 16\%$$

7. The selling price of a pen is $\frac{6}{5}$ of the cost price. What is the gain percent?

Answer:

Let the cost price = Rs x.

Selling price = ₹ $\frac{6x}{5}$

$$\text{Gain} = \frac{6x}{5} - x = \frac{6x - 5x}{5} = \frac{x}{5}$$

$$\text{Gain percent} = \frac{\frac{x}{5}}{x} \times 100 = \frac{x}{5} \times \frac{1}{x} \times 100 = 20\%$$

8. Mohit borrowed ₹ 20000 from his friend at 12% per annum simple interest. He lent it to Ankit at the same rate but compounded annually. Find his gain after 2 years.

Answer:

$$\text{Simple Interest} = \frac{20000 \times 2 \times 12}{100} = ₹\,4800$$

$$A = P\left(1 + \frac{r}{100}\right)^n$$

$$A = 20000\left(1 + \frac{12}{100}\right)^2 = 20000 \times \frac{112}{100} \times \frac{112}{100}$$

$$= ₹\,25088$$

C.I. = ₹ (25088 – 20000) = ₹ 5088

Gain = ₹ (5088 – 4800) = ₹ 288

9. What is the compound interest on ₹ 31250 at 8% per annum for 2 years.?

Answer:

P = ₹ 31250

$$A = P\left(1 + \frac{R}{100}\right)^n$$

$$= 31250\left(\frac{1+8}{100}\right)^2$$

$$= 31250\left(\frac{27}{25}\right)^2$$

$$= 36450$$

C.I. = 36450 – 31250 = 5200

10. In what time will ₹ 1000 amount to ₹ 1331 at 10% per annum compounded annually?

Answer:

$$A = P\left(1 + \frac{r}{100}\right)^n$$

$$1331 = 1000\left(1 + \frac{10}{100}\right)^n$$

$$\Rightarrow \quad \frac{1331}{1000} = \left(\frac{11}{10}\right)^n$$

$$\Rightarrow \quad \left(\frac{11}{10}\right)^3 = \left(\frac{11}{10}\right)^n \Rightarrow n = 3 \text{ years.}$$

Algebraic Expressions and Their Identities — 7

Learning Objectives : In this chapter, students will learn about:
- ✓ Algebraic Expressions
- ✓ Operations on Algebraic Expression
- ✓ Factorisation of Algebraic Expressions

CHAPTER SUMMARY

Algebraic Expression
An expression in which numbers and literal numbers are combined by the signs of fundamental operations is called an algebraic expression.

Types of Expressions
Monomial
An expression which contains only one term is called a monomial.
e.g., $-2x, 5x, 6xy$, etc.

Binomial
An expression which contains two terms is called a binomial.
e.g., $2x + 3, 5x + 3y, 5pq - 8p^3, 5x^2 + 3xy$, etc.

Trinomial
An expression which contains three terms is called a trinomial.
e.g., $2ab + a^2 + b^2, 5x - 3y + 8, 2xy + 3pq + 7$, etc.

Operations on Algebraic Expressions
1. Multiplication of Monomials
Monomials are multiplied, using the commutative and associative properties of numbers. after we multiply the respective coefficients to get the product.

Example 1: Find the product of $2xy$ and $5x^3 y^2$.
Solution: We have
$2xy \times 5x^3 y^2 = 2 \times x \times y \times 5 \times x^3 \times y^2$
$= (2 \times 5) \times (x \times x^3) \times (y \times y^2)$
$= 10 \times x^4 \times y^3 = 10x^4 y^3$
[commutative property]

2. Multiplication of a Binomial/Trinomial by a Monomial
If A, B and C are three expressions, then
(i) $A \cdot (B + C) = A \cdot B + A \cdot C$ (Distributive Property).
(ii) $A \cdot (B - C) = A \cdot B - A \cdot C$

3. Multiplication of a Binomial/Trinomial by a Binomial
If A, B, C and D are four monomials, then
$(A + B) \cdot (C + D) = A \cdot (C + D) + B \cdot (C + D)$ [Distributive property]
$= A \cdot C + A \cdot D + B \cdot C + B \cdot D$

Example 2: Find the product of :
$(5x^2 + 3xy + 2)$ and $(2x + 3y + 6)$
Solution: $(5x^2 + 3xy + 2) \cdot (2x + 3y + 6) = 5x^2 \cdot (2x + 3y + 6) + 3xy \cdot (2x + 3y + 6) + 2 \cdot (2x + 3y + 6)$
$= (5x^2)(2x) + (5x^2) \cdot (3y) + (5x^2) 6 + (3xy) 2x + (3xy)(3y) + (3xy)(3y) + 2(2x) + 2(3y) + 2 \times 6$
$= 10x^3 + 15x^2 y + 30x^2 + 6x^2 y + 18xy + 9xy^2 + 4x + 6y + 12$
$= 10x^3 + 21x^2 y + 9xy^2 + 30x^2 + 18xy + 4x + 6y + 12$

Standard Identities
1. $(a+b)^2 = (a+b) \times (a+b) = a(a+b) + b(a+b)$
$= a^2 + 2ab + b^2$

2. $(a-b)^2 = (a-b) \times (a-b)$
   $= a(a-b) - b(a-b) = a^2 - 2ab + b^2$
3. $(a+b)^2 + (a-b)^2 = 2(a^2 + b^2)$
4. $(a+b)^2 - (a-b)^2 = 4ab$
5. $x^2 - y^2 = (x+y)(x-y)$
6. $(x+y)(x+z) = x^2 + (y+z)x + yz$
7. $(x-a)(x+b) = x^2 + (b-a)x - ab$
8. $(x+a)(x-b) = x^2 + (a-b)x - ab$
9. $(x-a)(x-b) = x^2 - (a+b)x + ab$

Example 3: Simplify
(a) 999×1001 (b) 98×98

Solution:
(a) $999 \times 1001 = (1000 - 1) \times (1000 + 1)$
   $= (1000)^2 - (1)^2$ $\quad [(a+b)(a-b) = a^2 - b^2]$
   $= 1,000,000 - 1$
   $= 999,999$

(b) $98 \times 98 = (100 - 2) \times (100 - 2)$
   $= (100-2)^2 = (100)^2 + (2)^2 - 2 \times 100 \times 2$
   $= 10000 + 4 - 400$
   $= 9604$

Example 4: If $x - \dfrac{1}{x} = \sqrt{5}$, then, find the value of $\left(x^4 + \dfrac{1}{x^4}\right)$.

Solution: Given $x - \dfrac{1}{x} = \sqrt{5}$,

Squaring both sides,
$\left(x - \dfrac{1}{x}\right)^2 = (\sqrt{5})^2$

$\Rightarrow x^2 + \dfrac{1}{x^2} - 2 \times x \times \dfrac{1}{x} = 5$

$\Rightarrow x^2 + \dfrac{1}{x^2} = 7$

Again squaring both sides, $\left(x^2 + \dfrac{1}{x^2}\right)^2 = (7)^2$

$\Rightarrow x^4 + \dfrac{1}{x^4} + 2 = 49$

$\Rightarrow x^4 + \dfrac{1}{x^4} = 47$

Example 5: If $x + y = 7$ and, $xy = 3$, then find the value of $\sqrt{x^4 + y^4 + 2x^2 y^2}$.

Solution: $(x + y) = 7$
$\Rightarrow (x+y)^2 = (7)^2 \Rightarrow x^2 + y^2 + 2xy = 49$
$\Rightarrow x^2 + y^2 = 49 - 6 = 43$
$\Rightarrow \sqrt{x^4 + y^4 + 2x^2 y^2} = \sqrt{(x^2 + y^2)^2} = 43$

TRIVIA

Octothorpe is the another term for the hashtag sign or the no. sign (#).

Division of Monomials

Dividing a monomial x by a monomial y means find a monomial such that, $x = yz$

Here, x is called the dividend, y is called the divisor and z is called the quotient. Similarly, an algebraic expression is divided by a monomial.

Polynomial

An algebraic expression which contains only non-negative integral powers of the variables in them is called a polynomial.

Example 6: $5x^2 - 3x + 2$, $2x^2 + 5x + 1$, $5x + 3$, $5x^4 + 3x^2 + 3x + 4$, etc.

$x^{-1/2} + \sqrt{x} + 3$, $4\sqrt{x} + x + 3$, etc. are not polynomials.

Degree of a Polynomial

The highest power of the variable involved in the polynomial is called the degree of the polynomial.

Division of Polynomial by a Monomial/Binomial/Trinomial

Example 7: Divide $x^3 - 2x - 21$ by $x - 3$.

Solution:
$$\begin{array}{r}
x^2 + 3x + 7 \\
x-3 \overline{)\, x^3 - 2x - 21} \\
\underline{x^3 - 3x^2 } \\
3x^2 - 2x \\
\underline{3x^2 - 9x } \\
7x - 21 \\
\underline{7x - 21} \\
0
\end{array}$$

Example 8: Find the quotient and remainder when $-10y^3 + 12y^4 - 22y$ is divided by $2y^2$.

Solution:
$$\begin{array}{r}
-6y^2 + 5y \\
2y^2 \overline{)\, 12y^4 - 10y^3 - 22y} \\
\underline{12y^4 } \\
-10y^3 \\
\underline{-10y^3 } \\
-22y
\end{array}$$

∴ quotient = $5y - 6y^2$, remainder = $-22y$.

In case of division of a polynomial by another polynomial, the relation will be

Dividend = Divisor × Quotient + Remainder.

Factorisation of Algebraic Expressions

Every algebraic expression in the product will be a factor. Finding factors of a given expression is called factorisation.

Factorisation is done by several methods and one should carefully memorise the standard identities of algebraic expressions for factorising a given polynomial.

For factorising a given polynomial of homogenous degree, i.e., degree of every term is equal, can be solved using following method,

Let, $p(x) = a x^n + b x^{n-1} y + c y^n$, is a polynomial of degree 'n'. Let two numbers, l and m be such that $l + m = by$ and $lm = a \times cy^n$, and, break the middle term (by) in the form ($l + m$) and proceed.

Example 9: Factorise : $p^4 + 16q^2 - 9p^2 - 81q^4$.

Solution: $p^4 + 16q^2 - 9p^2 - 81q^4$

$= p^4 - 81q^4 - 9p^2 + 16q^2$

$= \left[(p^2)^2 - (9q^2)^2\right] - \left[(3p)^2 - (4q)^2\right]$

$= (p^2 + 9q^2)(p^2 - 9q^2) - (3p + 4q)(3p - 4q)$

$= (p^2 + 9q^2)(p + 3q)(p - 3q) - (3p + 4q)(3p - 4q)$.

Example 10: Factorise : $x^4 + x^2 + 1$.

Solution: $x^4 + x^2 + 1 = (x^2)^2 + 1 + x^2$

$= (x^4 + 2x^2 + 1) - x^2 = (x^2 + 1)^2 - x^2$

$= (x^2 + 1 - x)(x^2 + 1 + x)$.

Example 11: Factorise : $x^2 + 6\sqrt{3}x - 48$

Solution: $x^2 + 6\sqrt{3}x - 48$

$= x^2 + (8\sqrt{3}x - 2\sqrt{3}x) - 48$

{∵ $8\sqrt{3}x$ and $-2\sqrt{3}x$ gives $6\sqrt{3}x$ sum and $-48x^2$ as a product.}

$= x^2 + 8\sqrt{3}x - 2\sqrt{3}x - 48 = x(x + 8\sqrt{3}) - 2\sqrt{3}(x + 8\sqrt{3})$

$= (x - 2\sqrt{3})(x + 8\sqrt{3})$.

Example 12: Factorise : $36x^2 + 12xyz - 15y^2z^2$.

Solution: $l + m = 12xyz$, $lm = 36x^2 \times -15y^2z^2$

$= -540 x^2y^2z^2$

$\Rightarrow l = 30xyz$, $m = -18xyz$

∴ $36x^2 + 12xyz - 15y^2z^2 = 36x^2 + 30xyz - 18xyz - 15y^2z^2$

$= 6x(6x + 5yz) - 3yz(6x + 5yz)$

$= (6x - 3yz)(6x + 5yz)$.

MUST REMEMBER

- An expression in which numbers and literal numbers are combined by the signs of fundamental operations is called an algebraic expression.
- An expression which contains two terms is called a binomial.
- An expression which contains three terms is called a trinomial.
- An algebraic expression which contains only non-negative integral powers of the variables in them is called a polynomial.
- The highest power of the variable involved in the polynomial is called the degree of the polynomial.

MULTIPLE CHOICE QUESTIONS

1. What are the factors of the expression $ab - a - b + 1$?
   (a) $(a-1)(b-1)$ (b) $(1-a)(b-1)$
   (c) $(a-1)(1-b)$ (d) $(1+a)(1-b)$

2. If $(2x - 3)$ is a factor of $6x^2 - 7x - 3$, then what is the other factor?
   (a) $(1 - 3x)$ (b) $(3x + 1)$
   (c) $(x - 3)$ (d) $(3 - x)$

3. What are the factors of $(g + h)^2 - 4gh$?
   (a) $(g-h)(g+h)$ (b) $(g-h)(g-h)$
   (c) $(g+h)(g+h)$ (d) None of these

4. If one of the factors of $25(x + y)^2 - 36(x - 2y)^2$ is $(17y - x)$, then what is the other factor?
   (a) $(7x - 11y)$ (b) $(11x - 7y)$
   (c) $(11x + 7y)$ (d) $(7x + 11y)$

5. Find the value of $(a + 1)(a - 1)(a^2 + 1)$.
   (a) $a^4 + 1$ (b) $a^4 - 2a^2 - 1$
   (c) $a^4 - 1$ (d) $a^4 - a^2 - 1$

6. If $x + y = 12$ and $xy = 14$ then what is the value of $x^2 + y^2$?
   (a) 116   (b) 114
   (c) 112   (d) 118

7. If $x + \dfrac{1}{x} = 11$ then what is the value of $x^2 + \dfrac{1}{x^2}$?
   (a) 123   (b) 119
   (c) 117   (d) 121

8. If $x + y = 10$ and $xy = 9$, what is the value of $x^2 - y^2$?
   (a) 40   (b) 60
   (c) 80   (d) 90

9. If $x + \dfrac{1}{x} = 7$ then find the value of $x^4 + \dfrac{1}{x^4}$.
   (a) 2209   (b) 2207
   (c) 2211   (d) 2205

10. The perimeter of a triangle is $6m^2 - 4m + 9$ and two of the sides are $m^2 - 2m + 1$ and $2m^2 + 3m + 5$. What is the third side?
    (a) $3m^2 - 5m + 3$
    (b) $3m^2 + 5m - 3$
    (c) $5m^2 - 3m + 3$
    (d) $5m^2 - 3m + 3$

11. What is the remainder when $7 + 15x - 13x^2 + 5x^3$ is divided by $4 - 3x + x^2$?
    (a) $x - 1$ (b) $x + 1$
    (c) $1 - x$ (d) None of these

12. What is the quotient if $x^4 - 2x^3 + 2x^2 + x + 4$ is divided by $x^2 + x + 1$?
    (a) $x^2 - 3x + 4$ (b) $x^2 - 3x + 2$
    (c) $x^2 + 3x - 4$ (d) None of these

13. What is the quotient if $5x^3 - 4x^2 + 3x + 18$ is divided by $3 - 2x + x^2$?
    (a) $5x - 6$ (b) $5x + 6$
    (c) $6x - 5$ (d) $6x + 5$

14. If $x - \dfrac{1}{x} = 6$ then what is the value of $x^2 + \dfrac{1}{x^2}$?
    (a) 38   (b) 36
    (c) 34   (d) None of these

15. $8a^2 b^3 \div (-2ab)$?
    (a) $4a^2 b$ (b) $-4ab^2$
    (c) $-4a^2 b$ (d) $4ab^2$

16. What is the value of $\dfrac{198 \times 198 - 102 \times 102}{96}$?
    (a) 200   (b) 300
    (c) 400   (d) None of these

17. What is the numerical coefficient in the product of $2abc$, $-16a^2bc$ and $3ab^2c^2$?
    (a) 64   (b) 96
    (c) −96   (d) −64

18. If $x + \dfrac{1}{x} = 2$, what is the value of $x^4 + \dfrac{1}{x^4}$?
    (a) 4   (b) 2
    (c) 1   (d) None of these

Algebraic Expressions and Their Identities

19. What is the value of $\dfrac{8.37 \times 8.37 - 1.63 \times 1.63}{0.674}$?

    (a) 10 (b) 100
    (c) 1000 (d) None of these

20. What is the remainder when $6x^2 - 11x + 15$ is divided by $2x - 5$?

    (a) 15 (b) 25
    (c) 35 (d) -25

21. What is the quotient if $15p^4 + 16p^3 + \dfrac{10p}{3} - 9p^2 - 6$ is divided by $3p - 2$?

    (a) $5p^3 + \dfrac{26}{9}p^2 + \dfrac{25}{8}p + \dfrac{80}{27}$
    (b) $5p^3 + \dfrac{16}{3}p^2 + \dfrac{15}{9}p + \dfrac{80}{27}$
    (c) $5p^3 + \dfrac{26}{9}p^2 + \dfrac{25}{3}p + \dfrac{80}{27}$
    (d) $5p^3 + \dfrac{26}{3}p^2 + \dfrac{25}{9}p + \dfrac{80}{27}$

22. What is the H.C.F. of $11\,abc^3$, $13\,a^2b^2c$ and $17\,ab^3c^2$?

    (a) abc (b) ab^2c
    (c) a^2bc (d) $3abc$

23. If one of the factors of $x^2 - y^2 + 2yz - z^2$ is $(x + y - z)$ then what is the other factor?

    (a) $(x + y - z)$ (b) $(x - y + z)$
    (b) $(x + y + z)$ (d) $(x - y - z)$

24. If one of the factors of $x^4 + x^2 + 1$ is $(x^2 + x + 1)$ then what is the other factor?

    (a) $x^2 - x + 1$ (b) $x^2 + x - 1$
    (c) $x^2 + x + 1$ (d) None of these

25. What are the factors of $11a^2 + 54a + 63$?

    (a) $(11a + 21)(a + 3)$ (b) $(11a + 21)(a - 3)$
    (c) $(11a + 9)(a + 7)$ (d) $(11a + 7)(a + 9)$

26. What is the degree of the polynomial?
    $$1 - \dfrac{5}{3}x + 9x^2 - 6x^3 - x^4\ ?$$

    (a) 1 (b) 2
    (c) 3 (d) 4

27. Find the remainder when $x^4 + 4x^2 + 10$ is divided by $x^2 - 2x + 4$.

    (a) -6 (b) 6
    (c) 4 (d) -4

28. Which of the following is not a polynomial?

    (a) $x^2 - x + 1$ (b) $x^2 + \sqrt{x} - 2$
    (c) $x^3 - x^2 - 1$ (d) $x^4 - x + 3$

29. Find the product:
    $$\dfrac{1}{4}x^2y^2z^2 \times 3x \times \dfrac{3}{2}y^2z\ ?$$

    (a) $\dfrac{3}{4}x^3y^2z^2$ (b) $\dfrac{3}{4}x^3y^3z^3$
    (c) $\dfrac{9}{8}x^3y^4z^3$ (d) $\dfrac{9}{8}x^3y^4z^2$

30. If $\left(x - \dfrac{1}{x}\right)^2 = 36$ then what is the value of $x^4 + \dfrac{1}{x^4}$?

    (a) 1442 (b) 1440
    (c) 1444 (d) 1438

HOTS

1. What is the value of x if
$$\frac{(x+3)(7-2x)}{(x+4)(5-x)} = 2$$
   (a) 17   (b) –17
   (c) 19   (d) –19

2. $9x^2 + 25 - 30x$ is the square of
   (a) $3x - 5$ (b) $-3x - 5$
   (c) $3x + 5$ (d) $-3x^2 + 5$

3. One of the factors of $x^2 + 17x + 60$ is
   (a) $x + 12$ (b) $x - 5$
   (c) $5x - 1$ (d) $x - 12$

4. If we add, $7xy + 5yz - 3zx$, $4yz + 9zx - 4y$ and $-3xz + 5x - 2xy$, then the answer is:
   (a) $5xy + 9yz + 3zx + 5x - 4y$
   (b) $5xy - 9yz + 3zx - 5x - 4y$
   (c) $5xy + 10yz + 3zx + 15x - 4y$
   (d) $5xy + 10yz + 3zx + 5x - 6y$

5. If we subtract $4a - 7ab + 3b + 12$ from $12a - 9ab + 5b - 3$, then the answer is:
   (a) $8a+2ab+2b+15$
   (b) $8a+2ab+2b-15$
   (c) $8a-2ab+2b-15$
   (d) $8a-2ab-2b-15$

SUBJECTIVE QUESTIONS

1. If $\dfrac{2x+7}{5} - \dfrac{3x+11}{2} = \dfrac{2x+8}{3} - 5$, then what is the value of x?

   Answer:
   $$\Rightarrow \frac{2x+7}{5} - \frac{3x+11}{2} = \frac{2x+8}{3} - 5$$
   $$\Rightarrow \frac{4x+14-15x-55}{10} = \frac{2x+8-15}{3}$$
   $$\Rightarrow \frac{-11x-41}{10} = \frac{2x-7}{3}$$
   $$\Rightarrow -33x - 123 = 20x - 70$$
   $$\Rightarrow -53x = -70 + 123$$
   $$-53x = 53 \Rightarrow x = \frac{53}{-53} = -1$$

2. If $\dfrac{P+6}{4} + \dfrac{P-3}{5} = \dfrac{5P-4}{8}$ then find P.

   Answer:
   $$\frac{P+6}{4} + \frac{P-3}{5} = \frac{5P-4}{8}$$
   $$\Rightarrow \frac{5P+30+4P-12}{20} = \frac{5P-4}{8}$$
   $$\Rightarrow \frac{9P+18}{20} = \frac{5P-4}{8}$$
   $$\Rightarrow 72P + 144 = 100P - 80$$
   $$\Rightarrow 28P = 224$$
   $$P = \frac{224}{28}$$
   $$\Rightarrow P = 8$$

3. In a hostel, 75 students has food provision for 36 days. If 15 students leave the hostel, for how many days would the food provision last?

   Answer:
   75 students had food provision for 36 days.
   1 student has food provision for 36×75
   60 students has food provision for
   $$\frac{36 \times 75}{60} = 45 \text{ days}$$

4. A and B can do a piece of work in 12 days, B and C in 15 days and A and C in 20 days. How much time will B alone take to finish the job?

   Answer:
   In 1 day $(A + B)$ can do $\dfrac{1}{12}$ work.

In 1 day $(B + C)$ can do $\dfrac{1}{15}$ work.

In 1 day $(A + C)$ can do $\dfrac{1}{20}$ work.

$\therefore \quad A + B + C = \dfrac{1}{12} + \dfrac{1}{15} + \dfrac{1}{20}$

$\qquad = \dfrac{5 + 4 + 3}{60} = \dfrac{12}{60} = \dfrac{1}{5}$

1 day work of $B = \dfrac{1}{5} - \dfrac{1}{20} = \dfrac{4 - 1}{20} = \dfrac{3}{20}$.

B will finish the work in $\dfrac{20}{3} = 6\dfrac{2}{3}$ days

5. Subtract $3x - 4y - 7z$ from the sum of $x - 3y + 2z$ and $-4x + 9y - 11z$.

   Answer:
   The sum of $x - 3y + 2z$ and $-4x + 9y - 11z$ is
   $(x - 3y + 2z) + (-4x + 9y - 11z)$
   Upon rearranging
   $x - 4x - 3y + 9y + 2z - 11z$
   $-3x + 6y - 9z$
   Now, Let us subtract the given expression from $-3x + 6y - 9z$
   $(-3x + 6y - 9z) - (3x - 4y - 7z)$
   Upon rearranging
   $-3x - 3x + 6y + 4y - 9z + 7z$
   $-6x + 10y - 2z$

Linear Equations in One Variable   8

Learning Objectives : In this chapter, students will learn about:
- Concept of Linear equation in one variable

CHAPTER SUMMARY

Linear Equation

An equation is a statement of equality of two algebraic expressions involving one or more unknown quantities called variables.

An equation having only linear polynomials is called a linear equation.

Example: $x + 3 = 7$

Example 1: Solve the equation $\dfrac{4x + 7}{9 - 3x} = \dfrac{1}{4}$.

Solution: The given equation can be written as
$4(4x + 7) = 1(9 - 3x)$
$\Rightarrow 16x + 28 = 9 - 3x$
$\Rightarrow 16x + 3x = 9 - 28$
$\Rightarrow 19x = -19$
$\Rightarrow x = \dfrac{-19}{19} = -1$

Example 2: Simplify $\dfrac{2 - 7x}{1 - 5x} = \dfrac{3 + 7x}{4 + 5x}$.

Solution: We have $(2 - 7x)(4 + 5x) = (3 + 7x)(1 - 5x)$
$\Rightarrow 8 + 10x - 28x - 35x^2 = 3 - 15x + 7x - 35x^2$
$\Rightarrow 8 - 18x = 3 - 8x$
$\Rightarrow -18x + 8x = 3 - 8$
$\Rightarrow -10x = -5 \Rightarrow x = \dfrac{-5}{-10} = \dfrac{1}{2}$

Example 3: If 10 is added to four times a number, the result is 5 less than five times the number. What is the number?

Solution: Let the number be x.
$\therefore \quad 10 + 4x = 5x - 5$
$\Rightarrow 5x - 4x = 10 + 5$
$\Rightarrow x = 15$

Example 4: Find three consecutive even numbers whose sum is 348.

Solution: Let three numbers be $x, x + 2, x + 4$
$\therefore \quad x + x + 2 + x + 4 = 348$
$\Rightarrow 3x + 6 = 348$
$\Rightarrow 3x = 342$
$\Rightarrow x = \dfrac{342}{3} = 114$
$\therefore$ Numbers are 114, 116, 118.

TRIVIA

29 is the number of short straight lines needed to make the number 29 when it is written as words: TWENTY NINE

Example 5: Two angles of a triangle are in the ratio 4 : 5. If the sum of these angles is equal to 3rd angle, what are the angles of triangle ?

Solution: Let the two angles be $4x$ and $5x$.
$\therefore \quad 4x + 5x + 9x = 180°$
$\Rightarrow 18x = 180°$

⇒ $x = \dfrac{180°}{18}$

⇒ $x = 10°$

∴ angles are 40°, 50°, 90°.

Example 6: Solve $\dfrac{x+b}{a+b} = \dfrac{x-b}{a-b}$.

Solution: Given $(x+b)(a-b) = (x-b)(a+b)$
⇒ $ax - bx + ab - b^2 = ax + bx - ab - b^2$
⇒ $2bx = 2ab$
⇒ $x = \dfrac{2ab}{2b} = a$

Example 7: Shankar is 24 years older than his daughter. In 4 years, Shankar will be thrice as old as his daughter. What are their present ages?

Solution: Let the daughter's age be x years.

∴ Shankar's age $= x + 24$

Now, in 4 years,

Daughter's age $= x + 4$

Shankar's age $= x + 24 + 4 = x + 28$

∴ $x + 28 = 3(x + 4)$
⇒ $x + 28 = 3x + 12$
⇒ $2x = 28 - 12$
⇒ $2x = 16$
⇒ $x = 8$

∴ Daughter's age = 8 years
and Shankar's age = 8 + 24 = 32 years

Example 8: The perimeter of a rectangle is 52 cm. How long is each side if the width is 2 cm more than one third of the length ?

Solution: Let the length of rectangle be x cm.

∴ Width $= \dfrac{x}{3} + 2$

∴ Perimeter of rectangle = 52
⇒ 2(length + width) = 52
⇒ $2(x + \dfrac{x}{3} + 2) = 52$
⇒ $x + \dfrac{x}{3} + 2 = 26$.
⇒ $3x + x + 6 = 78$
⇒ $4x = 78 - 6$
⇒ $4x = 72$
⇒ $x = \dfrac{72}{4} = 18$ cm

Length $= x = 18$ cm.

Width $= \dfrac{x}{3} + 2 = \dfrac{18}{3} + 2 = 8$ cm.

MUST REMEMBER

➡ An equation is a statement of equality of two algebraic expressions involving one or more unknown quantities called variables.
➡ An equation having only linear polynomials is called a linear equation.

MULTIPLE CHOICE QUESTIONS

1. A boat goes downstream and covers the distance between two ports in 4 hours, while it covers the same distance upstream in 5 hours. If the speed of the stream is 2km/hour, what is the speed of boat in still water?
   (a) 18 km/hour (b) 16 km/hour
   (c) 20 km/hour (d) 15 km/hour

2. The ages of Mohan and Sohan are in the ratio 9 : 7. Ten years ago their ages were in the ratio 7 : 5. What is the difference between their present ages?
   (a) 5 years (b) 10 years
   (c) 15 years (d) 20 years

3. The sum of two numbers is 360. If 65% of one number is equal to 85% of the other., which is the largest number among them?
   (a) 204 (b) 156
   (c) 256 (d) 214

4. A certain number of workers can finish a piece of work in 70 days. If there are 20 men less, it would take 10 days more for the same work to be finished. How many workers were there initially?
   (a) 150 (b) 160
   (c) 140 (d) 152

5. The sum of three consecutive multiples of 11 is 363. Which of these multiple is greatest?
   (a) 121 (b) 131
   (c) 132 (d) 122

6. Arun's age is three times his son's age. 10 years ago he was 5 times his son's age. What is the sum of their present ages?
   (a) 60 years (b) 70 years
   (c) 80 years (d) 90 years

7. Nirmal thinks of a number and subtracts 2½ from it. He multiplies the result by 8. The result now obtained is 3 times the same number he thought of. Find the number.
   (a) 4 (b) 5
   (c) 6 (d) 8

8. The difference between the digits of a two-digit number is 3. If the digits are interchanged and the resulting number is added to the original number we get 143. What was the original number?
   (a) 58 (b) 85 9
   (c) 78 (d) 87

9. A grand father is ten times older than his grandson. He is then also 54 years older than him. What is the sum of their present ages?
   (a) 66 yeas (b) 45 years
   (c) 50 years (d) 52 years

10. An altitude of a triangle is five-thirds the length of its corresponding base. If the altitude is increased by 4 cm and the base is decreased by 2 cm, the area of triangle remains the same. Find the base and altitude of the triangle respectively.
    (a) 100 cm, 24 cm (b) 24 cm, 10 cm
    (c) 20 cm, 12 cm (d) 12 cm, 20 cm

11. A field can be ploughed in 18 days. If everyday an additional area of 16 hectares is ploughed, the field can be ploughed in 12 days. What is the area of the field?
    (a) 512 hectares (b) 576 hectares
    (c) 528 hectares (d) None of these

12. The sum of the digits of a two digit number is 9. If 9 is subtracted from the number its digits are interchanged. What is the number?
    (a) 54 (b) 63
    (c) 72 (d) 45

13. What is the value of x in the given equatiom?
    $$\frac{5(x+6)-15(2-x)}{3x-1}=10$$
    (a) $x=1$ (b) $x=-1$
    (c) $x=2$ (d) $x=-2$

14. What is the value of x in the given equation?
    $$\frac{3x+1}{16}+\frac{2x-3}{7}=\frac{x+3}{8}+\frac{3x-1}{14}$$
    (a) 2 (b) 3
    (c) 4 (d) 5

Linear Equations in One Variable

15. What is the value of x if
$$\frac{x-n}{m+n} = \frac{x+n}{m-n}?$$
    (a) m (b) n
    (c) $-m$ (d) $-n$

16. A shirt is sold for ₹1498 and the seller gains 7% on it. What is the cost price of the shirt?
    (a) 1600 (b) 1500
    (c) 1400 (d) 1450

17. Half of a herd of deer are grazing in the field and three fourth of remaining are playing nearby. The rest nine are drinking water from the river. What is the number of deer in the herd?
    (a) 72 (b) 62
    (c) 74 (d) 80

18. The ages of Raju and Rajan are in the ratio 5 : 8. If Raju was 5 years older and Rajan 4 years younger, the age of Raju would have been the same as that of Rajan. What is the age of Raju?
    (a) 15 years (b) 16 years
    (c) 24 years (d) 13 years

19. If $\frac{1}{2}$ is subtracted from a number and the difference is multiplied by 8, the result is 12. What is the number?
    (a) 2 (b) 3
    (c) 4 (d) 8

20. Mahesh travelled $\frac{1}{8}$th of his journey by bus, $\frac{1}{4}$th by taxi, $\frac{3}{5}$th by train and remaining $\frac{8}{}$ km by foot. What is the distance of his total journey?
    (a) 120 km (b) 240 km
    (c) 220 km (d) 320 km

HOTS

1. The age of the father is three times the age of the son. If the age of the son is 15 years old, then the age of the father is:
    (a) 50 years (b) 55 years
    (c) 40 years (d) 45 years

2. The difference between two whole numbers is 66. The ratio of the two numbers is 2 : 5. The two numbers are:
    (a) 60 and 6 (b) 100 and 33
    (c) 110 and 44 (d) 99 and 33

3. If a number is divided by 8 it gives 6 as the value. Find the number.
    (a) 36 (b) 42
    (c) 48 (d) 56

4. When 75% of a number is added to 75 the result is the number again. What is the number?
    (a) 150 (b) 300
    (c) 100 (d) 450

5. A student has to secure 40% marks to pass. He got 30 marks and failed by 50 marks. What is the maximum number of marks?
    (a) 160 (b) 180
    (c) 200 (d) 320

SUBJECTIVE QUESTIONS

Solve each of the following equations and also check your results in each case:

1. $\dfrac{(2x+5)}{3} = 3x - 10$

Answer:
$\dfrac{(2x+5)}{3} = 3x - 10$

Let us simplify,
$\dfrac{(2x+5)}{3} - 3x = -10$

By taking LCM
$\dfrac{(2x+5-9x)}{3} = -10$

$\dfrac{(-7x+5)}{3} = -10$

By using cross-multiplication, we get,
$-7x + 5 = -30$
$-7x = -30 - 5$
$-7x = -35$
$x = \dfrac{-35}{-7} = 5$

Let us verify the given equation now,
$(2x+5)/3 = 3x - 10$
By substituting the value of 'x', we get,
$\dfrac{(2x+5)}{3} = 3x - 10$

$\dfrac{(10+5)}{3} = 15 - 10$

$\dfrac{15}{3} = 5$

Hence, the given equation is verified

2. $\dfrac{(a-8)}{3} = \dfrac{(a-3)}{2}$

Answer:
$\dfrac{(a-8)}{3} = \dfrac{(a-3)}{2}$

By using cross-multiplication, we get,
$(a-8)2 = (a-3)3$
$2a - 16 = 3a - 9$
$2a - 3a = -9 + 16$
$-a = 7$
$a = -7$

Let us verify the given equation now,
$\dfrac{(a-8)}{3} = \dfrac{(a-3)}{2}$

By substituting the value of 'a' we get,
$\dfrac{(-7-8)}{3} = \dfrac{(-7-3)}{2}$

$\dfrac{-15}{3} = \dfrac{-10}{2}$

$-5 = -5$

Hence, the given equation is verified

3. $\dfrac{(7y+2)}{5} = \dfrac{(6y-5)}{11}$

Answer:
$\dfrac{(7y+2)}{5} = \dfrac{(6y-5)}{11}$

By using cross-multiplication, we get,
$(7y + 2)11 = (6y - 5)5$
$77y + 22 = 30y - 25$
$77y - 30y = -25 - 22$
$47y = -47$
$y = \dfrac{-47}{47}$
$y = -1$

Let us verify the given equation now,
$\dfrac{(7y+2)}{5} = \dfrac{(6y-5)}{11}$

By substituting the value of 'y', we get,
$\dfrac{(7(-1)+2)}{5} = \dfrac{(6(-1)-5)}{11}$

$\dfrac{(-7+2)}{5} = \dfrac{(-6-5)}{11}$

$\dfrac{-5}{5} = \dfrac{-11}{11}$

$-1 = -1$

Hence, the given equation is verified

4. $x - 2x + 2 - \dfrac{16}{x} + 5 = 3 - \dfrac{7}{2x}$

   Answer:

   $x - 2x + 2 - \dfrac{16}{x} + 5 = 3 - \dfrac{7}{2x}$

   Let us rearrange the equation

   $x - 2x - \dfrac{16x}{3} + \dfrac{7x}{2} = 3 - 2 - 5$

   By taking LCM for 2 and 3, which is 6

   $\dfrac{(6x - 12x - 32x + 21x)}{6} = -4$

   $\dfrac{-17x}{6} = -4$

   By cross-multiplying

   $-17x = -4 \times 6$

   $-17x = -24$

   $x = \dfrac{-24}{-17}$

   $x = \dfrac{24}{17}$

   Let us verify the given equation now,

   $x - 2x + 2 - \dfrac{16}{3x} + 5 = 3 - \dfrac{7}{2x}$

   By substituting the value of 'x', we get,

   $\dfrac{24}{17} - 2\left(\dfrac{24}{17}\right) + 2 - \left(\dfrac{16}{3}\right)\left(\dfrac{24}{17}\right) + 5$

   $= 3 - \left(\dfrac{7}{2}\right)\left(\dfrac{24}{17}\right)$

   $\dfrac{24}{17} - \dfrac{48}{18} + 2 - \dfrac{384}{51} + 5 = 3 - \dfrac{168}{34}$

   By taking 51 and 17 as the LCM we get,

   $\dfrac{(72 - 144 + 102 - 384 + 255)}{51}$

   $= \dfrac{(102 - 168)}{34}$

   $\dfrac{-99}{51} = \dfrac{-66}{34}$

   $\dfrac{-33}{17} = \dfrac{-33}{17}$

   Hence, the given equation is verified

5. $\dfrac{1}{2x} + 7x - 6 = 7x + \dfrac{1}{4}$

   Answer:

   $\dfrac{1}{2x} + 7x - 6 = 7x + \dfrac{1}{4}$

   Let us rearrange the equation

   $\dfrac{1}{2x} + 7x - 7x = \dfrac{1}{4} + 6$ (by taking LCM)

   $\dfrac{1}{2x} = \dfrac{(1 + 24)}{4}$

   $\dfrac{1}{2x} = \dfrac{25}{4}$

   By cross-multiplying

   $4x = 25 \times 2$

   $4x = 50$

   $x = \dfrac{50}{4}$

   $x = \dfrac{25}{2}$

   Let us verify the given equation now,

   $\dfrac{1}{2x} + 7x - 6 = 7x + \dfrac{1}{4}$

   By substituting the value of 'x', we get,

   $\left(\dfrac{1}{2}\right)\left(\dfrac{25}{2}\right) + 7\left(\dfrac{25}{2}\right) - 6 = 7\left(\dfrac{25}{2}\right) + \dfrac{1}{4}$

   $\dfrac{25}{4} + \dfrac{175}{2} - 6 = \dfrac{175}{2} + \dfrac{1}{4}$

   By taking LCM for 4 and 2 is 4

   $\dfrac{(25 + 350 - 24)}{4} = \dfrac{(350 + 1)}{4}$

   $\dfrac{351}{4} = \dfrac{351}{4}$

   Hence, the given equation is verified

Quadrilaterals 9

Learning Objectives: In this chapter, students will learn about:
- Basics of quadrilateral and its related concept
- Trapezium

CHAPTER SUMMARY

For a regular polygon of n sides, we have each exterior angle $= \left(\dfrac{360}{n}\right)^\circ$

Each interior angle = 180°− (each exterior angle)
In a polygon of n sides, we have sum of all exterior angles = 4 × right angle.
Sum of all interior angles = $(2n - 4)$ right angle.
Number of diagonals in a polygon of n sides
$= \dfrac{n(n-3)}{2}$.

Example 1: What is the measure of each exterior angle of a regular polygon of 9 sides?

Solution: Each exterior angle $= \dfrac{360°}{9} = 40°$

Example 2: What is the measure of each interior angle of regular octagon?

Solution: Each exterior angle $= \dfrac{360}{8} = 45°$

Each interior angle = 180° − 45° = 135°.

Example 3: What is the number of diagonals in a polygon of 10 sides?

Solution: No. of diagonals
$= \dfrac{10(10-3)}{2} = \dfrac{10 \times 7}{2} =$ **35**

Example 4: What is the number of sides in a regular polygon whose each exterior angle measures 45°?

Solution: No. of sides in the given polygon
$= \dfrac{360}{45} = 8$

Quadrilateral

Let A, B, C, D be four points in a plane such that no three of them are collinear and the line segment AB, BC, CD and AD do not intersect except at their end points. Then the closed figure ABCD is called a quadrilateral.

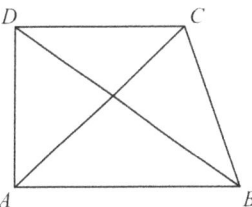

The points A, B, C, D are called its vertices. The line segments AB, BC, CD, DA are sides of quadrilateral.

Adjacent Side
Two sides of a quadrilateral which have a common end point are called adjacent sides.
Example: (AB, BC), (BC, CD).

Opposite Side
Two sides of a quadrilateral are called its opposite sides if they do not have a common end point.
Example: (AB, DC) and (AD, BC).
Sum of the angles of a quadrilateral is 360°.

Example 5: Three angles of a quadrilateral are 54°, 80° and 116°. What is the measure of fourth angle?

Solution: Let x is the fourth angle then
$54° + 80° + 116° + x = 360°$
$\Rightarrow 250 + x = 360 \Rightarrow x = 360 - 250 = 110°$.

Example 6: The angles of a quadrilateral are in the ratio 3: 5: 7:9. What is the measure of each of these angle?

Solution: If the angles are $3x$, $5x$, $7x$ and $9x$ respectively then

$3x + 5x + 7x + 9x = 360°$

$\Rightarrow 24x = 360°$

$\Rightarrow x = \left(\dfrac{360}{24}\right)° = 15°$

∴ Angles are $3x = 3 \times 15 = 45°$
$5x = 5 \times 15 = 75°$
$7x = 7 \times 15 = 105°$
$9x = 9 \times 15 = 135°$

TRIVIA

206 is the smallest number that when written in words contains all five vowels exactly once: TWO HUNDRED AND SIX

Trapezium

A quadrilateral having exactly one pair of parallel sides is called a trapezium.

In a parallelogram, the opposite sides are equal.

The opposite angles are equal and the diagonals bisect each other.

The diagonals of a rhombus bisect each other at right angles.

The diagonals of a square are equal and bisect each other at right angles.

Two adjacent angles of a parallelogram are supplementary.

Example 7: The perimeter of a parallelogram is 140 cm. If one of the sides is longer than the other by 10 cm, find the length of each of its sides.

Solutions : Let the side be x cm.

∴ Other side $= (x + 10)$ cm.

Hence Perimeter $= x + x + (x + 10) + (x + 10)$

$\Rightarrow 4x + 20 = 140$

$\Rightarrow 4x = 120$

$\Rightarrow x = \dfrac{120}{4} = 30$ cm

∴ Sides are 30 cm, 30 cm, 40 cm, 40 cm.

Example 8: The sum of two opposite angles of a parallelogram is 130°. Find the measure of each of angle.

Solution: Given sum of two opposite angles are 130°.

∴ $x + x = 130°$

$\Rightarrow 2x = 130° \Rightarrow x = \dfrac{130°}{2} = 65°$

So, the angles are 65°, 115°, 65°, 115°.

➡ Two sides of a quadrilateral which have a common end point are called adjacent sides.
➡ A quadrilateral having exactly one pair of parallel sides is called a trapezium.

MULTIPLE CHOICE QUESTIONS

1. The four angles of a quadrilateral are in the ratio 2 : 3 : 5 : 8. Then what is the difference between largest and smallest angle of the quadrilateral?
   (a) 80° (b) 100°
   (d) 110° (d) 120°

2. In the given figure the bisector of ∠A and ∠B meet at a point P. If ∠C = 100°, ∠D = 60°, what is the the measure of ∠APB?

   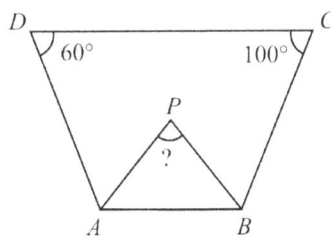

   (a) 60° (b) 80°
   (c) 90° (d) 100°

3. Three angles of a quadrilateral are equal and the measure of fourth angle is 120°. What is the measure of each of the equal angle?
   (a) 40° (b) 60°
   (c) 80° (d) 90°

4. The length of diagonals of a rhombus are 16 cm and 12 cm respectively. What is the length of each of its sides?
   (a) 10 cm (b) 12 cm
   (c) 14 cm (d) 16 cm.

5. The sum of two opposite angles of a parallelogram is 130°. What is the difference between largest and smallest angle of parallelogram?
   (a) 65° (b) 50°
   (c) 115° (d) 100°

6. The bisectors of any two adjacent angles of a parallelogram intersect at
   (a) 30° (b) 45°
   (c) 60° (d) 90°

7. If one angle of a parallelogram is 24° less than twice the smallest angle then what is the value of largest angle of the parallelogram?

   (a) 102° (b) 112°
   (c) 116° (d) 120°

8. The ratio of two sides of a parallelogram is 4 : 3. If its perimeter is 56 cm, what is the difference between largest and smallest side?
   (a) 8 cm (b) 4 cm
   (c) 12 cm (d) 16 cm

9. In the given Fig. ABCD is a rhombus. If ∠DMC = 90°, ∠DAB = 110°, what is ∠BDC ?

   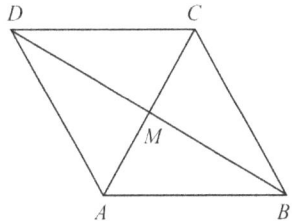

   (a) 30° (b) 35°
   (c) 40° (d) 45°.

10. Two adjacent sides of a parallelogram are 5 cm and 7 cm long what is the perimeter of parallelogram?
    (a) 24 cm (b) 28 cm
    (c) 22 cm (d) 26 cm

11. Of any two adjacent sides of a parallelogram one is longer than the other by 3 cm. If the perimeter is 36 cm, then what is the length of smaller side of parallelogram?
    (a) 10.5 cm (b) 7.5 cm
    (c) 6 cm (d) 12 cm

12. ABCD is a rhombus, AC = 24 cm and BD = 10 cm, then what is the measure of BC?

    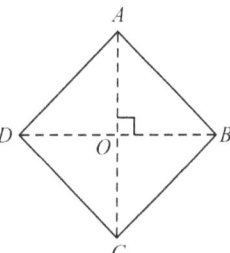

    (a) 13 cm (b) 12cm
    (c) 9 cm (d) 11 cm

Quadrilaterals

13. In △BCE, BE = EC, and ABCD is a square, and ∠BEC = 60°, then the measure of ∠BEA will be :

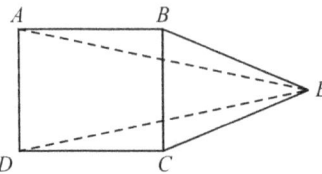

   (a) 45°   (b) 35°
   (c) 15°   (d) 25°

14. From the adjoining figure, find the measure of ∠EFD if AB ∥ CD, EF ∥ BC.

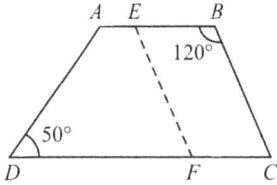

   (a) 40°   (b) 70°
   (c) 50°   (d) 60°

15. In the adjoining figure ABCD, AD = DC and AB = BC and, ∠ADC = 40° and ∠BCD = 140°, then, ∠ABC =

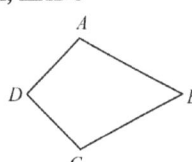

   (a) 60°   (b) 70°
   (c) 40°   (d) 50°

16. ABCD is a parallelogram having its sides, AB = 3x + 1 BC = 2y + 3, CD = 25, DA = y + 28, then, x + y =
   (a) 29   (b) 21
   (c) 25   (d) 33

17. PQRS is a parallelogram and ∠SPR = 50°, then find y.

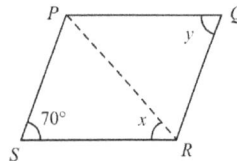

   (a) 70°   (b) 110°
   (c) 50°   (d) 130°

18. If α < 90°, then, ABCD, may be a : (Given : ABCD is a parallelogram and ∠B = 90°)

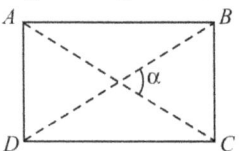

   (a) Rectangle   (b) Trapezium
   (c) Square   (d) Rhombus

19. If θ = 90°, and, ∠A = ∠C = 110°, then, ABCD is :

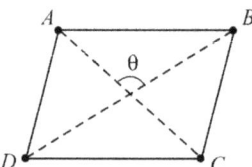

   (a) Square   (b) Rectangle
   (c) Rhombus   (d) None of these

20. ABCD is an isosceles trapezium, i.e., AD = BC, then

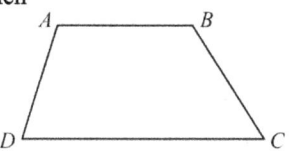

   (a) AD = CD   (b) ∠A = ∠B
   (c) ∠A = ∠D   (d) ∠C = ∠A

21. In the given figure, OS = OQ and PR = 2OP = 2OR, and also, OR = OS, then, PQRS is not a

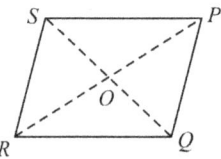

   (a) Rhombus   (b) Rectangle
   (c) Square   (d) Parallelogram.

22. In the adjoining figure, AD ∥ BC and AB and DC are not parallel, then ∠B =

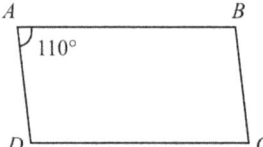

   (a) 110°   (b) 70°
   (c) 80°   (d) 40°

23. Find x and y:

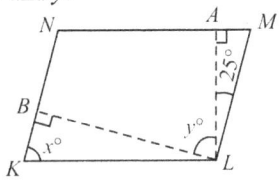

KLMN is a parallelogram.
(a) $x = 55°, y = 55°$ (b) $x = 65°, y = 55°$
(c) $x = 60°, y = 65°$ (d) None of these

24. ABCD is a parallelogram.

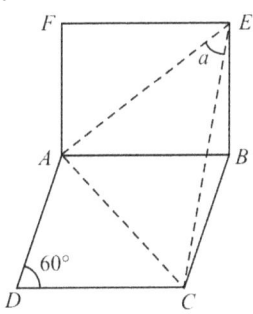

The measure of $\angle ADO$ is :
(a) 55° (b) 45°
(c) 35° (d) 75°

25. The quadrilateral formed by joining the mid-points of a given quadrilateral will be (surely) :
(a) Parallelogram (b) Rectangle
(c) Rhombus (d) Square

26. ABCD is a rhombus and ABEF is a square find 'a'.

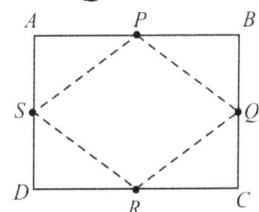

(a) 30° (b) 45°
(c) 60° (d) 75°

27. ABCD is a rectangle, $ED = DC$, $\angle BOC = 120°$, $\angle CED = 30°$, find the value of x.

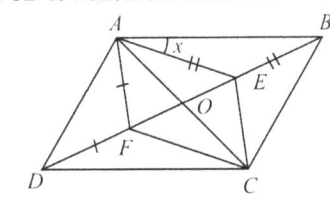

(a) 75° (b) 65°
(c) 90° (d) 120°

28. The adjacent sides of a rectangle are in the ratio 5: 3 and its area is 135 cm^2. The perimeter of the rectangle is :
(a) 135 cm (b) 54 cm
(c) 81 cm (d) 48 cm

29. ABCD is a rhombus and $\angle AEF = 50°$. Find x.

(a) 15° (b) 20°
(c) 35° (d) 25°

30. ABCD is a square, P, Q, R, S are the mid-points of AB, BC, CD and DA respectively. If the perimeter of ABCD is $16\sqrt{2}$ cm, then perimeter of PQRS is :

(a) $16\sqrt{2}$ cm (b) $8\sqrt{2}$ cm
(c) 8 cm (d) 16 cm

HOTS

1. In a parallelogram ABCD, angle A and angle B are in the ratio 1:2. Find the angle A.
   (a) 30° (b) 45°
   (c) 60° (d) 90°

2. The angles of a quadrilateral are in ratio 1:2:3:4. Which angle has the largest measure?
   (a) 120° (b) 144°
   (c) 98°   (d) 36°

3. The diagonals of a rectangle are $2x + 1$ and $3x - 1$, respectively. Find the value of x.
   (a) 1 (b) 2
   (c) 3 (d) 4

4. ABCD is a parallelogram. If angle A is equal to 45°, then find the measure of its adjacent angle.
   (a) 135° (b) 120°
   (c) 115° (d) 180°

5. If angles P, Q, R and S of the quadrilateral PQRS, taken in order, are in the ratio 3:7:6:4, what is PQRS?
   (a) A rhombus
   (b) A parallelogram
   (c) A trapezium
   (d) A kite

SUBJECTIVE QUESTIONS

1. What is the measure of each interior angle of a regular octagon?

   Answer:

   Each exterior angle of a regular Octagon
   $$= \frac{360°}{8} = 45°.$$
   Each interior angle = 180° − 45° = 135°.

2. What is the number of diagonals in a hexagon?

   Answer:

   Number of diagonals in a hexagon
   $$= \frac{6(6-3)}{2} = \frac{6 \times 3}{2} = 9.$$

3. Find the value of x in the following diagram:

   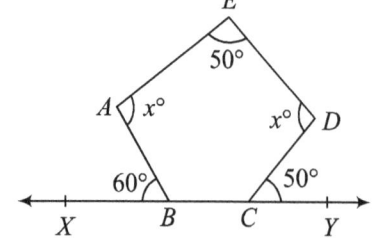

   Answer:

   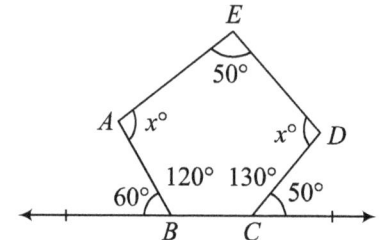

   Sum of all interior angles of a pentagon
   $$= (2 \times 5 - 4) \times 90°$$
   $$= 6 \times 90° = 540°$$
   $\Rightarrow 50 + x + x + 120 + 130 = 540$
   $\Rightarrow 300 + 2x = 540 \Rightarrow 2x = 240$
   $\Rightarrow x = 120$

4. What is the number of sides of a regular polygon whose each exterior angle measures 45°?

   Answer:

   Let n be the number of sides of polygon.
   $$45° = \frac{360°}{n} \Rightarrow n = \frac{360°}{45} = 8$$

5. A quadrilateral has three acute angles each measuring 75°. What is the measure of fourth angle?

Answer:

Let Fourth angle = x

For a quadrilateral,

$75° + 75° + 75° + x = 360°$

$\Rightarrow \quad 225° + x = 360°$

$\Rightarrow \quad x = 360° - 225° = 135°$.

6. Two adjacent angles of a parallelogram are as 2 : 3. What is the measure of each angle of quadrilateral?

Answer:

For a parallelogram,

$2x + 3x = 180°$

$\Rightarrow \quad 5x = 180 \Rightarrow x = \dfrac{180}{5} = 36°$.

$\therefore \qquad 2x = 2 \times 36° = 72°$

and $\qquad 3x = 3 \times 36° = 108°$

Hence the angles are 72°, 108°, 72°, 108°.

Mensuration   10

Learning Objectives : In this chapter, students will learn about:
- Basics of Mensuration

CHAPTER SUMMARY

Volume of cuboid = Length × Breadth × Height.
$V = l \times b \times h$
1 ml = 1 cu cm
1 l = 1000 cu cm.
1 kl = 1000 litre = 1 cu m.
Volume of cube = $l \times l \times l = l^3$
Surface area of cuboid = $2(l \times b + b \times h \times l \times h)$
Lateral surface area of the cuboid = $2(l + b)h$.
Surface area of cube = $6l^2$.
Volume of cylinder = $\pi r^2 h$.
Lateral surface of cylinder = $2\pi rh$
Total surface area of cylinder = $2\pi r^2 + 2\pi rh = 2\pi r(r+h)$

Example 1: Find the volume of a cuboid cake whose length is 12 cm, breadth 4 cm and height 3 cm.
Solution: Here $l = 12$ cm
$b = 4$ cm
$h = 3$ cm
$\therefore$ Volume = $l \times b \times h = 12 \times 4 \times 3 = 144$ cm^3

Example 2: A tank measuring 15 m long, 10 m wide and 6m deep is full of water. Find the volume of the water in the tank?
Solution: Here $l = 15$ m
$b = 10$ m
$h = 6$ m
Volume = $15 \times 10 \times 6 = 900$ cu m
= 900 kilo litres

Example 3: The volume of a cube is 343 cu m. What is the measure of its side?
Solution: Let side of the cube be x then
$x^3 = 343$
$\Rightarrow x^3 = 7^3 \Rightarrow x = 7$ m

Example 4: How many litres of water can a cubical tank of side 10 m hold?
Solution: Volume of tank = $10 \times 10 \times 10 = 1000$ m^3
= $1000 \times 1000 = 1000000$ litres.

Example 5: What is the surface area of a tin which is 40 cm long, 30 cm broad and 40 cm high?
Solution: Given $l = 40$ cm.
$b = 30$ cm
$h = 40$ cm
$\therefore$ Surface area of tin
= $2(40 \times 30 + 30 \times 40 + 40 \times 40)$
= $2(1200 + 1200 + 1600)$
= $2 \times 4000 = 8000$ sq. cm.

TRIVIA
$12 + 3 - 4 + 5 + 67 + 8 + 9$ equals 100.

Example 6: Find the lateral surface area of a cuboid having length 6 cm, breadth 5 cm and height 4 cm.
Solution: Here $l = 6$ cm
$b = 5$ cm
$h = 4$ cm

Lateral surface area of cuboid = 2 (l + b)h
= 2 (6 + 5) × 4
= 2 × 11 × 4
= 88 cm^2

Example 7: Find the surface area of cube if its edge is 5 cm.
Solution: Here l = 5 cm
∴ Surface area of cube = 6l^2
= 6 × 5^2
= 6 × 25
= 150 cm^2

Example 8: What is the volume of the cylinder if the diameter of the base of cylinder is 14 cm and height 6 cm ?

Solution: Here $r = \dfrac{14}{2} = 7$ cm

and h = 6 cm.
∴ Volume = $\pi r^2 h = \dfrac{22}{7} \times 7^2 \times 6$
$= \dfrac{22}{7} \times 7 \times 7 \times 6$
= 22 × 42
= 924 cm^3

Example 9: What is the lateral surface area of the cylinder having radius 7 cm and height 6 cm.
Solution: Given r = 7 cm.
h = 6 cm.
∴ Lateral surface area = $2\pi rh$
$= 2 \times \dfrac{22}{7} \times 7 \times 6$
= 22 × 12
= 264 cm^2

MUST REMEMBER

➡ Mensuration is the branch of mathematics that studies the measurement of geometric figures and their parameters like length, volume, shape, surface area, lateral surface area, etc.
➡ If a shape is surrounded by three or more straight lines in a plane, then it is a 2D shape.
➡ If a shape is surrounded by a no. of surfaces or planes then it is a 3D shape.

MULTIPLE CHOICE QUESTIONS

1. A piece of ductile metal is in the form of a cylinder of radius 0.5 cm and length 6 cm. It is drawn out into a wire of diameter 1 mm. What will be the length of the wire?
   (a) 6 m   (b) 12 m
   (c) 9 m   (d) 3 m

2. How many cubic metres of earth must be dug out to sink a well of 22.5 m deep and diameter 7 m ?
   (a) 866.25 cu m   (b) 826.25 cu m
   (c) 16.25 cu m   (d) None of these

3. The circumference of the base of a cylinder is 198 cm and its height is 30 cm. What is the curved surface area of the cylinder?
   (a) 5240 cm^2 (b) 5940 cm^2
   (c) 5640 cm^2 (d) 5340 cm^2

4. The volume of a metallic pipe is 1408 cm^3. Its length is 14 cm and its internal radius is 7 cm. What is the thickness of the pipe?
   (a) 3 cm   (b) 4 cm
   (c) 2 cm   (d) 2.5 cm

5. What is the total surface area of a cylinder having base radius 10.5 cm and length 18 cm?
   (a) 1188 cm^2 (b) 1818 cm^2
   (c) 1881 cm^2 (d) None of these

6. A cylindrical tank has capacity of 5632 m^3. Its diameter is 16 m. What is its depth?
   (a) 24 m   (b) 26 m
   (c) 28 m   (d) 32 m

7. The volume of a cylinder of height 8 cm is 1232 cm^3. What is the difference between its curved surface area and total surface area?
   (a) 352 cm^2 (b) 308 cm^2
   (c) 316 cm^2 (d) 332 cm^2

8. What is the volume of a cube whose total surface area is 486 cm^2 ?
   (a) 729 cm^3 (b) 572 cm^3
   (c) 343 cm^3 (d) None of these

9. A beam of wood is 5 m long and 36 cm thick. It is made of 1.35 m^3 of wood. What is the width of the beam?
   (a) 15 cm   (b) 25 cm
   (c) 75 cm   (d) None of these

10. How many planks of size 2m × 25 cm × 8 cm can be prepared from a wooden block 5 m long 70 cm broad and 32 cm thick ?
    (a) 28   (b) 32
    (c) 36   (d) 42

11. The radius and height of a cylinder are in the ratio 3 : 7. Its volume is 1584 cu cm. What is the radius of the cylinder?
    (a) 2 cm   (b) 4 cm
    (c) 6 cm   (d) 8 cm

12. How many bricks of size 22 cm × 10 cm × 7 cm are required to construct a wall 33 m long 3.5 m high and 40 cm thick and sand used in the construction occupy $\frac{1}{10}$ th part of the wall?
    (a) 24000   (b) 25000
    (c) 26000   (d) 27000

13. A rectangular sheet of paper 44 cm × 18 cm is rolled along its length and a cylinder is formed. What is the volume of that cylinder?
    (a) 2772 cm^3 (b) 2722 cm^3
    (c) 2727 cm^3 (d) 2277 cm^3

14. The area of the base of a cone is 180 cm^2. If the height of the cone is 8 cm what is its volume?
    (a) 420 cm^3 (b) 480 cm^3
    (c) 460 cm^3 (d) 520 cm^3

15. The radii of two cylinders are in the ratio 2: 3 and their heights are in the ratio 5 : 3. What is the ratio of their volumes?
    (a) 20 : 27   (b) 27 : 20
    (c) 10 : 9   (d) 9 : 10

16. A swimming pool is 260 m long and 140 m wide. If 54600 cubic metres of water is pumped into it, what is the height of the water level in it ?
    (a) 1 m   (b) 1·5 m
    (c) 2 m   (d) 1·0 m

17. A rectangular piece of paper 22 cm × 6 cm is folded without overlapping to make a cylinder of height 6 cm. What is the volume of the cylinder?
    (a) 221 cm^3 (b) 231 cm^3
    (c) 214 cm^3 (d) 243 cm^3

18. The lateral surface area of a cylinder is 11440 cm^3. If its height is 65 cm then what is its circumference?
    (a) 174 cm (b) 176 cm
    (c) 184 cm (d) 186 cm

19. In the given figure the outer dimension is 24 cm × 28 cm and the inner dimension 16 cm × 20 cm. What is the difference between two adjacent section of the frame if the width of each section is same?
    (a) 20 cm^2
    (b) 24 cm^2
    (c) 16 cm^2
    (d) 28 cm

    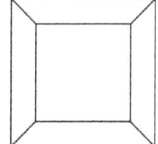

20. The area of a trapezium is 480 m^2. The distance between two parallel sides is 15 m and one of the parallel side is 20 m. What is the length of other parallel side?
    (a) 42 m (b) 44 m
    (c) 48 m (d) 52 m

21. A rectangular piece of paper 11 cm × 4 cm is folded without overlapping to make a cylinder of height 4 cm. What is its volume?
    (a) 32·5 cm^3 (b) 36·5 cm^3
    (c) 38·5 cm^3 (d) None of these

22. The total surface area of a cube is 486 m^2. Then what is the measure of its side?
    (a) 7 cm (b) 8 cm
    (c) 9 cm (d) 12 cm

23. The parallel sides of a trapezium are 25 cm and 11 cm and its non-parallel sides are 15 cm and 13 cm. What is the area of trapezium?
    (a) 216 cm^2 (b) 242 cm^2
    (c) 226 cm^2 (d) 256 cm^2

24. The area of a trapezium is 384 cm^2. Its parallel sides are in the ratio 5 : 3 and the distance between them is 12 cm. What is the length of longer of the parallel sides?

    (a) 36 cm (b) 40 cm
    (c) 42 cm (d) 44 cm

25. In the given figure $ST = SR$, $PQ = QR = RT = TP = 25$ m and its 5 total height is 41 m. What is its total area?

    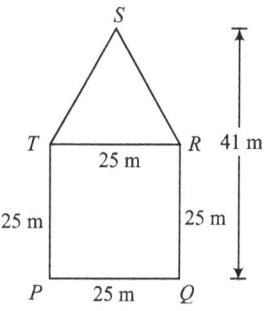

    (a) 825 m^2 (b) 815 m^2
    (c) 845 m^2 (d) None of these

26. $ABCD$ is a quadrilateral field in which the diagonal BD is 36 m. $AL \perp BD$ and $CM \perp BD$ such that $AL = 19$ m and $CM = 11$ m. What is the area of the field?
    (a) 520 m^2 (b) 540 m^2
    (c) 560 m^2 (d) 570 m^2

27. If the length of each side of a cube is doubled then by how many times does its surface area increase?
    (a) 4 times (b) 8 times
    (c) 16 times (d) None of these

28. The edges of a cuboid are in the ratio 1 : 2 : 3 and its surface area is 88 cm^2. What is the volume of the cuboid?
    (a) 48 cm^3 (b) 64 cm^3
    (c) 56 cm^3 (d) 64 cm^3

29. The curved surface area of a cylinder is 220 cm^2 and then volume of the cylinder is 770 cm^3 then what is the diameter of cylinder?
    (a) 7 cm (b) 14 cm
    (c) 21 cm (d) 28 cm

30. The circumference of the circular base of a cylinder is 44 cm and its height is 15 cm. What is the volume of the cylinder?
    (a) 1155 cm^3 (b) 1540 cm^3
    (c) 2310 cm^3 (d) None of these

Mensuration

HOTS

1. The area of the base of a cone is 180 cm². If the height of the cone is 8 cm what is its volume?
   (a) 480 cm³ (b) 1440 cm³
   (c) 6188 cm³ (d) 22.5 cm³

2. The curved surface area of a cylinder is 5940 cm². If its height is 30 cm, what is the diameter of the base?
   (a) 36 cm (b) 198 cm
   (c) 31.5 cm (d) 63 cm

3. A cuboid vessel is 20 cm long and 12 cm wide. How high must it be to hold 3 liters of water?
   (a) 12.5 cm (b) 12 cm
   (c) 14 cm (d) 4.5 cm

4. The perimeter of a rectangle is 54 cm. If its width is 2 cm more than one-fourth of its length, what is its length?
   (a) 12 cm (b) 16 cm
   (c) 20 cm (d) 24 cm

5. A well with internal diameter 8m is dug 7m deep. The earth taken out of it is spread around to a width of 2 m to form an embankment. The height of embankment will be :
   (a) 1.4 m (b) 2.8 m
   (c) 4.2 m (d) 5.6 m

SUBJECTIVE QUESTIONS

1. The area of a trapezium is 352 cm² and the distance between its parallel side is 16 cm. If length of one parallel side is 25 cm, what is the length of the other parallel side?

   Answer:

   Area of trapezium = 352

   $\Rightarrow \frac{1}{2} \times 16 (25 + x) = 352$

   $\Rightarrow 25 + x = \frac{2 \times 352}{16}$

   $\Rightarrow x = 44 - 25 = 19$ cm

2. A field is in the form of a right triangle with hypotenuse 50 m and one side 30 m. What is the area of the field?

   Answer:

   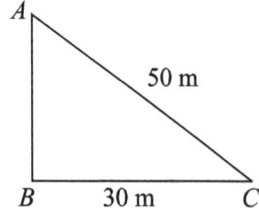

   $AB = \sqrt{50^2 - 30^2}$

   $= \sqrt{2500 - 900}$

   $= \sqrt{1600}$

   $= 40$ m.

   Area of field $= \frac{1}{2} \times BC \times AB = \frac{1}{2} \times 30 \times 40$

   $= 600$ m²

3. The volume of a cube is 729 cm³. What is its total surface area?

   Answer:

   Volume of a cube = 729 cm³

   $a^3 = 729 = 9^3 \Rightarrow a = 9$ χµ

   Total surface area = $6a^2 = 6(9^2) = 486$ cm²

4. There are 900 creatures in a zoo as per list given below.

Beat animals	Birds	Reptiles	Water animals	other land animals
150	175	50	125	400

   What is the central angle of the sector representing water animals?

Answer:

Total no. of creatures = 900

No. of water animals = 125.

Central angle $= \dfrac{125}{900} \times 360° = 50°$

5. A cylindrical tank has capacity of 5632 m³. If the diameter of the base is 16 m, what is its depth?

Answer:

Capacity of cylindrical tank = 5632 m³.

Radius of base $= \dfrac{16}{2} = 8$ m.

Let h be the depth.

Volume of the tank $= \pi r^2 h$.

$$\pi r^2 h = 5632$$

$$\dfrac{22}{7} \times 8^2 \times h = 5632$$

$$h = \dfrac{5632 \times 7}{22 \times 8 \times 8} = 28 \text{ m.}$$

Visualising Solid Shapes 11

Learning Objectives : In this chapter, students will learn about:
- ✓ Key points related to visualizing solid shapes
- ✓ Euler's formula
- ✓ Polyhedron

CHAPTER SUMMARY

Key Points

- 2-D shape is one whose two measurements, *i.e.,* length and breadth are possible.
- 3-D shape or a solid shape has three measurements, *i.e,* length, breadth and height.
- A solid object occupies some space, the measure of this space is known as volume.
- Any 2-D object can be extended to a 3-D object by means of extrusion or rotation.
- Every solid shape has some views. These views are top, side, front, bottom views. Further, side view is classified as right hand side view and left hand side view.
- 3-D shapes are classified into shapes with flat surfaces curved surfaces and flat as well as curved surfaces.
- 3-D shapes with flat surfaces only are further classified into prisms and pyramids.
- In prisms, all lateral surfaces are rectangles or parallelograms, whereas in pyramids all lateral surfaces are triangles.

TRIVIA

8,549,017,632 contains all of the digits in alphabetical order.

Euler's Formula

The number of faces (F), the number of edges (E) and the number of vertices (V) of a 3-D shape with flat surfaces satisfy the following relationship.
$$V + F - E = 2$$

Example 1: Identify 2-D and 3-D figures :

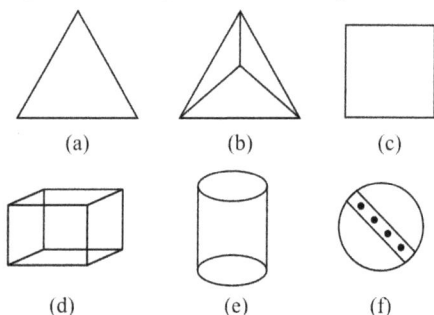

Solution: 2-D shapes : (a), (c);
3D shapes : (b), (d), (e), (f).

Example 2: Which of the following shapes are pyramids?

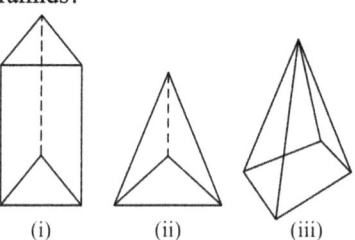

Solution: According to definition of pyramids, only (ii) and (iii) have all triangular lateral surfaces.

Polyhedron

A surface bounded by planes is called a polyhedron. The bounded planes are called the faces of polyhedron.

- If all the faces of a polyhedron are congruent, it is called a regular polyhedron. Example: cube, tetrahedron.
- If the faces of a polyhedron are not congruent, it is called a polyhedron having un-equal faces.

➡ A surface bounded by planes is called a polyhedron. The bounded planes are called the faces of polyhedron.

MULTIPLE CHOICE QUESTIONS

1. A cube has _____ vertices.
   (a) 8   (b) 12
   (c) 6   (d) 4

2. A cuboid has _____ edges.
   (a) 4   (b) 12
   (c) 8   (d) 6

3. A cube can be obtained by :
   (a) Extruding a square
   (b) Extruding a rectangle
   (c) Rotating a square about centre
   (d) None of these

4. Which of the following is not a 3-D shape?
   (a) Sphere   (b) Cylinder
   (c) Cuboid   (d) Circle

5. A sphere can be obtained by :
   (a) Extruding a circle
   (b) Rotating a rectangle
   (c) Rotating a square
   (d) Rotating a semicircle about its diameter.

6. A polyhedron such that its base and top are congruent polygons and other faces (lateral) are parallelograms in shape will be a
   (a) Pyramid   (b) Cylinder
   (c) Prism   (d) Tetrahedron

7. A regular polyhedron has :
   (a) Congruent faces
   (b) Non-congruent faces
   (c) Vertices are formed by different number of faces
   (d) None of these

8. A cylinder has :
   (a) 2 surfaces   (b) 3 surfaces
   (c) 4 surfaces   (d) 5 surfaces

9. A tetrahedron has :
   (a) 3 equilateral triangles
   (b) 4 equilateral triangles
   (c) 5 equilateral triangles
   (d) 4 isosceles triangles

10. A hexahedron has :
    (a) 8 squares
    (b) 6 squares
    (c) 6 rectangles
    (d) 6 parallelograms

11. A paraboloid is formed by :
    (a) Extruding a parabola.
    (b) Rotating a parabola about its vertex.
    (c) Rotating a parabola about its axis.
    (d) None of these.

12. The number of edges of a octahedron are :
    (a) 16   (b) 17
    (c) 18   (d) 20

13. A dodecahedron has 12 regular
    (a) Equilateral triangles
    (b) Pentagons
    (c) Squares
    (d) Rectangles

14. The number of faces of an icosahedron are :
    (a) 14   (b) 16
    (c) 18   (d) 20

15. A solid is formed by rotating right-angled triangle about any of its altitudes. The solid will be :
    (a) Cylinder (Right circular)
    (b) Sphere
    (c) Cone (Right Circular)
    (d) Hemisphere

16. If two equal tetrahedrons are joined through their base triangles, by sticking, then the shape generated will be a :
    (a) Tetrahedron   (b) Hexahedron
    (c) Dodecahedron   (d) Decahedron

17. While drawing an isometric view of a cube, the sides should be inclined at :
    (a) 30° to the horizontal
    (b) 30° to the vertical
    (c) $(30° + 30°) = 60°$, to the vertical
    (d) both (a) and (c)

18. The front view of a tetrahedron will be :

(a) 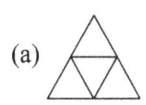   (b)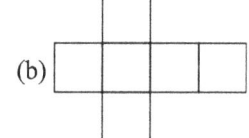

(c) 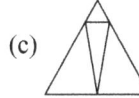   (d) None of these

19.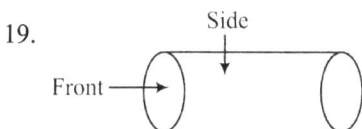

The front and side views of a right circular cylinder are :
(a) Circular, Triangular
(b) Circular, Rectangular
(c) Curved, straight
(d) None of these.

20. A solid shape is generated by rotating a rectangle about any of its sides. The shape will be :
(a) Cuboid
(b) Cone
(c) Sphere
(d) Cylinder (right circular)

21. A solid shape is generated by extruding a rectangle, out of its plane. The shape will be :
(a) Cube   (b) Cuboid
(c) Cylinder   (d) Cone

22. The top view will contain :

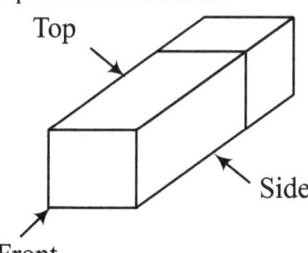

(a) 1 rectangle, 1 square (joined)
(b) 2 squares (joined)
(c) 2 rectangles (joined)
(d) 1 rectangle.

23.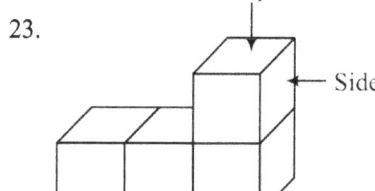

The above figure is generated from 4 cubes; The number of squares in front view = x, number of squares in top view = y then $(x + y) =$
(a) 7   (b) 6
(c) 5   (d) 8

24.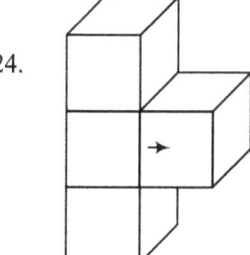

A cube is extracted from a well-arranged vertical cubes, which are 3 in number. When viewed from top, the number of edges will be :
(a) 8   (b) 6
(c) 7   (d) 10

25.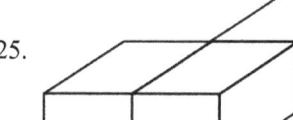

The above solid contain 3 cubes. The number of edges will be : (cubes are of same dimensions)
(a) 30   (b) 32
(c) 28   (d) 36

26. Number of vertices in Q – 25 are : (cubes are of same dimension)
(a) 24   (b) 12
(c) 18   (d) 20

Visualising Solid Shapes

27.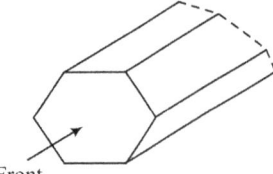
Front

The front view of the given shape will have ____ edges.
(a) 5 (b) 6
(c) 7 (d) 4

28.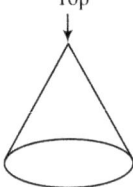

The top view of a cone will be :
(a) Square (b) Rectangular
(c) Triangle (d) Circular

29. A parallelogram is extruded outwards with the axis inclined at some angle with the vertical. The resulting figure will be :
(a) Cuboid (b) Parallelopiped
(c) Parallelex (d) None of these.

30.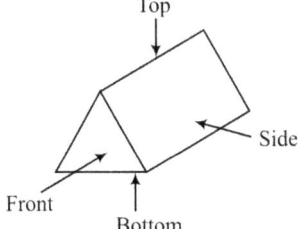

The number of vertices in front view + number of vertices in top view − number of vertices in bottom view =
(a) 4 (b) 6
(c) 5 (d) 9

HOTS

1. A solid is of the shape given. Which is its top view?

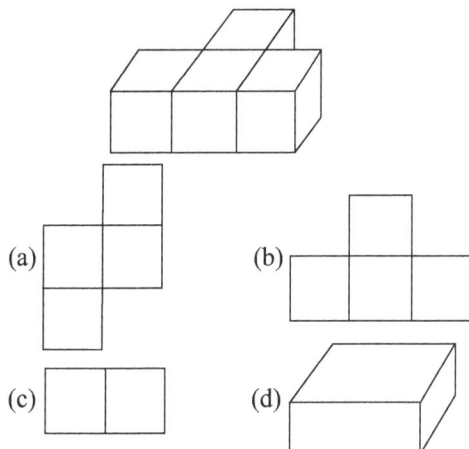

2. Observe the following solid.

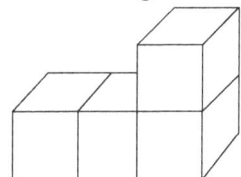

The following box has a figure which is a view of the given solid.

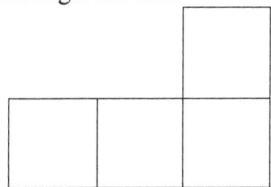

Which view of the solid is shown in the box?
(a) Side view (b) Top view
(c) Back view (d) Front view

3. Which one of the following cubes can be formed by the net given?

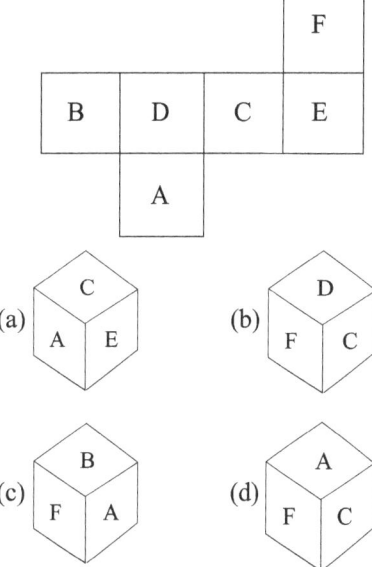

4. If two cubes of dimensions 3 cm × 3 cm × 3 cm are placed side by side, what would the dimensions of the resulting cuboid be?
(a) 6 cm × 6 cm × 6 cm
(b) 12 cm × 12 cm × 12 cm
(c) 9 cm × 6 cm × 3 cm
(d) 6 cm × 3 cm × 3 cm

5. How many triangles can be seen in this figure?

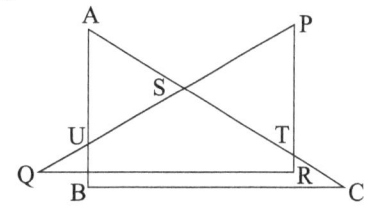

(a) 5   (b) 8
(c) 10   (d) 11

Visualising Solid Shapes

SUBJECTIVE QUESTIONS

1. Can a polyhedron have for its faces 3 Triangles?

   Answer:
   No, such polyhedrons are not possible. A polyhedron should have a minimum of 4 faces.

2. Which are prisms among the following:

   (i)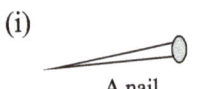
   A nail

   (ii)
   Unsharpened pencil

   (iii)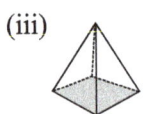
   A table weight

   (iv)
   A box

   Answer:
   (i) A nail: It is not a prism.
   (ii) Unsharpened pencil: It is a prism.
   (iii) A table weight: It is not a prism.
   (iv) A box: It is a prism.

3. Verify Euler's formula for the given solid.

   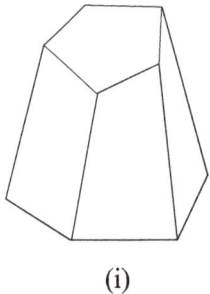
   (i)

   Answer:
   Number of faces, F = 7
   Number of edges, E = 15
   Number of vertices, V = 10
   As per formula, F + V – E = 2
   Substitute the values, we have
   F + V – E = 7 + 10 – 15
   = 2
   Hence, verified.

4. Using Euler's formula, find the unknown:

Faces	?	5	20
Vertices	6	?	12
Edges	12	9	?

   Answer:
   Euler's formula: F + V – E = 2
   Where, F = Faces, V = Vertices and E = Edges
   (i) F + 6 – 12 = 2
   F = 2 + 6
   $\Rightarrow$ F = 8
   (ii) 5 + V – 9 = 2
   V – 4 = 2
   $\Rightarrow$ V = 4 + 2
   $\Rightarrow$ V = 6
   (iii) 20 + 12 – E = 2
   32 – E = 2
   $\Rightarrow$ E = 32 – 2
   $\Rightarrow$ E = 30

5. Can a polyhedron have 10 faces, 20 edges and 15 vertices?

   Answer:
   From the given data, we have
   F = 10
   E = 20
   V = 15
   Every polyhedron satisfies Euler's formula, which is stated as, F + V – E = 2
   For the given polygon,
   F + V – E = 10 + 15 – 20 = 25 – 20 = 5, which is not equal to 2.
   Therefore, a polyhedron cannot have 10 faces, 20 edges and 15 vertices, as Euler's formula is not satisfied.

Data Handling 12

Learning Objectives : In this chapter, students will learn about:
- ✓ Types of Data
- ✓ Random Probability Concepts

CHAPTER SUMMARY

Statistics is the formal science of making effective use of numerical data relating to group of individuals or experiments, with all aspects, including the collection, analysis and interpretation of data and also the planning of the collection of data in terms of the design of surveys and experiments. A statistician is someone who is particularly versed in the ways of thinking necessary for the successful application of statistical analysis. Often such people have gained this experience after starting work in number of fields. This is also a discipline called Mathematical Statistics, which is concerned with the theoretical basis of the subject,

Types of Data

The data may be in the form of raw or grouped. The data which is not arranged in any form is known as the raw data and data which is arranged in a definite pattern is known as the grouped data.

Data is normally classified into two types, Primary data and Secondary data. The primary data is that data which is collected by the person himself for his own personal use, while secondary data is that data which is collected by others and used by someone else for his or her use. It may be data collected form the books/ newspaper/ internet or any other sources.

Pie Chart

A pie chart is the pictorial representation of the given data with the help of non- intersecting sectors of different areas and different central angles. The magnitude of the central angles depend on the magnitude of the data. In a pie chart, the arc length of each sector and consequently its central angles and area, is directly proportional to the quantity it represents. It is named for its resemblance to a pie which has been sliced.

The following pie chart represents the populations of English native speakers in different countries.

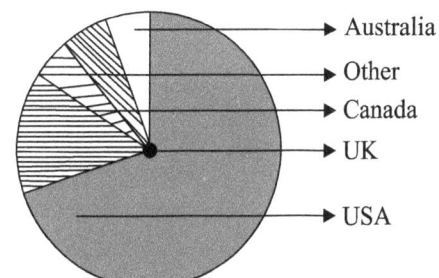

Co-ordinates of a Point

The pair of points which is used to describe the location of a point in two dimensional system are called co-ordinates of a point. The x- coordinate of a point is horizontal distance of the point from origin and y-coordinate of the point is the vertical distance from the origin.

Line Graph

A line graph is very useful for displaying data or information which changes continuously over a certain period of time. A line graph compares two variables. One variable is plotted along x-axis while another variable is plotted along y-axis.

Linear Graph

A linear graph is a graph which is used to represent the linear relationship between two variables. To draw a linear graph we use co-ordinates along x and y axis. The difference between a line graph or linear graph is that a line graph displays information as a series of points joined by line segments while a linear graph is always a straight line.

TRIVIA

TWELVE PLUS ONE = ELEVEN PLUS TWO
The left side of this equation is an anagram of the right side!

Basics of Probability

- Experiment: An experiment is a situation involving chance or probability that leads to results called outcomes.

- Outcome: An outcome is the result of a single trial of an experiment.

- Event: An event is one or more outcomes of an experiment.

- Probability: Probability is the measure of how likely an event is.

    The probability of event A is the number of ways A can occur divided by the total number of possible outcomes.

    P(A) = (The number of ways event A can occur)/ (The total number of possible outcomes) when the outcomes are equally likely.

- Random experiment: A random experiment is one whose outcomes cannot be predicted exactly in advance.

- Equally likely outcomes: The outcomes of an event with the same probability of occurrence are known as equally likely outcomes.

MUST REMEMBER

➡ The data which is not arranged in any form is known as the raw data and data which is arranged in a definite pattern is known as the grouped data.

➡ A pie chart is the pictorial representation of the given data with the help of non- intersecting sectors of different areas and different central angles.

➡ The x- coordinate of a point is horizontal distance of the point from origin and y-coordinate of the point is the vertical distance from the origin.

MULTIPLE CHOICE QUESTIONS

1. From a well shuffled deck of 52 cards, one card is drawn at random. What is the probability that the card drawn is a diamond?
   (a) $\frac{1}{2}$ (b) $\frac{1}{3}$
   (c) $\frac{1}{4}$ (d) $\frac{1}{13}$

2. A bag contains 4 red balls, 5 green balls and 7 black balls. They are mixed thoroughly and one ball is drawn at random. What is the probability of getting a black ball?
   (a) $\frac{7}{16}$ (b) $\frac{5}{16}$
   (c) $\frac{1}{4}$ (d) $\frac{1}{16}$

3. The following data shows the agricultural production in India during a certain year.

Foodgrains	Rice	Wheat	Pulses	Maize
Production in million of tons	57	76	19	38

   What is the central angle for Rice in a pie chart?
   (a) 120°   (b) 108°
   (c) 90°   (d) 144°

4. The electricity bill in Rupees of 24 houses of a certain locality for a month are given below. 472, 763, 312, 630, 584, 324, 700, 617, 754, 776, 596, 745, 565, 780, 378, 570, 685, 400, 356, 365, 435, 506, 548, 736. Arrange the data in increasing order and find the frequency of the group 700-800.
   (a) 3   (b) 4
   (c) 5   (d) 7

5. The monthly income of a family is ₹ 14, 400 and the central angle for the rent on a pie chart is 100°. What amount shows the rent?
   (a) ₹ 5400   (b) ₹ 1800
   (c) ₹ 4000   (d) ₹ 3600

6. In a pie-chart for expenditure in percent incurred in the construction of a house in a city, the central angle for cement is 72°. What is the percentage of cement expenditures ?
   (a) 15%   (b) 20%
   (c) 25%   (d) 30%

7. In a lottery there are 10 prizes and 20 blanks. A ticket is chosen at random. What is the probability of not getting a prize?
   (a) $\frac{1}{2}$ (b) $\frac{2}{3}$
   (c) $\frac{3}{13}$ (d) $\frac{1}{13}$

8. From a well shuffled deck of 52 cards, one card is drawn at random. What is probability of getting a red card?
   (a) $\frac{1}{2}$ (b) $\frac{1}{4}$
   (c) $\frac{3}{13}$ (d) $\frac{1}{13}$

9. In a box of 100 electric bulbs, 8 bulbs are defective. One bulb is taken out at random from the box. What is the probability that the bulb drawn is not defective?
   (a) $\frac{2}{25}$ (b) $\frac{1}{4}$
   (c) $\frac{23}{25}$ (d) $\frac{1}{25}$

10. One card is drawn at random from a well shuffled deck of 52 cards. What is the probability that the card drawn is a queen?
    (a) $\frac{1}{4}$ (b) $\frac{1}{3}$
    (c) $\frac{1}{13}$ (d) $\frac{2}{13}$

Data Handling

11. A die is thrown. What is the probability of getting 6?
    (a) 1 (b) $\frac{1}{2}$
    (c) $\frac{1}{4}$ (d) $\frac{1}{6}$

12. From a well shuffled deck of 52 cards, one card is drawn at random. What is the probability of getting a card of black 6?
    (a) $\frac{1}{26}$ (b) $\frac{1}{52}$
    (c) $\frac{1}{13}$ (d) $\frac{3}{26}$

13. The ages of 50 members of the Junior cricket club in a town are as given below. 15, 17, 14, 13, 14, 13, 14, 17, 17, 16, 17, 16, 15, 16, 15, 14, 13, 14, 15, 13, 18, 13, 15, 14, 15, 13, 14, 13, 13, 17, 15, 14, 14, 17, 16, 17, 15, 14, 17, 16, 16, 16, 14, 16, 13, 18, 16, 15, 14, 14.
    What percentage of members are in the 15-16 age group?
    (a) 28% (b) 30%
    (c) 32% (d) 36%

14. The pie-chart represents the amount spent on different sports by a sport club in a year. If the total money spent by the club is ₹ 10,800, find the amount spent on cricket.

    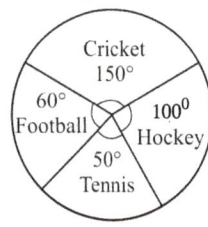

    (a) 3000 (b) 4500
    (c) 5000 (d) 6000

15. Mohan spends 40% of his monthly income on food items, 20% on house rent and 30% on miscellaneous items. He saves 10% of his income every month. What is the central angle for house rent on pie-chart?
    (a) 144° (b) 36°
    (c) 72° (d) 108°

16. One of letters from the word PHYSICS is chosen at random. What is the probability that this letter is S?
    (a) $\frac{1}{7}$ (b) $\frac{2}{7}$
    (c) $\frac{3}{7}$ (d) None of these

17. One of letters from the word "MOVEMENT" is chosen at random. What is the probability that this letter is M?
    (a) $\frac{1}{2}$ (b) $\frac{1}{4}$
    (c) $\frac{2}{7}$ (d) $\frac{1}{8}$

18. An 8-faced fair dice with numbers 1 to 8 is rolled. What is the probability of getting an even number?
    (a) $\frac{1}{2}$ (b) $\frac{1}{3}$
    (c) $\frac{1}{4}$ (d) $\frac{1}{6}$

19. A survey of 400 families of a town was conducted to find out how many children are there in a family?

No. of Children.	0	1	2	3	4	5
No. of family	56	82	123	95	18	26

    What is the probability that a family has 3 children?
    (a) $\frac{19}{80}$ (b) $\frac{19}{400}$
    (c) $\frac{3}{95}$ (d) None of these

20. Numbers 1 to 10 are written on ten separate slips (one number on one slip), kept in a box and mixed well. One slip is chosen from the box without looking into it. What is the probability of getting a number greater than 6?
    (a) $\frac{3}{5}$ (b) $\frac{2}{5}$
    (c) $\frac{4}{7}$ (d) $\frac{2}{7}$

HOTS

1. A bag has 4 red balls and 2 yellow balls. (The balls are identical in all respect other than colour). A ball is drawn from the bag without looking into the bag. The probability of getting a red ball is _____.
   (a) 12   (b) 23
   (c) 14   (d) 15

2. The histogram representing the marks obtained by 60 students in a Mathematics examination. What is the total number of students who obtained more than or equal to 80 marks in the examination?

   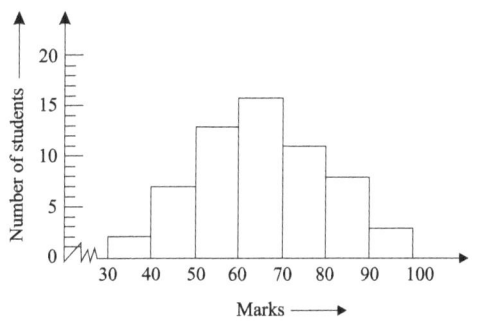

   (a) 13   (b) 3
   (c) 8   (d) 11

3. From the given table, the number of students who got more than or equal to 50 marks, is _____.

Marks (class-interval)	No. of students
30-40	12
40-50	13
50-60	4
60-70	15
70-80	6

   (a) 15   (b) 21
   (c) 25   (d) 29

4. The given pie chart gives the marks scored in an examination by a student in English, Hindi, Science and Technology, Social Science and Mathematics. If the total marks obtained by the student were 540, then the subject in which the student scored 105 marks, is_____.

   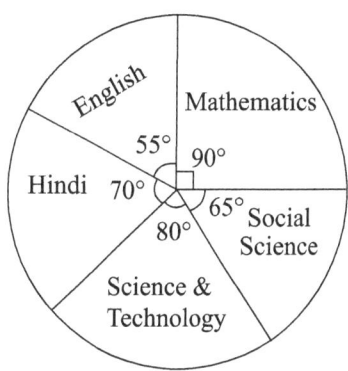

   (a) English   (b) Mathematics
   (c) Social Science (d) Hindi

5. Study the graph carefully and answer the questions given below it.

   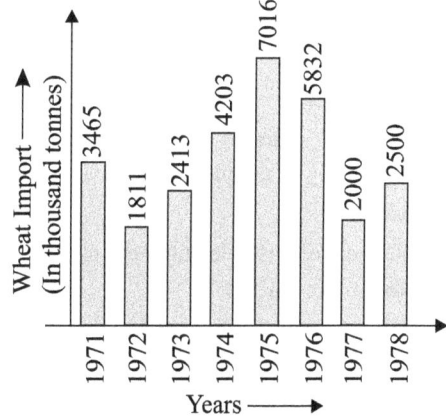

   In which year did the wheat import register highest increase over its preceding year?
   (a) 1973   (b) 1974
   (c) 1975   (d) 1978

Data Handling

SUBJECTIVE QUESTIONS

1. A solid rectangular piece of iron measures 1.05 cm × 70 cm × 1.5 cm. What is the weight of this piece in kilogram if 1 cm³ of iron weigh 8 gram?

   Answer:
   Volume = 1.05 × 70 × 1.5 = 110.25 cm³
   1 cm³ = 8 gram.
   110.25 cm³ = 8 × 110.25 gram.
   = 882 gram.
   $= \dfrac{882}{1000} = 0.882$ kg

2. There are 35 students in a class of which 20 are boys and 15 are girls. One student is chosen at random. What is the probability that the chosen student is a girl?

   Answer:
   Total number of students = 35.
   No. of boys = 20
   No. of girls = 15.
   P(student is a girl) $= \dfrac{15}{35} = \dfrac{3}{7}$

3. From a well shuffled pack of 52 cards, one card is drawn at random. What is the probability of getting a face card?

   Answer:
   Total no. of possible outcomes = 52
   No. of face cards = 12.
   P(getting a face card) $= \dfrac{12}{52} = \dfrac{3}{13}$.

4. When two coins are tossed simultaneously what is the probability of getting at least one head?

   Answer:
   Total no. of possible outcomes = 4.
   event of getting atleast one head
   = HT, HH, TH
   P(getting at least one head) $= \dfrac{3}{4}$.

5. The marks obtained by 40 students of class VIII in an examination are given below:

   16, 17, 18, 3, 7, 23, 18, 13, 10, 21, 7, 1, 13, 21, 13, 15, 19, 24, 16, 3, 23, 5, 12, 18, 8, 12, 6, 8, 16, 5, 3, 5, 0, 7, 9, 12, 20, 10, 2, 23.

   Divide the data into five groups namely 0-5, 5-10, 10-15, 15-20 and 20-25 and prepare a grouped frequency table.

   Answer:
   The frequency table for the marks of 40 students of class VIII in an examination is shown below:

Range of Marks	No. of Students
0-5	9
5-10	9
10-15	7
15-20	9
20-25	6

6. The following is the distribution of weights (in kg) of 52 persons:

Weight in kg	Persons
30-40	10
40-50	15
50-60	17
60-70	6
70-80	4

   (i) What is the lower limit of class 50-60?
   (ii) Find the class marks of the classes 40-50, 50-60.
   (iii) What is the class size?

   Answer:
   (i) The lower limit of the class 50-60 is 50.
   (ii) Class mark for the class 40-50:
   i.e., (40+50) / 2 = 90/2 = 45
   Again, Class mark for the class 50-60:
   i.e., (50+60) / 2 = 110/2 = 55
   (iii) Here the class size is 40-30, i.e. 10.

7. Construct a frequency table for the following weights (in gm) of 35 mangoes using the equal class intervals, one of them is 40-45 (45 not included):

30, 40, 45, 32, 43, 50, 55, 62, 70, 70, 61, 62, 53, 52, 50, 42, 35, 37, 53, 55, 65, 70, 73, 74, 45, 46, 58, 59, 60, 62, 74, 34, 35, 70, 68.

(i) What is the class mark of the class interval 40-45?
(ii) What is the range of the above weights?
(iii) How many classes are there?

Answer:

Weight (in grams)	No: of Mangoes
30 – 35	5
35 – 40	2
40 – 45	4
45 – 50	3
50 – 55	5
55 – 60	3
60 – 65	5
65 – 70	5
70 – 75	3

(i) Class mark for the class interval 40 – 45:
Class mark = (40+45) / 2 = 85/2 = 42.5
(ii) Range of the above weights:
Range = Highest value – Lowest value
Range = 74 – 30 = 44
(iii) Number of classes = 9

8. Construct a frequency table with class-intervals 0-5 (5 not included) of the following marks obtained by a group of 30 students in an examination:

0, 5, 7, 10, 12, 15, 20, 22, 25, 27, 8, 11, 17, 3, 6, 9, 17, 19, 21, 29, 31, 35, 37, 40, 42, 45, 49, 4, 50, 16.

Answer:
The frequency table with class intervals 0 – 5, 5 – 10, 10 – 15, . . . , 45 – 50 is shown below:

Marks	No: of Students
0 – 5	3
5 – 10	5
10 – 15	3
15 – 20	5
20 – 25	3
25 – 30	3
30 – 35	1
35 – 40	2
40 – 45	2
45 – 50	2
50 – 55	1

Data Handling

Direct and Inverse Variations   13

Learning Objectives : In this chapter, students will learn about:
- ✓ Direct Variation and related concepts

CHAPTER SUMMARY

Direct Variation

Two quantities a and b are said to be in direct variation, if whenever the value of a increases or decreases then the value of b also increases or decreases in a manner that their ratio $\dfrac{a}{b}$ remains constant.

$$\dfrac{a}{b} = \text{constant}$$

Hence $\dfrac{a_1}{b_1} = \dfrac{a_2}{b_2} = \dfrac{a_3}{b_3} = \ldots\ldots\ldots = \text{Constant}$

Example 1: If P and Q are directly proportional then find the value of P_1 and Q_1.

P	8	P_1	14
Q	96	36	Q_1

Solution:
Here $\dfrac{8}{96} = \dfrac{P_1}{36} \Rightarrow P_1 = \dfrac{8 \times 36}{96} = 3$

Then $\dfrac{8}{96} = \dfrac{14}{Q_1} \Rightarrow Q_1 = \dfrac{14 \times 96}{8} = 168$

Example 2: A train is moving at a uniform speed of 90 km/hr. In how much time will it cover a distance of 270 km?

Solution: If x is required time then

Distance (km)	90	270
Time (hour)	1	x

It is case of direct variation.

$\therefore \dfrac{90}{1} = \dfrac{270}{x} \Rightarrow x = \dfrac{270}{90} = 3$ hours.

Example 3: A bus covers 680 km in 51 litres of diesel. How much distance would it cover in 30 litres of diesel ?

Solution: If x is required distance then

Distance (km)	680	x
Diesel (litre)	51	30

It is the case of direct variation.

$\therefore \quad \dfrac{680}{51} = \dfrac{x}{30}$

$\Rightarrow \quad 51 \times x = 680 \times 30$

$\Rightarrow \quad x = \dfrac{680 \times 30}{51}$

$\Rightarrow \quad x = 400$ km

Example 4: Sohan walks at the uniform rate of 12 km/hr. What distance would be cover in 2 hours 15 minutes?

Solution: If x is required distance then

Distance (km)	12	x
Time (Minute)	60	135

It is the case of direct variation.

$\therefore \quad \dfrac{12}{60} = \dfrac{x}{135}$

$\Rightarrow \quad 60 \times x = 12 \times 135$

$\Rightarrow \quad x = \dfrac{12 \times 135}{60} = 27$ km.

TRIVIA

Here are the only temperatures that are prime integers in both Celsius and Fahrenheit:
−5°C is equal to 23°F and 5°C is equal to 41°F.

Inverse Variation

Two variables a and b are said to be in inverse proportion if $ab = k$
where k is a constant
So, $a_1 b_1 = a_2 b_2 = a_3 b_3 = \ldots\ldots = k$

Example 5: If L and M are inversely proportional then find the value of L_1 and M_1?

L	16	L_1	48
M	6	12	M_1

Solution: Here $16 \times 6 = L_1 \times 12$

$\Rightarrow \qquad L_1 = \dfrac{16 \times 6}{12} = 8$

and $\qquad 16 \times 6 = 48 \times M_1$

$\Rightarrow \qquad M_1 = \dfrac{16 \times 6}{48} = 2$

Example 6: If 12 men can do a work in 9 days then how many men can do it in 4 days?

Solution: If x is required no. of men then

No. of men	12	x
No. of days	9	4

It is the case of inverse variation.

$12 \times 9 = x \times 4$

$x = \dfrac{12 \times 9}{4} = 27$ men

Example 7: A train is running at 72 km/hr. If it crosses a pole in 25 seconds, what is its length?

Solution: Here 72 km/hour = $72 \times \dfrac{5}{18} = 20$ m/sec

Now if x is the length of train then

Distance (m)	20	x
Time (seconds)	1	25

It is the case of direct variation.

$\therefore \quad \dfrac{20}{1} = \dfrac{x}{25}$

$\Rightarrow \quad x = 20 \times 25 = 500$ m.

Example 8: 6 taps of equal capacity can fill a tank in 45 minutes. How many taps can fill it in 15 minutes?

Solution: If x is required no. of taps, then

No. of taps	6	x
Time (minutes)	45	15

It is the case of inverse variation.

$6 \times 45 = x \times 15$

$\Rightarrow \quad x = \dfrac{6 \times 45}{15} = 18$ taps

MUST REMEMBER

➡ Two quantities a and b are said to be in direct variation, if whenever the value of a increases or decreases then the value of b also increases or decreases in a manner that their ratio $\dfrac{a}{b}$ remains constant.

➡ Two variables a and b are said to be in inverse proportion if $ab = k$, where k is a constant.

Direct and Inverse Variations

MULTIPLE CHOICE QUESTIONS

1. A train is running at 36 km/hour. If it crosses a pole in 25 seconds, then what is its length?
   (a) 250 m (b) 225 m
   (c) 275 m (d) 300 m

2. A garrison of 1500 men had provision for 38 days. However a reinforcement of 400 men arrived. For how many days will the provision last?
   (a) 28 days (b) 30 days
   (c) 32 days (d) 34 days

3. Manish can pack 260 bundles in 5 days. How many bundles can he pack in 7 days?
   (a) 264 (b) 364
   (c) 384 (d) 324

4. A worker is paid ₹ 280 for 8 days work. If the total income of the month was ₹ 945, for how many days did he work?
   (a) 25 days (b) 26 days
   (c) 27 days (d) 28 days

5. A bus is travelling at an average speed of 56 km/hour. How much distance will it travel in 15 minutes?
   (a) 14 km (b) 12 km
   (c) 13 km (d) 16 km

6. In 15 days, the earth picks up 1.2×10^8 kg of dust from the atmosphere. In how many days will it pick up 4.8×10^8 kg of dust?
   (a) 40 days (b) 50 days
   (c) 30 days (d) 60 days

7. Suppose L and M vary inversely. When L is 10, M is 6. Which of the following is not a possible pair of corresponding values of L and M?
   (a) 12 and 5 (b) 15 and 4
   (c) 45 and 1.3 (d) 25 and 2.4

8. If 28 people can do a piece of work in 65 days, how many people can do it in 35 days?
   (a) 48 (b) 46
   (c) 52 (d) 56

9. A 270 m long train is running at 81 km/hr. How much time will it take to cross a 225 m long platform?
   (a) 18 sec (b) 21 sec
   (c) 22 sec (d) 24 sec

10. By working 8 hours a day Ankur can copy a book in 18 days. How many hours a day should he work so as to finish the work in 12 days?
    (a) 10 hours (b) 12 hours
    (c) 14 hours (d) 16 hours

11. If 6 men can do a job in 8 days, in how many days can 8 men do it?
    (a) 4 days (b) 5 days
    (c) 6 days (d) 8 days

12. A factory requires 42 machines to produce a given number of articles in 56 days. How many machines would be required to produce the same number of articles in 48 days?
    (a) 40 (b) 46
    (c) 48 (d) 49

13. A photograph of a bacteria enlarged 70000 times attains a length of 7 cm. What is the actual length of the bacteria?
    (a) 10^3 cm (9) 10^{-3} cm
    (c) 10^{-2} cm (d) 10^{-4} cm

14. If 5 men or 7 women can earn ₹ 1372 per day, how much would 10 men and 5 women earn per day?
    (a) ₹ 3724 (b) ₹ 3624
    (c) ₹ 3524 (d) ₹ 3124

15. 11 people can dig $6\frac{3}{4}$ m long trench in one day. How many men should be employed for digging 27 m trench of the same type in one day?
    (a) 42 men (b) 43 men
    (c) 44 men (d) 46 men

16. The scale of a map is $1:3 \times 10^7$. Two cities are 5cm apart on the map. What is the actual distance between them in kilometer ?
    (a) 1000 km	(b) 1200 km
    (c) 1500 km	(d) None of these
17. A loaded truck covers 18 km in 35 minutes. At the same speed how far can it travel in 7 hours?
    (a) 196 km	(b) 216 km
    (c) 212 km	(d) 192 km
18. 6 cows can graze a field in 28 days. How long would 21 cows take to graze the same field?
    (a) 6 days	(b) 8 days
    (c) 7 days	(d) 12 days
19. A car is travelling at a uniform speed of 84 km/hr. How much distance will it cover in 15 minutes?
    (a) 16 km	(b) 18 km
    (c) 19 km	(d) 21 km
20. Ranjna types 510 words in half an hour. How many words would she type in 10 minutes?
    (a) 153	(b) 150
    (c) 170	(d) 85
21. 14 workers can build a wall in 42 days. In how many days can 21 workers build it?
    (a) 21 days	(b) 28 days
    (c) 14 days	(d) 7 days
22. A can do a piece of work in 25 days and B can finish it in 20 days. They work together for 5 days and then A leaves. In how many days will B finish the remaining work?
    (a) 8 days	(b) 10 days
    (c) 11 days	(d) None of these
23. Amar, Rajesh and Mohan can do a piece of work in 10 days, 12 days and 15 days respectively. How long will it take to finish it if they work together ?
    (a) 5 days	(b) 4 days
    (c) 6 days	(d) 3 days
24. A pipe can fill a cistern in 9 hours. Due to a leak in its bottom, the cistern fills up in 10 hours. If the cistern is full, in how much time will it be emptied by the leak?
    (a) 60 hours	(b) 70 hours
    (c) 80 hours	(d) 90 hours
25. Mohit deposited a sum of ₹ 12000 in a Bank at a certain rate of interest for 2 years and earns an interest of ₹ 900. How much interest would be earned for a deposit of ₹ 15000 for the same period cand at the same rate of interest?
    (a) ₹ 840	(b) ₹ 1175
    (c) ₹ 1125	(d) ₹ 1714

HOTS

1. If the weight of 12 sheets of thick paper is 40 grams, how many sheets of the same paper would weigh 2500 grams?
   (a) 750	(b) 800
   (c) 850	(d) 950
2. The scale of a map is given as 1:300. Two cities are 4 km apart on the map. The actual distance between them is:
   (a) 1000 km	(b) 1100 km
   (c) 1200 km	(d) 1300 km
3. 6 pipes are required to fill a tank in 1 hour 20 minutes. If we use 5 such types of pipes, how much time it will take to fill the tank?
   (a) 120 minutes	(b) 96 minutes
   (c) 80 minutes	(d) 85 minutes
4. A man walks 20 km in 5 hours. How much time it will take for him to walk 32 km?
   (a) 3 hours	(b) 4 hours
   (c) 6 hours	(d) 8 hours
5. If 300 kg of coal cost 6000₹, then find the cost of 120 kg of coal?
   (a) 1200₹	(b) 2400₹
   (c) 3200₹	(d) 4200₹

Direct and Inverse Variations

SUBJECTIVE QUESTIONS

1. What is the range of the following data which represent the weight of 15 persons ?

   59, 68, 47, 85, 64, 76, 92, 107, 58, 62, 71, 93, 87, 128, 49

   Answer:

   Range = Maximum value – Minimum value
   = 128 – 47 = 81

2. Explain the concept of direct variation.

   Answer:

   If the values of two quantities depend on each other in such a way that a change in one quantity results in corresponding change in other, therefore if the ratio between the two variables remains constant, it is said to be in direct variation.

3. Which of the following quantities vary directly with each other?
   (i) Number of articles (x) and their price (y).
   (ii) Weight of articles (x) and their cost (y).
   (iii) Distance x and time y, speed remaining the same.
   (iv) Wages (y) and number of hours (x) of work.
   (v) Speed (x) and time (y) distance covered remaining the same).
   (vi) Area of a land (x) and its cost (y).

   Answer:
   (i) Number of articles (x) and their price (y)
   If number of articles is increasing then cost will also increase. So it is a case of direct proportion
   (ii) Weight of articles (x) and their cost (y).
   When weight of the article is increasing then cost also increase. So it is a case of direct proportion
   (iii) Distance x and time y, speed remaining the same.
   Time increases when distance increases, if speed remains constant. So it is a case of direct proportion
   (iv) Wages (y) and number of hours (x) of work.
   Wages increases if the number of working hours increases. So it is a case of direct proportion
   (v) Speed (x) and time (y) distance covered remaining the same).
   For same distance time taken will reduce if speed is increased. So it is not a case of direct proportion
   (vi) Area of a land (x) and its cost (y).
   Cost of the land increases if its area increases. So it is a case of direct proportion

4. In which of the following tables x and y vary directly?

   (i)

a	7	9	13	21	25
b	21	27	39	63	75

   (ii)

a	10	20	30	40	46
b	5	10	15	20	23

   (iii)

a	2	3	4	5	6
b	6	9	12	17	20

   (iv)

a	12	22	32	42	52
b	13	23	33	43	53

   Answer:
   (i) Directly proportional.
   In this table, value of 'b' is thrice the value of 'a' in all the columns. Therefore 'a' and 'b' are directly proportional.
   (ii) Directly proportional.
   In this table, value of 'b' is half of the value of 'a' in all the columns. Therefore 'a' and 'b' are directly proportional.
   (iii) Not directly proportional.

In this table, value of 'b' is not thrice the value of 'a' in all the columns. Therefore 'a' and 'b' are not directly proportional.

(iv) Not directly proportional.

In this table, value of 'b' is not varying in the same ratio as the value of 'a' in all the columns. Therefore 'a' and 'b' are not directly proportional.

5. Fill in the blanks in each of the following so as to make the statement true:
   (i) Two quantities are said to vary.... with each other if they increase (decrease) together in such a way that the ratio of the corresponding values remains same.
   (ii) x and y are said to vary directly with each if for some positive number k, ...= k.
   (iii) if $u = 3v$, then u and v vary.... with each other.

Answer:
   (i) Two quantities are said to vary **directly** with each other if they increase (decrease) together in such a way that the ratio of the corresponding values remains same.
   (ii) x and y are said to vary directly with each if for some positive number k, $k = \dfrac{x}{y}$ where k is a positive number.
   (iii) If $u = 3v$, then u and v vary directly with each other.

6. Complete the following tables given that x varies directly as y.

(i)
x	2.5	...	...	15
y	5	8	12	...

(ii)
x	5	...	10	35	25	...
y	8	12	...	...	...	32

(iii)
x	6	8	10	...	20	...
y	15	20	...	40	...	

(iv)
x	4	9	...	...	3	...
y	16	...	48	36	...	4

(v)
x	3	5	7	9
y	...	20	28	...

Answer:

(i) We know $k = \dfrac{x}{y}$

$$\dfrac{25.5}{5} = \dfrac{x_1}{8}$$

By cross-multiplying
8(2.5) = 5 × 1
20 = 5x_1

$$x_1 = \dfrac{20}{5} = 4$$

We know $k = \dfrac{x}{y}$

$$\dfrac{4}{8} = \dfrac{x_2}{12}$$

By cross-multiplying
12(4) = 8x_2
48 = 8x_2

$$x_2 = \dfrac{48}{8} = 6$$

We know $k = \dfrac{x}{y}$

$$\dfrac{6}{12} = \dfrac{15}{y_1}$$

By cross-multiplying
6y_1 = 15(12)
6y_1 = 180

$$y_1 = \dfrac{180}{6} = 30$$

x	2.5	**4**	**6**	15
y	5	8	12	**30**

(ii) We know $k = \dfrac{x}{y}$

Direct and Inverse Variations

$\dfrac{5}{8} = \dfrac{x_1}{12}$

By cross-multiplying
$12(5) = 8x_1$
$60 = 8x_1$
$x_1 = \dfrac{60}{8} = 7.5$

We know $k = \dfrac{x}{y}$

$\dfrac{7.5}{12} = \dfrac{10}{y_1}$

By cross-multiplying
$7.5y_1 = 10(12)$
$7.5y_1 = 120$
$y_1 = \dfrac{120}{7.5} = 16$

We know $k = \dfrac{x}{y}$

$\dfrac{10}{16} = \dfrac{35}{y_2}$

By cross-multiplying
$10y_2 = 35(16)$
$10y_2 = 560$
$y_2 = \dfrac{560}{10} = 56$

We know $k = \dfrac{x}{y}$

$\dfrac{35}{56} = \dfrac{25}{y_3}$

By cross-multiplying
$35y_3 = 56(25)$
$35y_3 = 1400$
$y_3 = \dfrac{1400}{35} = 40$

We know $k = \dfrac{x}{y}$

$\dfrac{25}{40} = \dfrac{x_2}{32}$

By cross-multiplying
$25(32) = 40x_2$
$800 = 40x_2$
$x_2 = \dfrac{800}{40} = 20$

x	5	**7.5**	10	35	25	**20**
y	8	12	**16**	**56**	**40**	32

(iii) We know $k = \dfrac{x}{y}$

$\dfrac{8}{20} = \dfrac{10}{y_1}$

By cross-multiplying
$8y_1 = 10(20)$
$8y_1 = 200$
$y_1 = \dfrac{200}{8} = 25$

We know $k = \dfrac{x}{y}$

$\dfrac{10}{25} = \dfrac{x_1}{40}$

By cross-multiplying
$10(40) = 25x_1$
$400 = 25x_1$
$x_1 = \dfrac{400}{25} = 16$

We know $k = \dfrac{x}{y}$

$\dfrac{16}{40} = \dfrac{20}{y_2}$

By cross-multiplying
$16y_2 = 20(40)$
$16y_2 = 800$
$y_2 = \dfrac{800}{16} = 50$

x	6	8	10	**16**	20
y	15	20	**25**	40	**50**

(iv) We know $k = \dfrac{x}{y}$

$\dfrac{4}{16} = \dfrac{9}{y_1}$

By cross-multiplying
$4y_1 = 9(16)$
$= 144$
$y_1 = \dfrac{144}{4} = 36$

We know $k = \dfrac{x}{y}$

$\dfrac{9}{36} = \dfrac{x_1}{48}$

By cross-multiplying
$9(48) = 36x_1$
$432 = 36x_1$
$x_1 = \dfrac{432}{36} = 12$

We know $k = \dfrac{x}{y}$

$\dfrac{12}{48} = \dfrac{x_2}{36}$

By cross-multiplying
$12(36) = 48x_2$
$432 = 48x_2$
$x_2 = \dfrac{432}{48} = 9$

We know $k = \dfrac{x}{y}$

$\dfrac{9}{36} = \dfrac{3}{y_2}$

By cross-multiplying
$9y_2 = 3(36)$
$= 108$

$y_2 = \dfrac{108}{9} = 12$

We know $k = \dfrac{x}{y}$

$\dfrac{3}{12} = \dfrac{x_3}{4}$

By cross-multiplying
$3(4) = 12x_3$
$12 = 12x_3$
$x_3 = \dfrac{12}{12} = 1$

x	4	9	**12**	9	3	**1**
y	16	**36**	48	36	**12**	4

(v) We know $k = \dfrac{x}{y}$

$\dfrac{3}{y_1} = \dfrac{5}{20}$

By cross-multiplying
$3(20) = 5y_1$
$60 = 5y_1$
$y_1 = \dfrac{60}{5} = 12$

We know $k = \dfrac{x}{y}$

$\dfrac{7}{28} = \dfrac{9}{y_2}$

By cross-multiplying
$7y_2 = 9(28)$
$= 252$
$y_2 = \dfrac{252}{7} = 36$

x	3	5	7	9
y	**12**	20	28	**36**

Direct and Inverse Variations

Factorisation 14

Learning Objectives : In this chapter, students will learn about:
- ✓ Degree of the Polynomials

CHAPTER SUMMARY

The process of writing an algebraic expression as the product of two or more algebraic expressions is called factorisation. When we factories an expression, we write it as a product of factors. These factors may be numbers, algebraic variables or algebraic expressions. An irreducible factor is that which cannot be expressed further as a product of factors. A systematic way of factorising an expression is the common factor method.

It consists of three steps:
(a) Write each term of the expression as a product of irreducible factors.
(b) Look for and separate the common factors.
(c) Combine the remaining factors in each term in accordance with the distributive law.
(d) Sometimes, all the terms in a given expression do not have a common factor; but the terms can be grouped in such a way that all the terms in each group have a common factor. When we do this, there emerges a common factor across all the groups leading to the required factorisation of the expression. This is the method of regrouping.

TRIVIA

The two sentences, "twelve plus one" and "eleven plus two", both have 13 letters.

Degree of the Polynomials

The degree of the polynomials is the highest of power of the variable in the given polynomials. If the degree of the polynomial is zero then it is called constant polynomial.

If the degree of the polynomial is one then it is called linear polynomial and if the degree of the polynomial is two then it is called quadratic polynomial. For cubic polynomial the degree is three and if the degree is four then it is called biquadrate polynomial.

MUST REMEMBER

- The process of writing an algebraic expression as the product of two or more algebraic expressions is called factorisation. When we factories an expression, we write it as a product of factors.
- The degree of the polynomials is the highest of power of the variable in the given polynomials. If the degree of the polynomial is zero then it is called constant polynomial.
- For cubic polynomial the degree is three and if the degree is four then it is called biquadrate polynomial.

MULTIPLE CHOICE QUESTIONS

1. The factorisation of $12a^2b+15ab^2$ gives:
   (a) $3ab(4ab + 5)$ (b) $3ab(4a + 5b)$
   (c) $3a(4a + 5b)$ (d) $3b(4a + 5b)$

2. The factorisation of $12x + 36$ is
   (a) $12(x + 3)$ (b) $12(3x)$
   (c) $12(3x + 1)$ (d) $x(12 + 36x)$

3. On factorising $14pq + 35pqr$, we get:
   (a) $pq(14 + 35r)$
   (b) $p(14q + 35qr)$
   (c) $q(14p + 35pr)$
   (d) $7pq(2 + 5r)$

4. The factors of $6xy – 4y + 6 – 9x$ are:
   (a) $(3x + 2)(2y + 3)$
   (b) $(3x – 2)(2y – 3)$
   (c) $(3x – 2)(2y + 3)$
   (d) $(3x –+2)(2y – 3)$

5. The factors of $x^2 + xy + 8x + 8y$ are:
   (a) $(x + y)(x + 8)$
   (b) $(2x + y)(x + 8)$
   (c) $(x + 2y)(x + 8)$
   (d) $(x + y)(2x + 8)$

6. The factors of $4y^2 – 12y + 9$ is:
   (a) $(2y + 3)^2$
   (b) $(2y – 3)^2$
   (c) $(2y – 3)(2y + 3)$
   (d) None of the above

7. The factors of $49p^2 – 36$ are:
   (a) $(7p + 6)^2$
   (b) $(7p – 6)^2$
   (c) $(7p – 6)(7p + 6)$
   (d) None of the above

8. The factors of $m^2 – 256$ are:
   (a) $(m + 4)^2$
   (b) $(m – 4)^2$
   (c) $(m – 4)(m + 4)$
   (d) None of the above

9. When we factorise $x^2 + 5x + 6$, then we get:
   (a) $(x +2)(x + 3)$ (b) $(x – 2)(x – 3)$
   (c) $(x \times 2) + (x \times 3)$ (d) $(x \times 2) – (x \times 3)$

10. The factors of $3m^2 + 9m + 6$ are:
    (a) $(m + 1)(m + 2)$
    (b) $3(m + 1)(m + 2)$
    (c) $6(m + 1)(m + 2)$
    (d) $9(m + 1)(m + 2)$

11. The common factor of a^3b^3 and ab^2 is:
    (a) a^2b^2 (b) ab^2
    (c) a^2b (d) ab

12. The common factor of a^3b^2 and a^4b is:
    (a) a^4b^2 (b) a^4b
    (c) a^3b^2 (d) a^3b

13. The common factor $12a$ and 30 is:
    (a) 6 (b) 12
    (c) 30 (d) $6a$

14. The common factors of $10a$, $20b$ and $30c$ are:
    (a) ab (b) ac
    (c) $10abc$ (d) 10

15. The common factor of $6x^3y^4z^2$, $21x^2y$ and $15x^3$ is:
    (a) $3x^2$ (b) $3x^3$
    (c) $6x^3$ (d) $6x^2$

16. The common factor of $24a^3b^4$, $36a^4c^4$ and $48a^3b^2c$ is:
    (a) $12a^3$ (b) $24a3$
    (c) $36a^3$ (d) $48a3$

17. The factorisation of $12x^2y + 15xy^2$ is:
    (a) $3xy^2(4x + 5y)$
    (b) $3x^2y(4x + 5y)$
    (c) $3xy(4x + 5y)$
    (d) $3x^2y^2(4x + 5x)$

18. The factorisation of $5x – 20$ is:
    (a) $5(x – 5)$ (b) $5(x – 4)$
    (c) $5(x – 3)$ (d) $5(x– 20)$

19. The factorisation of $8x + 4y$ is:
    (a) $8(x + 4y)$ (b) $4(2x + 4y)$
    (c) $8(x + y)$ (d) $4(2x + y)$

20. The factors of xyz are:
    (a) x (b) y
    (c) z (d) All of the above

HOTS

1. Which of the following is the common factor of $25a^2b$ and $55ab^2$?
   (a) $5ab^2$ (b) $5a^2b$
   (c) $5ab$ (d) $5a^2b^2$

2. The common factor of $6a^2b4c^2$, $21a^2b$ and $15a^3$ is
   (a) $3a^3$ (b) $6a^3$
   (c) $6a^2$ (d) $3a^2$

3. The factorisation of $12a^2b + 15ab^2$ is
   (a) $3ab(4a + 5b)$
   (b) $3a^2b(4a + 5b)$
   (c) $3ab^2(4a + 5b)$
   (d) $3a^2b^2(4a + 5b)$

4. The factorisation of $10x^2 - 18x^3 + 14x^4$ is
   (a) $2x^3 (7x^2 - 9x + 5)$
   (b) $2x (7x^2 - 9x + 5)$
   (c) $2x^2 (7x^2 - 9x + 5)$
   (d) $2(7x^2 - 9x + 5)$

5. The value of $3.5 \times 3.5 - 2.5 \times 2.5$ is
   (a) -6 (b) 6
   (c) 60 (d) 1

SUBJECTIVE QUESTIONS

1. Find the common factors of the given terms.
   (i) $12x, 36$
   (ii) $2y, 22xy$
   (iii) $14pq, 28p^2q^2$
   (iv) $2x, 3x^2, 4$
   (v) $6abc, 24ab^2, 12a^2b$
   (vi) $16x^3, -4x^2, 32x$
   (vii) $10pq, 20qr, 30rp$
   (viii) $3x^2y^3, 10x^3y^2, 6x^2y^2z$

   Answer:
   (i) Factors of $12x$ and 36
   $12x = 2 \times 2 \times 3 \times x$
   $36 = 2 \times 2 \times 3 \times 3$
   Common factors of $12x$ and 36 are $2, 2, 3$
   and , $2 \times 2 \times 3 = 12$

   (ii) Factors of $2y$ and $22xy$
   $2y = 2 \times y$
   $22xy = 2 \times 11 \times x \times y$
   Common factors of $2y$ and $22xy$ are $2, y$
   and, $2 \times y = 2y$

   (iii) Factors of $14pq$ and $28p^2q^2$
   $14pq = 2 \times 7 \times p \times q$
   $28p^2q^2 = 2 \times 2 \times 7 \times p \times p \times q \times q$
   Common factors of $14pq$ and $28 p^2q^2$ are $2, 7, p, q$
   and, $2 \times 7 \times p \times q = 14pq$

   (iv) Factors of $2x, 3x^2$ and 4
   $2x = 2 \times x$
   $3x^2 = 3 \times x \times x$
   $4 = 2 \times 2$
   Common factors of $2x, 3x^2$ and 4 is 1.

   (v) Factors of $6abc, 24ab^2$ and $12a^2b$
   $6abc = 2 \times 3 \times a \times b \times c$
   $24ab^2 = 2 \times 2 \times 2 \times 3 \times a \times b \times b$
   $12a^2b = 2 \times 2 \times 3 \times a \times a \times b$
   Common factors of $6abc, 24ab^2$ and $12a^2b$ are $2, 3, a, b$
   and, $2 \times 3 \times a \times b = 6ab$

   (vi) Factors of $16x^3, -4x^2$ and $32x$
   $16x^3 = 2 \times 2 \times 2 \times 2 \times x \times x \times x$
   $-4x^2 = -1 \times 2 \times 2 \times x \times x$
   $32x = 2 \times 2 \times 2 \times 2 \times 2 \times x$
   Common factors of $16x^3, -4x^2$ and $32x$ are $2, 2, x$
   and, $2 \times 2 \times x = 4x$

   (vii) Factors of $10pq, 20qr$ and $30rp$
   $10pq = 2 \times 5 \times p \times q$
   $20qr = 2 \times 2 \times 5 \times q \times r$
   $30rp = 2 \times 3 \times 5 \times r \times p$

Factorisation

Common factors of $10pq$, $20qr$ and $30rp$ are 2, 5
and, $2 \times 5 = 10$

(viii) Factors of $3x^2y^3$, $10x^3y^2$ and $6x^2y^2z$
$3x^2y^3 = 3 \times x \times x \times y \times y \times y$
$10x^3y^2 = 2 \times 5 \times x \times x \times x \times y \times y$
$6x^2y^2z = 3 \times 2 \times x \times x \times y \times y \times z$
Common factors of $3x^2y^3$, $10x^3y^2$ and $6x^2y^2z$ are x^2, y^2
and, $x^2 \times y^2 = x^2y^2$

Factorise.
(i) $4p^2 - 9q^2$
(ii) $63a^2 - 112b^2$
(iii) $49x^2 - 36$
(iv) $16x^5 - 144x^3$ differ
(v) $(l+m)^2 - (l-m)^2$
(vi) $9x^2y^2 - 16$
(vii) $(x^2 - 2xy + y^2) - z^2$

Answer:
(i) $4p^2 - 9q^2$
$= (2p)^2 - (3q)^2$
$= (2p - 3q)(2p + 3q)$
Using the identity $x^2 - y^2 = (x+y)(x-y)$

(ii) $63a^2 - 112b^2$
$= 7(9a^2 - 16b^2)$
$= 7((3a)^2 - (4b)^2)$
$= 7(3a + 4b)(3a - 4b)$

Using the identity $x^2 - y^2 = (x+y)(x-y)$
(iii) $49x^2 - 36$
$= (7x)^2 - 6^2$
$= (7x + 6)(7x - 6)$
Using the identity $x^2 - y^2 = (x+y)(x-y)$

(iv) $16x^5 - 144x^3$
$= 16x^3(x^2 - 9)$
$= 16x^3(x^2 - 9)$
$= 16x^3(x - 3)(x + 3)$
Using the identity $x^2 - y^2 = (x+y)(x-y)$

(v) $(l+m)2 - (l-m)^2$
$= \{(l+m)-(l-m)\}\{(l+m)+(l-m)\}$
Using the identity $x^2 - y^2 = (x+y)(x-y)$
$= (l + m - l + m)(l + m + l - m)$
$= (2m)(2l)$
$= 4 ml$

(vi) $9x^2y^2 - 16$
$= (3xy)^2 - 4^2$
$= (3xy - 4)(3xy + 4)$
Using the identity $x^2 - y^2 = (x+y)(x-y)$

(vii) $(x^2 - 2xy + y^2) - z^2$
$= (x - y)^2 - z^2$
Using the identity $(x-y)^2 = x^2 - 2xy + y^2$
$= \{(x-y)-z\}\{(x-y)+z\}$
$= (x - y - z)(x - y + z)$
Using the identity $x^2 - y^2 = (x+y)(x-y)$

Introduction to Graphs   15

Learning Objectives : In this chapter, students will learn about:
- ✓ Basics of bar diagrams and pie charts
- ✓ Different types of graphs
- ✓ Advantages and disadvantages of various graphs

CHAPTER SUMMARY

Bar diagrams and pie charts are used extensively in mathematics to demonstrate the statistical data. Bar Diagrams represent information using a sequence of bars while pie charts represent information in circular form. Let us know briefly about different types of graphs:

- **Histogram:** Representation that shows data in intervals.
- **Line graph:** It shows data that changes continuously over periods of time.
- **Linear graph:** A straight line graph is called a linear graph.
- **The Cartesian system:** (i) A plane is divided into 4 quarters (called quadrants) by two perpendicular lines, intersecting at 0(called origin). The horizontal line is called the X-axis and the vertical line is called the Y-axis. (ii) A point is represented by the horizontal distance from the origin called the *x*-coordinate and by the vertical distance from the origin called the *y*-coordinate.(ii) A point is represented by an ordered pair (*x*, *y*) where *x* is the *x*-coordinate and *y* is the *y*-coordinate.

TRIVIA

William Shanks, a renowned Mathematician, spent a large amount of his life calculating Mathematical constants, but he made a mistake on the 528th digit.

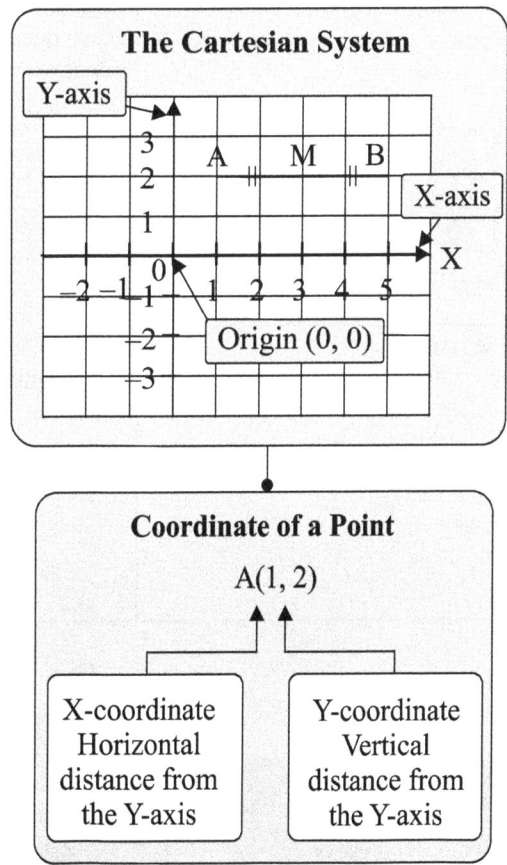

A graph shows the relation between two variables, one of which is an independent variable (or control variable) and the other a dependent variable.

Advantages and disadvantages of various graphs:

Representation of data	Advantages	Disadvantages
Pictogram Sales of Fruits Stall A 🍎🍎 Stall B 🍎🍎🍎 Stall C 🍎🍎 Key:1 Represents 50 Apples	Data is represented in an attractive manner.	Not accurate Difficult and time consuming to draw data involving fractions.
Bar Chart Number of students enrolled in three years (bar chart showing Boys and Girls)	Easy to construct Shows the exact quantities of each data category.	Does not how comparisons between the categories of data. the categories of data.
Pie chat 	Shows Clearly the Difference in magnitude between the categories.	Long calculations are needed. Not suitable if too many categories of Data are involved. Actual quantities are not displayed.

MUST REMEMBER

➡ Bar Diagrams represent information using a sequence of bars while pie charts represent information in circular form.
➡ A graph shows the relation between two variables, one of which is an independent variable (or control variable) and the other a dependent variable.
➡ The horizontal line is called the X-axis and the vertical line is called the Y-axis.

MULTIPLE CHOICE QUESTIONS

1. A _____ is a bar graph that shows data in intervals.
   (a) Bar-graph (b) Pie-chart
   (c) Histogram (d) Line Graph

2. A graph that displays data that changes continuously over periods of time is called:
   (a) Bar-graph (b) Pie-chart
   (c) Histogram (d) Line Graph

3. A line graph which is a whole unbroken line is called a:
   (a) Linear graph (b) Pie-chart
   (c) Histogram (d) Bar-graph

4. Which point lies only on y-axis?
   (a) (–2, 0) (b) (2, 0)
   (c) (0, –2) (d) (2, –2)

5. If we join (–3, 2), (–3, –3) and (–3, 4), then we obtain:
   (a) A triangle
   (b) Straight-line without passing through origin
   (c) Straight-line passing through origin
   (d) None of the above

6. The point (4, 0) lies on which of the following?
   (a) x-axis (b) y-axis
   (c) origin (d) None of the above

7. The point (–2, –2) is:
   (a) near to x-axis
   (b) near to y-axis
   (c) near to origin
   (d) Equidistant from x-axis and y-axis.

8. The point (–2, 5) is nearer to:
   (a) x-axis (b) y-axis
   (c) origin (d) None of the above

9. The point (-5, 2) is nearer to:
   (a) x-axis (b) y-axis
   (c) origin (d) None of the above

10. The point (0, 0) lies at:
    (a) x-axis (b) y-axis
    (c) origin (d) None of the above

Observe the diagram, given below and find the correct answer to the following MCQs.

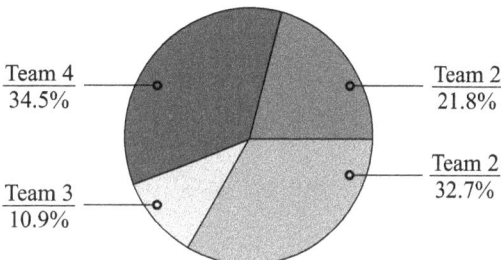

Points scored

11. Which team has the highest score?
    (a) Team 1 (b) Team 2
    (c) Team 3 (d) Team 4

12. Which team has the lowest score?
    (a) Team 1 (b) Team 2
    (c) Team 3 (d) Team 4

13. Which team is coloured green?
    (a) Team 1 (b) Team 2
    (c) Team 3 (d) Team 4

14. What is the average score of all the teams?
    (a) 22% (b) 25%
    (c) 27% (d) 29%

15. Which team has the second-highest score?
    (a) Team 1 (b) Team 2
    (c) Team 3 (d) Team 4

Below is the data of the number of men and women in a village for different years. Now based on this data answer the following MCQs with the correct option.

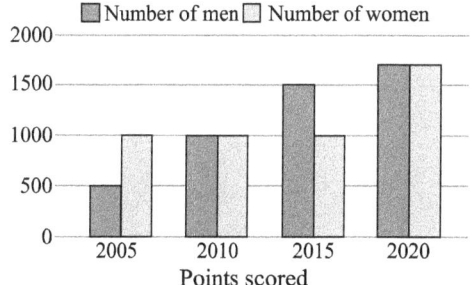

Points scored

Introduction to Graphs

16. How many men were there in the village in 2010?
    (a) 500   (b) 1000
    (c) 1500   (d) 2000
17. The population of men and women in 2020 is the same?
    (a) True   (b) False
18. In which year the population of women is the highest?
    (a) 2005   (b) 2010
    (c) 2015   (d) 2020
19. When is the population of men, the minimum?
    (a) 2005   (b) 2010
    (c) 2015   (d) 2020
20. In which year population of men is more than women?
    (a) 2005   (b) 2010
    (c) 2015   (d) 2020

HOTS

1. Which of the following points lies on y-axis?
   (a) (–4, 0)   (b) (4, 0)
   (c) (0, –4)   (d) (–4, 4)
2. By joining (–3, 2) (–3, 3) and (–3, 4), which of the following is obtained?
   (a) Triangle
   (b) A straight line not passing through origin
   (c) A straight line passing through origin.
   (d) None of these
3. By joining (1, 1), (0, 0) and (3, 3), which of the following is obtained?
   (a) A triangle
   (b) A straight line passing through origin
   (c) A curved line
   (d) A straight line not passing through origin
4. **DIRECTION:** The following graph shows the temperature of a patient admitted in a hospital, recorded every 2 hours.

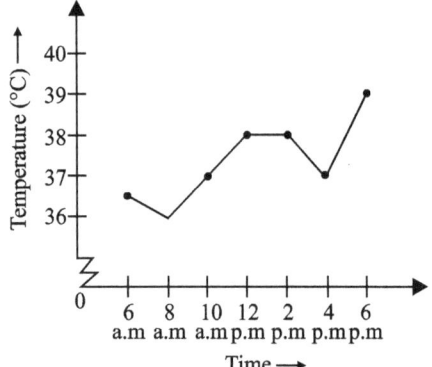

   What was the patient's temperature at 3 p.m.?
   (a) 37.5°C   (b) 38°C
   (c) 36°C   (d) 37°C
5. Based on above graph, when was the patient's temperature highest?
   (a) 10 a.m.   (b) 6 p.m.
   (c) 4 p.m.   (d) 2 p.m.

SUBJECTIVE QUESTIONS

1. Locate the points :
   (i)   (1, 1), (1, 2), (1, 3), (1, 4)
   (ii) (2, 1), (2, 2), (2, 3), (2, 4)
   (iii) (1, 3), (2, 3), (3, 3), (4, 3)
   (iv) (1, 4), (2, 4), (3, 4), (4, 4,)

   Answer:
   (i) (1, 1), (1, 2), (1, 3), (1, 4)
   To plot these points,
   Take point O on a graph paper and draw horizontal and vertical lines OX and OY, respectively.
   Then, let on the x-axis and y-axis, 1 cm represents 1 unit.
   To plot the point (1, 1), we start from the origin O and move 1 cm along X-axis and 1 cm along Y-axis. The point we arrive at is (1, 1).
   To plot the point (1, 2), we move 1 cm along X-axis and 2 cm along Y-axis. The point we arrive at is (1, 2).
   To plot the point (1, 3), we move 1 cm along X-axis and 3 cm along Y-axis. The point we arrive at is (1, 3).
   To plot the point (1, 4), we move 1 cm along X-axis and 4 cm along Y-axis. The point we arrive at is (1, 4)

   (ii) (2, 1), (2, 2), (2, 3), (2, 4)
   To plot these points,
   Take point O on a graph paper and draw horizontal and vertical lines OX and OY, respectively.
   Then, let on the x-axis and y-axis, 1 cm represents 1 unit.
   To plot the point (2, 1), we move 2 cm along X-axis and 1 cm along Y-axis. The point we arrive at is (2, 1).
   To plot the point (2, 2), we move 2 cm along X-axis and 2 cm along Y-axis. The point we arrive at is (2, 2).
   To plot the point (2, 3), we move 2 cm along X-axis and 3 cm along Y-axis. The point we arrive at is (2, 3).
   To plot the point (2, 4), we move 2 cm along X-axis and 4 cm along Y-axis. The point we arrive at is (2, 4).

   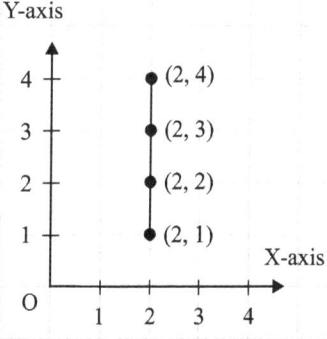

   (iii) (1, 3), (2, 3), (3, 3), (4, 3)
   To plot these points,
   Take point O on a graph paper and draw horizontal and vertical lines OX and OY, respectively.
   Then, let on the x-axis and y-axis, 1 cm represents 1 unit.
   To plot the point (1, 3), we move 1 cm along X-axis and 3 cm along Y-axis. The point we arrive at is (1, 3).

Introduction to Graphs

To plot the point (2, 3), we move 2 cm along X-axis and 3 cm along Y-axis. The point we arrive at is (2, 3).
To plot the point (3, 3), we move 3 cm along X-axis and 3 cm along Y-axis. The point we arrive at is (3, 3).
To plot the point (4, 3), we move 4 0 cm along X-axis and 3 cm along Y-axis. The point we arrive at is (4, 3).

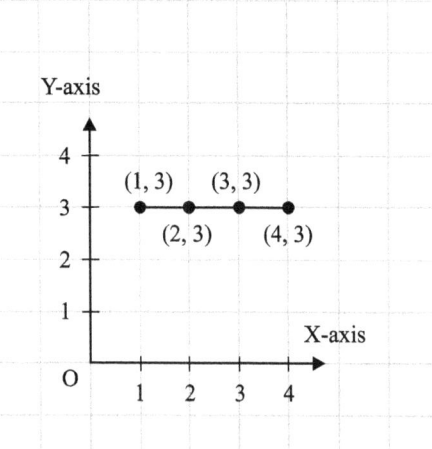

(iv) (1, 4), (2, 4), (3, 4), (4, 4,)

To plot these points,

Take point O on a graph paper and draw horizontal and vertical lines OX and OY, respectively.

Then, let on the x-axis and y-axis, 1 cm represents 1 unit.

In order to plot the point (1, 4), we move 1 cm along X-axis and 4 cm along Y-axis. The point we arrive at is (1, 4).
To plot the point (2, 4), we move 2 cm along X-axis and 4 cm along Y-axis. The point we arrive at is (2, 4).
To plot the point (3, 4), we move 3 cm along X-axis and 4 cm along Y-axis. The point we arrive at is (3, 4).
To plot the point (4, 4), we move 4 cm along X-axis and 4 cm along Y-axis. The point we arrive at is (4, 4).

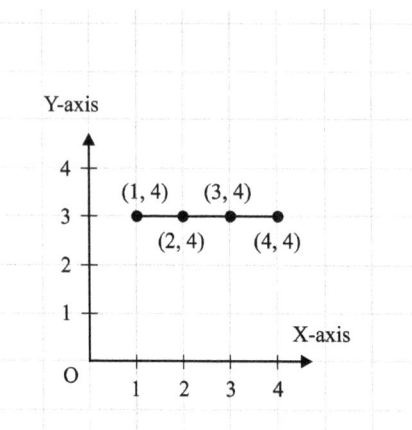

2. Find the coordinates of points P, Q, R and S in Figure below.

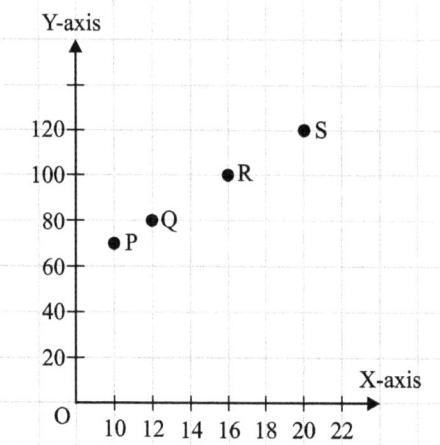

Answer:

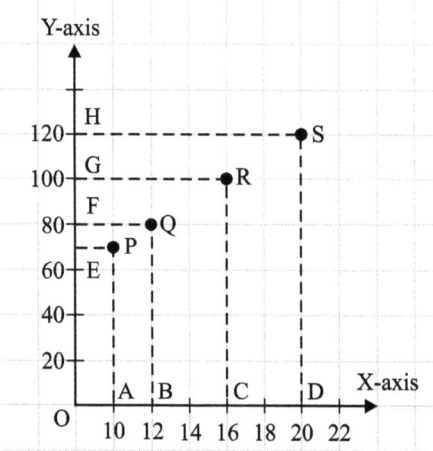

Draw perpendiculars PA, QB, RC and SD from vertices P, Q, R and S on the X-axis. Also, draw perpendiculars PE, QF, RG, and SH on the Y-axis from these points.
PE = 10 units and PA = 70 units
So, the coordinates of vertex P are (10, 70).
QF = 12 units and QB = 80 units
So, the coordinates of vertex Q are (12, 80).
RG = 16 units and RC = 100 units
So, the coordinates of vertex R are (16, 100).
SH = 20 units and SD = 120 units
So, the coordinates of vertex S are (20, 120).

3. Write the coordinates of each of the vertices of each polygon in Figure below.

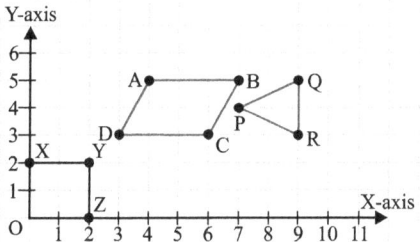

Answer:

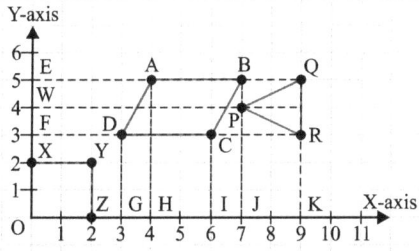

From the figure, we have the following:
In Quadrilateral OXYZ:
O lies on the origin, and the coordinates of the origin are (0, 0). So, the coordinates of O are (0, 0).
X lies on the Y – axis. So, the X – coordinate is 0. Hence, the coordinate of X is (0, 2).
Also, YX is equal to 2 units, and YZ is equal to 2 units. So, the coordinates of vertex Y are (2, 2).
Z lies on the X-axis. So, the Y-coordinate is 0. Hence, the coordinates of Z are (2, 0).

In polygon ABCD:
Draw perpendiculars DG, AH, CI and BJ from A, B, C and D on the X-axis.
Also, draw perpendiculars DF, AE, CF and BE from A, B, C and D on the Y-axis.
Now, from the figure:
DF = 3 units and DG = 3 units
So, the coordinates of D are (3, 3).
AE = 4 units and AH = 5 units
So, the coordinates of A are (4, 5).
CF = 6 units and CI = 3 units
So, the coordinates of C are (6, 3).
BE = 7 units and BJ = 5 units
So, the coordinates of B are (7, 5).

In polygon PQR:
Draw perpendiculars PJ, QK and RK from P, Q and R on the X-axis.
Also, draw perpendiculars PW, QE and RF from P, Q and R on the Y-axis.
Now, from the figure:
PW = 7 units and PJ = 4 units
So, the coordinates of P are (7, 4).
QE = 9 units and QK = 5 units
So, the coordinates of Q are (9, 5).
RF = 9 units and RK = 3 units
So, the coordinates of R are (9, 3).

4. Decide which of the following statements is true and which is false. Give reasons for your answer.
   (i) A point whose x-coordinate is zero will lie on the y-axis.
   (ii) A point whose y-coordinate is zero will lie on the x-axis.
   (iii) The coordinates of the origin are (0, 0).
   (iv) Points whose x and y coordinates are equal lie on a line passing through the origin.

Answer:
(i) A point whose x-coordinate is zero will lie on the y-axis.

Introduction to Graphs

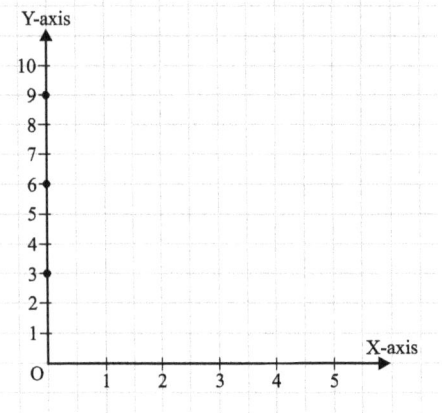

From the figure,

For $x = 0$, we have x-coordinates as zero.

For example, $(0, 3), (0, 6), (0, 9)$

These points will lie on the y-axis. Hence, we say that our given statement is true.

(ii) A point whose y-coordinate is zero will lie on the x-axis.

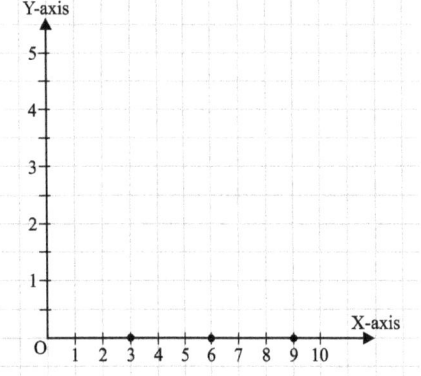

A point whose y-coordinate is zero will lie on the x-axis.

For $y = 0$, we have y-coordinates as zero.

For example, $(3, 0), (6, 0), (9, 0)$

These points will lie on the x-axis. Hence, we say that our given statement is true.

(iii) The coordinates of the origin are $(0, 0)$.

Origin is the intersection of the x-axis and y-axis. This means that the coordinates of the origin will be the intersection of lines $y = 0$ and $x = 0$.

Hence, the coordinates of the origin are $(0, 0)$.

∴ The given statement is true.

(iv) Points whose x and y coordinates $(0, 0)$, $(1, 1), (2, 2)$ etc., are equal and lie on a line passing through the origin.

For the above statement, we can conclude that our statement satisfies the equation $x = y$.

For $x = 0$ and $y = 0$, this equation gets satisfied.

∴ The given statement is true.

SECTION 2
LOGICAL REASONING

Alphabet Test

Learning Objectives : In this chapter, students will learn about:
- ✓ Alphabet Order
- ✓ Alphabet Quibble
- ✓ Alphabet series

CHAPTER SUMMARY

Alphabetical Order

Alphabetical order means arrangement of words as they appear in English dictionary. Alphabetical order is the order in which the beginning letters of these words appear in the English alphabet.

First consider the first letter of each word, arrange the words in the order in which these letters appear in English alphabet.

Example 1: Arrange the given words in alphabetical order.

Moment, Artist, Cricket, Patient, Worship, Neck

Solution: The order of words as per English dictionary is as follows ;

Artist, Cricket, Moment, Neck, Patient, Worship

In some cases, two or more than two words begin with the same letter. Each word should be arranged in the order of second letters in the alphabet.

Example 2: Bucket, Parrot, Mirror, Memory, Crown, Crowd, Cancel, Work, Nose

Solution: The alphabetical order of the given words are as follows :

Bucket, Cancel, Crowd, Crown, Memory, Mirror, Nose, Parrot, Work

If both the first and second letters of two or more words are the same, then arrange these words considering their third letters and so on. If the first, second, third letters of two or more words are the same, then arrange these words considering their fourth letter and so on. This is the way in which the words are arranged.

Example 3: Arrange the given words as per dictionary.

Mountain, Module, Middle, Miracle, Modem.

Solution: The words are arranged as Middle, Miracle, Modem, Module, Mountain.

Example 4: If the following words are arranged in alphabetical order, which word will come in middle?

Lucky, Letter, Light, Life, Luxury.

Solution: The given words are arranged as Letter, Life, Light, Lucky, Luxury.

The word in the middle is Light.

Alphabetical Quibble

In these questions, a letter series is given, be it the English alphabet from A to Z or a randomized sequence of letters. We have to trace the letter satisfying certain given condition as per their position in the given sequence or the sequence obtained by performing certain given operations on the given sequence.

Some alphabetical sequences are based on some particular rule. We have to detect the rule. In this type, number of letters skipped in between adjacent letters in the series increases by one, two or decrease by one, two or so on.

Example 5: If MAT = 34, AT = 21 then what is the value of LATE?

Solution: MAT = 13 + 1 + 20 = 34

AT = 1 + 20 = 21,

LATE = 12 + 1 + 20 + 5 = 38.

Example 6: In alphabet series A B C D E F G H I J K L M N O P Q R S T U V W X Y Z, which letter is exactly midway between F and P?

Solution: Between F and P there are 9 letters namely G H I J K L M N O, in which K is the midway between F and P.

Alphabet Series

In this type, a series of single, pairs or group of letters or combination of letters is given which follows a particular pattern or rule as regards the position of letters in English alphabet. We have to find the certain pattern and find the missing term.

Example 7: ABD, CEH, EHL, ?

Solution:

1st letter $A \xrightarrow{+2} C \xrightarrow{+2} E \xrightarrow{+2} G$

2nd letter $B \xrightarrow{+3} E \xrightarrow{+3} H \xrightarrow{+3} K$

3rd letter $D \xrightarrow{+4} H \xrightarrow{+4} L \xrightarrow{+4} P$

The missing term is GKP.

MULTIPLE CHOICE QUESTIONS

1. If ZOO stands for 56, DEER stands for 32 then for which numerical value does LION stand for?
   (a) 48 (b) 49
   (c) 50 (d) 51

2. If JEANS = 49, COAT = 39 then SHIRT = ?
   (a) 71 (b) 72
   (c) 73 (d) 74

3. If BUD = 27, ROSE = 57 then FLOWER = ?
   (a) 77 (b) 78
   (c) 79 (d) 80

4. BMX, DNW, FOV, ?
   (a) HQS (b) HPU
   (c) HPS (d) IPT

5. UPI, SHJ, ODP, MBQ, ?
   (a) IAW (b) IBV
   (c) IAV (d) JAW

6. AYD, BVF, ? , GMJ.
   (a) DSH (b) CRH
   (c) DRH (d) DRI

7. BMZ, EPY, HSX, ?
   (a) KUW (b) KVW
   (c) KTV (d) KTW

8. DF, GJ, KM, NQ, ?
   (a) RT (b) RS
   (c) ST (d) None of these

9. GH, JL NQ, SW, YD, ?
   (a) FL (b) EL
   (c) FK (d) GK

10. WFB, TGD, QHF, ?
    (a) NHJ (b) NHK
    (c) NIH (d) MIJ

Direction (11 to 15): Arrange the given words in alphabetical order and choose the one that comes first.

11. (a) Quarter (b) Quality
    (c) Qualify (d) Quarrel

12. (a) Science (b) Security
    (c) Service (d) Secure

13. (a) Social (b) Society
    (c) Soil (d) Sock

14. (a) Discipline (b) Distill
    (c) Disney (d) Disorder

15. (a) Centre (b) Constant
    (c) Consent (d) Cotton

Direction (16 to 20): Arrange the given words in the alphabetical order and choose the word that comes last.

16. (a) Agriculture (b) Accurate
    (c) Assignment (d) Attention

17. (a) Resume (b) Registration
    (c) Registrar (d) Restriction

18. (a) Hill (b) Honest
    (c) Holiday (d) Hunter

19. (a) Train (b) Test
    (c) Triple (d) Treat

20. (a) Earn (b) Else
    (c) Empty (d) Eager

Direction (21 to 30): Each of the following question is based on the following alphabet series.
A B C D E F G H I J K L M N O P Q R S T U V W X Y Z.

21. Which letter is fifth to the right of ninth letter from the left end of the alphabet?
    (a) M (b) N
    (c) L (d) P

22. If the order of English alphabet is reversed then which letter would be exactly in the middle?
    (a) N (b) M
    (c) L (d) None of these

23. If only first half of the given alphabet is reversed, how many letters will be there between J and S?
    (a) 12 (b) 13
    (c) 14 (d) 15

24. Which letter in the alphabet is as far from G as T is from M?
    (a) M (b) N
    (c) D (d) P

International Mathematics Olympiad – 8

25. If the given alphabets are written in the reverse order then which letter would be sixth letter to the right of P?
    (a) L (b) K
    (c) J (d) J
26. If the second half of the given alphabet is reversed then which letter will be seventh letter to the right of K?
    (a) W (b) V
    (c) U (d) T
27. If first ten letters of the given alphabet is reversed then which letter will be 4th letter to the right of L?
    (a) O (b) P
    (c) Q (d) R
28. Which letter will be exactly midway between P and Z?
    (a) S (b) T
    (c) U (d) V
29. Which letter will be exactly midway between N and V if the alphabet is written in reverse order?
    (a) S (b) R
    (c) Q (d) P
30. Which letter will be the fifth to the left of 17th letter from the right end of the alphabet?
    (a) F (b) E
    (c) D (d) G

Odd One Out 2

Learning Objectives : In this chapter, students will learn about:
- ✓ Solving questions related to Odd one out

CHAPTER SUMMARY

In these types of questions, four words or numbers or pair of numbers are given. Out-of these three of them are almost similar to each other, but one is different. We have to choose the odd one from four options. In case of numbers, three numbers are related in some particular manner or rule but one does not fulfil that condition or rule. We have to choose the odd one from the various numbers or pair of numbers. The various examples are as follows :

Choose the odd one.

Example 1: (a) Broker (b) Customer
(c) Hawker (d) Salesman

Solution: (b) All others earn from the customer.

Example 2: (a) Walrus (b) Koala
(c) Alpaca (d) Beaver

Solution: (a) All others are fur-bearing animals.

Example 3: (a) Crank (b) Brakes
(c) Steering (d) Wheel

Solution: (a) All others are mechanical parts of a four wheeler vehicle.

Example 4: (a) Health (b) Sickness
(c) Illness (d) Disease

Solution: (a) All others are disorder of health.

Example 5: (a) 43 (b) 39
(c) 79 (d) 89

Solution: (b) All others are prime numbers.

Example 6: (a) 443 (b) 486
(c) 576 (d) 728

Solution: (c) All others are not a perfect square of a number but 576 is square of a number.

Example 7: (a) 7658 (b) 9674
(c) 6857 (d) 5683

Solution: (d) In all others, the sum of all digits is 26.

Example 8: (a) 198 – 22 (b) 225 – 25
(c) 239 – 23 (d) 117 – 13

Solution: (c) In all others, first number is 9 times the second number.

Example 9: (a) 13 (40) 8 (b) 18 (48) 12
(c) 22 (24) 19 (d) 27 (28) 23

Solution: (d) In all others, the middle number is 8 times the difference of outside numbers.

MULTIPLE CHOICE QUESTIONS

Direction : Choose the odd one from the given group.

1. (a) Spanner (b) Shovel
   (c) Spade   (d) Rave
2. (a) Harbour (b) Island
   (c) Coast   (d) Oasis
3. (a) Fibula   (b) Appendix
   (c) Pelvis   (d) Vertebra
4. (a) Siachen (b) Sambhar
   (c) Chilka   (d) Bail
5. (a) Optics   (b) Physics
   (c) Mechanics (d) Dyamics
6. (a) X-ray   (b) Computer
   (c) Telephone (d) Television
7. (a) Square   (b) triangle
   (c) Cube   (d) Rectangle
8. (a) Glue   (b) Paste
   (c) Cement   (d) Oil
9. (a) Town   (b) State
   (c) District (d) Metropolis
10. (a) Direct (b) Advice
    (c) Suggest (d) Counsel
11. (a) Natraj (b) Diana
    (c) Apollo (d) Olympus
12. (a) Declare (b) Depend
    (c) Confess (d) Admit
13. (a) Dock   (b) Park
    (c) Bus-Stand (d) Plat form
14. (a) Mizoram (b) Sikkim
    (c) Manipur (d) Kohima
15. (a) Cub   (b) Kitten
    (c) Doe   (d) Infant

Direction: Choose the odd numeral group

16. (a) 361   (b) 381   (c) 324   (d) 484
17. (a) 216   (b) 343   (c) 514   (d) 729
18. (a) 1315 (b) 2057 (c) 3216 (d) 5317
19. (a) 4625 (b) 3628 (c) 8352 (d) 8964
20. (a) 7894 (b) 9478 (c) 8259 (d) 8965
21. (a) 2356 (b) 7698 (c) 8574 (d) 9672
22. (a) 4678 (b) 2894 (c) 3786 (d) 4675
23. (a) 6538 (b) 4756 (c) 3475 (d) 7319

Direction: Choose the odd numeral pair/group.

24. (a) 7124 – 7421   (b) 8673 – 8763
    (c) 3259 – 9532   (d) 4582 – 2458
25. (a) (843, 924)   (b) (643, 481)
    (c) (962, 573)   (d) (673, 592)
26. (a) 36 – 216   (b) 48 – 342
    (c) 81 – 729   (d) 25 – 125
27. (a) 239 – 75   (b) 140 – 45
    (c) 170 – 55   (d) 110 – 35
28. (a) 119 – 17   (b) 147 – 21
    (c) 158 – 24   (d) 203 – 29
29. (a) 13 (48) 11   (b) 25 (141) 22
    (c) 17 (81) 14   (d) 35 (201) 32
30. (a) 17 (204) 6   (b) 24 (188) 6
    (c) 19 (266) 7   (d) 27 (270) 5

Coding Decoding 3

Learning Objectives : In this chapter, students will learn about:
- ✓ Letter Coding
- ✓ Number/Symbol coding
- ✓ Substitution coding

CHAPTER SUMMARY

Coding is a method of transmitting a message between the sender and receiver without a third person knowing it.

There are various types of coding like Letter coding, Direct letter coding, Number/Symbol coding, etc.

Letter Coding

In letter coding, the letters in a word are replaced by certain other letters according to a particular rule to form its code. The candidate is required to detect the coding pattern and answer the question according to that pattern.

Direct Letter Coding

In direct letter coding particular letters are made code for particular letters without there being any set patterns. In direct coding, the code letters occur in the same sequence as the corresponding letters occur in the words.

Number/Symbol Coding

In number/symbol coding numerical code values are assigned in a word or alphabetical code letters are assigned to the numbers. The candidate is required to analyze the rule as per the question.

Substitution Coding

In substitution, some particular words are assigned certain substituted names. The candidate has to analyze the given substitution properly and then answer carefully.

Example 1: If POND is coded as RSTL. How is HAIR coded in this language?

Solution:

$$P \xrightarrow{+2} O \xrightarrow{+4} N \xrightarrow{+6} D \xrightarrow{+8} \rightarrow R\ S\ T\ L$$

$$H \xrightarrow{+2} A \xrightarrow{+4} I \xrightarrow{+6} R \xrightarrow{+8} \rightarrow J\ E\ O\ Z$$

HAIR → JEOZ

Example 2: If the word PORTER can be coded as MBNZQN, how can REPORT be written?

Solution: P O R T E R
              ↓ ↓ ↓ ↓ ↓ ↓
              M B N Z Q N

R E P O R T → N Q M B N Z.

Example 3: If O = 16, FOR = 42 then what is MORAL equal to?

Solution: In this code, A = 2; B = 3; C = 4; ......
O = 16; .... Z = 27
MORAL = 14 + 16 + 19 + 2 + 13 = 64.

Example 4: If ENGLAND is written as 123456, FRANCE is written as 785291, what is the code for GREECE?

Solution:
E N G L A N D   F R A N C E
↓ ↓ ↓ ↓ ↓ ↓ ↓   ↓ ↓ ↓ ↓ ↓ ↓
1 2 3 4 5 2 6   7 8 5 2 9 1

then G R E E C E
       ↓ ↓ ↓ ↓ ↓ ↓
       3 8 1 1 9 1

Example 5: In a certain code ROAD is coded as URDG. What is the code for SMILE in that system?

Solution:

R O A D → U R D G (each letter +3)

S   M   I   L   E
↓+3 ↓+3 ↓+3 ↓+3 ↓+3
V   P   L   O   H

Example 6: If GO = 105; DO = 60 then what is the code for DEAR?

Solution: A = 1, B = 2, ... Z = 26.

GO = 7 × 15 = 105; DO = 4 × 15 = 60.

DEAR = 4 × 5 × 1 × 18 = 20 × 18 = 360.

360 is code for DEAR.

MULTIPLE CHOICE QUESTIONS

1. In a certain code, HAND is written as SZMW, then what will be the code of MILK?
   (a) NROP (b) NOPR
   (c) NORP (d) RNOP

2. In a certain code TURN is written as VWTP, then how is WALK written in that code?
   (a) VCMN (b) YCNM
   (c) YBMN (d) YCON

3. In a coding language GUAVA is coded as HVBWB, then how is JUICE written in that language?
   (a) KVHEF (b) KVJDF
   (c) KVIEG (d) KUJDT

4. In a certain code JUMP is written as ITLO, then how is ROUND written in that code?
   (a) QMSMB (b) QNTMC
   (c) QMTLB (d) QNTME

5. If AT = 21; CAT = 24 then what is code for MAT?
   (a) 34 (b) 35 (c) 33 (d) 36

6. If NAGPUR is written as GPAUNR, Then how STRONG is written in that code?
   (a) ROTSGN (b) ROTNSG
   (c) ROTNGS (d) RTONGS

7. In a certain code CONDEMN is written as CNODMEN. How will TEACHER be written in that code?
   (a) TAEHCER (b) TAECHRE
   (c) TAECEHR (d) TEACERH

8. In a coding system, SHEEP is written as GAXXR and BLEAT as HPXTN. How can SEAT be coded?
   (a) GXTN (b) GTXN
   (c) GNTX (d) GNXT

9. If AT = 20; CAT = 60 then what is the value of MAT in that language?
   (a) 260 (b) 250
   (c) 240 (d) 270

10. If ZIP = 198 and ZAP = 246 then how will you code VIP?
    (a) 222 (b) 220 (c) 122 (d) 102

11. If BAT = 40; CAT = 60 then how will you code GOAT?
    (a) 2100 (b) 1200 (c) 2050 (d) 1050

12. If ZOO = 25; GO = 32; then how will you code GOAL?
    (a) 73 (b) 35 (c) 37 (d) 71

13. If ZEAL = 44; MEAL = 31 then what is the value of SEAL in that code?
    (a) 47 (b) 37 (c) 27 (d) 57

14. If FAIR is coded as 1234, TAIL is coded as 7239 then what is code for TRIAL?
    (a) 72439 (b) 74239
    (c) 74329 (d) None of these

15. If MEDICINE is coded as EOJDJEFM then how is HONEST coded in that code?
    (a) TTFOPH (b) TFTOPH
    (c) TTOFPH (d) TTOFIT

16. In a certain coding, ROAST is coded as PQYUR then how will CROWD be coded in that coding language?
    (a) ATMYB (b) AMTYB
    (c) ATMBY (d) AMTBY

17. In a certain coding pattern, HEALTH is coded as GSKZDG then how will STARCH be written in that code?
    (a) GQBZSR (b) GBQZSR
    (c) GBQRSZ (d) GBQZRS

18. If BOMBAY is written as MYMYMY, how will MADRAS be written in that code?
    (a) SDSASD (b) DSDSDS
    (c) RDRDED (d) DRDRDR

19. If SYSTEM is coded as SYSMET and NEARER as AENRER then BRIGHT will be coded as
    (a) IRBTHG (B) IRBGHT
    (c) BRITHG (d) None of these

20. In a certain code RAIL is written as KCTN and SPEAK is written as CGRUM. How will NIGHT be coded in that code?
    (a) JIKVP (b) JHKPV
    (c) JIKPV (d) IJKPV

21. In a coding language STOVE is written as FNBLK then how will VOTES be coded in that language?
    (a) LBKNF
    (b) LBNKF
    (c) LNBKF
    (d) None of these

22. If MACHINE is coded as 19 – 7 – 9 – 14 – 15 – 20 – 11 then how will ORANGE be coded in that language?
    (a) 21 – 23 – 7 – 19 – 13 – 11
    (b) 21 – 24 – 7 – 20 – 13 – 11
    (c) 21 – 24 – 7 – 20 – 14 – 11
    (d) 22 – 24 – 8 – 19 – 13 – 11

23. In a code language EAT is written as 318 and PAINT as 71548 then how can PATIENT be coded?
    (a) 7185348
    (b) 7138348
    (c) 7158438
    (d) 7185483

24. In a certain code, FILE is coded as 7465, MAN is coded as 823, then how will FEMALE be coded in that code?
    (a) 785265
    (b) 785265
    (c) 758265
    (d) 758526

25. If ANSWER is coded as 5 and FOUNDER is coded as 6 then what is the code for COMMUNICATION?
    (a) 13   (b) 12   (c) 11   (d) 14

26. If L = 12, CAT = 8, then how will HOTEL be coded in that code?
    (a) 12   (b) 14   (c) 13   (d) 15

27. If HAIR = 8, EAGLE = 10 then what is the code for BUILDING?
    (a) 14   (b) 16   (c) 12   (d) 18

28. If COBRA is coded as 3152181 then what is the code for FARMER?
    (a) 611813518   (b) 611612518
    (c) 611712516   (d) None of these

29. In a certain code language, BEAT is written as YVZG, then what will be the code of MILD?
    (a) NROW   (b) NOWR
    (c) ONWR   (d) ONRW

30. If in a certain code, LUTE is written as MUTE and FATE is written as GATE, then how will BLUE be written in that code?
    (a) GLUE   (b) CLUE
    (c) FLUE   (d) SLUE

Direction Sense Test   4

Learning Objectives: In this chapter, students will learn about:
✓ Solving questions related to direction sense test

CHAPTER SUMMARY

As the name specifies, these type of questions are based on various directions. In other words, these questions are called direction puzzles. The adjoining figure shows four main directions namely North, South, East and West. There are four cardinal directions namely North-East (NE), North-West (NW), South-East (SE) and South-West (SW).

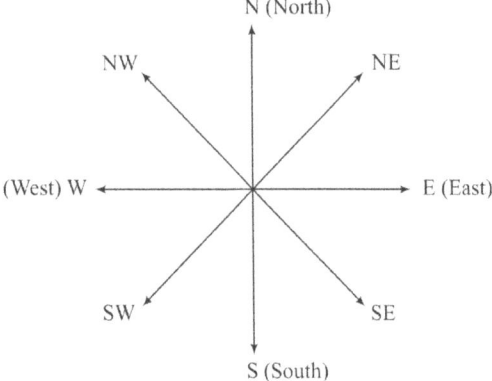

In these types of questions, a successive follow up of directions is formulated. The candidate is required to decide the final direction or distance between starting and ending points. Direction sense test check the candidate's ability to trace and sense the direction correctly.

The diagram is very essential in direction sense problems.

Example 1: Mohan faces towards North. Turning to his right he move 15 m, he then turns to his left and walks 20 m. Then he moves 30 m to his right. He then turns to his right and walks 45 m. Finally he turns to his right and moves 40 m. In which direction is he now from his starting point?

Solution: Here Starting point = A,
Ending point = F

Then final direction is in South-East from starting Point.

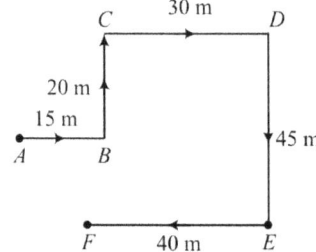

Example 2: Ankur walked 20 m towards East took a right turn and walked 30m, then again he took a right turn and walked 20m. In which direction is he now from the starting position?

Solution:

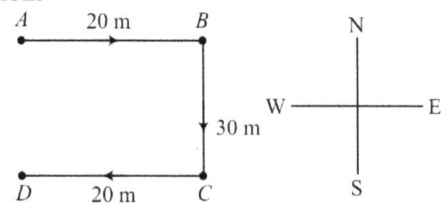

Here Starting point = A,
Ending point = D
Direction of D from A is in South.
Hence, Ankur is in South direction.

Example 3: It is 9 O' clock in the watch. If the hour hand point towards North then what is the direction of minute hand?

Solution:

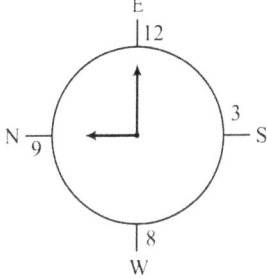

From figure it is clear that minute hand is in East direction.

Example 4: If South-East becomes North, North-East becomes West then what is new direction for West?

Solution:

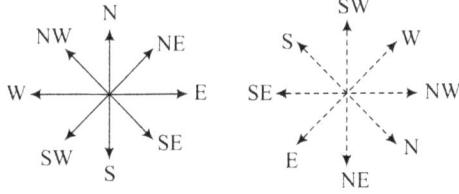

New direction for West is South-East.

Example 5: Mohan walks 10 m towards East and 20m towards South and 10m towards West. What distance and in which direction is he now from his starting position?

Solution:

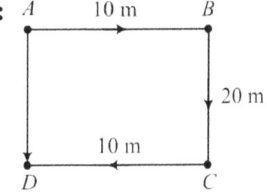

Final Position = D

which is 20 m towards South from starting point A.

MULTIPLE CHOICE QUESTIONS

1. Nitesh faces towards North. Turning to his right he walks 20 meters. He then turns to his left and walks 20 meters, then he moves 30 m to his right then turns to his right again and walks 45 meters. At last he turns to his right and moves 35 meters. In which direction is he now from the starting position?
   (a) South   (b) South-East
   (c) South-West   (d) North-East

2. Ranjan is looking for Ratan. He went 90m towards the East before turning to his right. He went 20m before turning to his right again to look, for Ratan at Mohan's position 30m from this point. Ratan was not there. From that point he went 100m to his North before meeting Ratan. What is the shortest distance between Ranjan's starting point and Ratan's position?
   (a) 60 m   (b) 80 m
   (c) 100 m   (d) 120 m

3. Dinesh walks 10m towards East and 10m to the right then turning to his left three times he walks 5m, 15m, 15 m respectively. How far is he from his starting position?
   (a) 5 m   (b) 10 m
   (c) 15 m   (d) None of these

4. Pritam walks 15m towards South then turning to his right he walks 30m then turning to his left he walks 20m. Again he turns to his left and walks 30m. How far is he from his starting position?
   (a) 25 m   (b) 35 m
   (c) 45 m   (d) 55 m

5. Ankit is facing East. He turns $100°$ in the clockwise direction and then $145°$ in the anticlockwise direction. In which direction is he facing now?
   (a) North East   (b) East
   (c) North-West   (d) South-West

6. Nishi walked 20m towards North, took a left turn and walked 10m. She again took a left turn and walked 20m. How far and in which direction is she from starting point?
   (a) 5 m, West   (b) 10 m, East
   (c) 5 m, East   (d) 10 m, West

7. Milan walks 10m towards North. From there he walks 6m towards South. Then he walks 3m toward East. How far and in which direction is he with reference to the starting point?
   (a) 5 m, North-West (b) 5 m, North-East
   (c) 7 km, East   (d) 7 m, West

8. Nitu leave from her house, she first walks 20 m in North-West direction and then 20 m in South West direction. Next she walks 20 m in South East direction. At last she turns towards her house. In which direction is she moving?
   (a) North West   (b) North-East
   (c) South-east   (d) None of these

9. Arman is facing South. Arman turns right and walk 20m. Then he turns right again and walk 10m. Then he turns left and walk 10m and then turning right walk 20m. Then he turns right again and walk some distance. In which direction is he from the initial point?
   (a) North-West   (b) East
   (c) North-East   (d) West

10. Mohit walked 30 m towards East, took a right turn and walked 50m then he took a left turn and walked 30m. In which direction is he now from initial point?
    (a) East   (b) South
    (c) South-East   (d) North-East

11. It is 3 O clock in a watch. If the minute hand points towards the North-East then what is the direction of hour hand?
    (a) South West   (b) South
    (c) South-East   (d) North-West

12. Hari is 40m South-West of Rohit. Sukeah is to the East of Rohit. Then Sukeah is in which direction of Hari?
    (a) South   (b) West
    (c) East   (d) North-East

13. Rata walked 30m towards South. Then he turn to his left and walked 25m. He then turned to his left and walked 30m. He again turned to his right and walked 35m. At what

International Mathematics Olympiad – 8

distance and in which direction is he from the starting point?
(a) 35 m, West (b) 35 m, East
(c) 60 m, West (d) 60 m, East

14. Kishan goes 30m North then turns right and walked 50m, then again turns right and walks 20m then again turns right and walks 50m. What is the distance of new position from original position?
(a) 5 m (b) 10 m
(c) 15 m (d) 20 m

15. Manas is facing South. He turns 135° in the anticlock-wise direction and then 180° in the clock-wise direction. Which direction is he facing now?
(a) West (b) South-West
(c) South (d) South-East

16. Rina walks 18m towards West then she turns to her right and walks 18m and then turns to her left and walks 13m. Again turning to her left she walks 18m. What is the shortest distance between her starting point and new position?
(a) 13 m (b) 18 m
(c) 15 m (d) 31 m

17. From his house, Mihir went 15km to the North then he turned West and covered 10km. Then he turned South and covered 5km. Finally turning to East he covered 10km. In which direction is he from his house?
(a) South (b) North
(c) East (d) West

18. Going 70m to the South of her house Madhu turns left and goes another 20m. Then she turns towards North and covers 40m and starts walking to her house. In which direction is she walking now?
(a) North (b) North-West
(c) East (d) South-East

19. Aman is facing North-West. He turns 90° in the clockwise direction and then 135° in the anti-clockwise direction. In which direction is he facing now?
(a) East (b) North
(c) West (d) South

20. John went 15km to the West from my house then turned left and walked 20km. He then turned East and walked 25km. And finally turning left he walked 20km. How far is he from his house?
(a) 10 km (b) 15 km
(c) 20 km (d) 40 km

21. A,B,C,D,E,F,G,H are sitting around a round table in the same order for group discussion at equal distances. Their positions are clockwise. If G sits in the North, then what will be the position of D?
(a) South-West (b) East
(c) South (d) South-East

22. Shankar wants to go to the college. He starts from his house which is in the East and reaches a crossing. The road to the left ends in a Hospital, straight ahead is the Library. In which direction is the college if all are in different directions?
(a) East (b) West
(c) South (d) North

23. A watch reads 4:30. If the hour hand points towards North-East, in which direction is the minute hand?
(a) East (b) West
(c) South (d) North

24. If North is called South-West, South-West is called East, North-West is called South then what is West called?
(a) South-East (b) North east
(c) South west (d) North west

25. Lalit is facing West. He turns 45° in the clockwise direction and then another 180° in the same direction and then 270° in the anti-clock wise direction. In which direction is he facing now?
(a) North west (b) South West
(c) West (d) South

Direction Sense Test

Series Completion 5

Learning Objectives : In this chapter, students will learn about:
- ✓ Solving questions related to series completion

CHAPTER SUMMARY

In series completion, a series of numbers or letters or combination of both numbers and letters are given. Each of the numbers and letters is called as term of the series. The terms of the series follow a particular pattern throughout the series. The candidate has to analyze the series and find out the certain pattern which is applied for whole of the series. Basically series completion is based on numbers. Each succeeding terms of the series may be obtained by adding, subtracting, multiplying or dividing by some number, which is same for whole of the series. Sometimes the alternate terms of the series obeys a certain pattern. So, we have to analyze the term of the series and then find out the missing term or wrong term in the given series. The candidate should study the given series, identify the pattern followed in the series and either complete the given series with most suitable alternative or find the wrong term in the given series.

In some series, there is a combination of two series. Candidate has to analyze the given series and answer the suitable answer.

Example 1: Find the next term in 895, 870, 821, 740, 619, 450, ……….
- (a) 220
- (b) 225
- (c) 230
- (d) 240

Solution: (b) 225

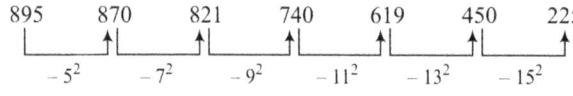

$450 - 225 = 225$

Example 2: Find the next term in 2, 6, 16, 38, 84, ……….
- (a) 176
- (b) 180
- (c) 178
- (d) 172

Solution: (c) 178

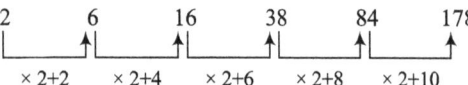

Example 3: Find the next term in 32, 36, 45, 61, 86, 122, 171, ……….
- (a) 235
- (b) 236
- (c) 234
- (d) 240

Solution: (a) 235

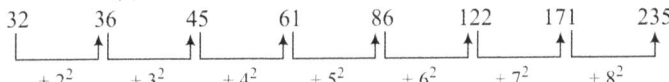

Example 4: Find the wrong term in the series 445, 221, 109, 46, 25, 11, 4.

    (a) 221   (b) 109

    (c) 25   (d) 46

Solution: (d) 46

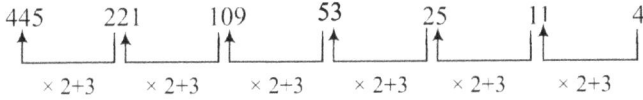

$25 \times 2 + 3 = 50 + 3 = 53$

So, 46 is the wrong term.

Example 5: Find the wrong term in the series 13, 16, 21, 28, 36, 48, 61.

    (a) 36   (b) 48

    (c) 28   (d) 61

Solution: (a) 36

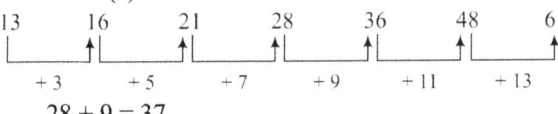

$28 + 9 = 37$

So, 36 is the wrong term.

Example 6: Find the wrong term in the series 2880, 480, 92, 24, 8, 4, 4

    (a) 92   (b) 480

    (c) 24   (d) 2880

Solution: (a) 92

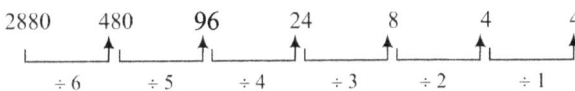

$24 \times 4 = 96$. So, 92 is wrong term.

MULTIPLE CHOICE QUESTIONS

Direction: Find the next term in the following series.

1. 6, 15, 28, 45, 66, ...?
   (a) 91   (b) 92
   (c) 93   (d) 94

2. 12, 19, 28, 39, 52, ?
   (a) 65   (b) 66
   (c) 67   (d)

3. 10, 22, 46, 94, ?
   (a) 189   (b) 190
   (c) 191   (d) 192

4. 15, 31, 63, 127, 255, ?
   (a) 508   (b) 510
   (c) 511   (d) 512

5. 40320, 5760, 960, 192, 48, ...?
   (a) 14   (b) 16
   (c) 18   (d) 22

6. 13, 25, 41, 61, 85, ?
   (a) 112   (b) 113
   (c) 114   (d) 115

7. 402, 325, 259, 204, 160, 127, ?
   (a) 102   (b) 103
   (c) 104   (d) 105

8. 8, 28, 116, 584, 3508, ?
   (a) 24560   (b) 24556
   (c) 24558   (d) 24562

9. 1, 4, 10, 22, 46, 94, ?
   (a) 190   (b) 192
   (c) 194   (d) 196

10. 168, 143, 120, 99, 80, 63, ?
    (a) 45   (b) 46
    (c) 47   (d) 48

11. 15, 16, 20, 29, 45, ?
    (a) 68   (b) 69
    (c) 70   (d) 71

12. 8, 14, 26, 50, 98, 194, ?
    (a) 386   (b) 384
    (c) 388   (d) 382

13. 325, 259, 204, 160, 127, 105, ?
    (a) 92   (b) 93
    (c) 94   (d) 95.

14. 7, 15, 31, 63, 127, ?
    (a) 253   (b) 254
    (c) 255   (d) 256

15. 5, 24, 61, 122, 213, ?
    (a) 338   (b) 339
    (c) 340   (d) None of these

16. 2, 5, 9, 14, 20, ?
    (a) 27   (b) 28
    (c) 29   (d) None of these

17. 28, 33, 31, 36, 34, ?
    (a) 31   (b) 38
    (c) 39   (d) 14.

18. 3, 4, 10, 33, 136, ?
    (a) 682   (b) 683
    (c) 684   (d) 685.

19. 25, 49, 81, 121, 169, 225, ?
    (a) 264   (b) 266
    (c) 288   (d) 289

20. 9, 27, 31, 155, 161, ?
    (a) 1123   (b) 1124
    (c) 1127   (d) None of these

21. 12, 23, 45, 78, 122, ?
    (a) 165   (b) 166
    (c) 177   (d) 168

22. 2, 3, 8, 27, 112, ?
    (a) 565   (b) 566
    (c) 567   (d) 568

23. 45, 68, 91, 114, ?
    (a) 135   (b) 136
    (c) 137   (d) 138.

24. 67, 92, 117, 142, 167, 192, ?
    (a) 223   (b) 214
    (c) 217   (d) 226

25. 125, 138, 151, 164, 177, ?
    (a) 190   (b) 191
    (c) 192   (d) 193

International Mathematics Olympiad – 8

Pattern 6

Learning Objectives : In this chapter, students will learn about:
- Solving questions related to pattern

CHAPTER SUMMARY

In these types of questions, a figure, set of figures, an arrangement or a matrix is given, each of which be it numbers, letters or a group or combination of letters or numbers, follows a certain pattern. The candidate is required to analyze the pattern and find the missing character in the figure.

In pattern, the missing character is obtained by adding, subtracting, multiplying or dividing by some number and by proper analyisation of pattern. In figure type, the middle term is the addition of all the given terms or addition of squares of each term or square of addition of all given terms. Sometimes the left part of figure has exactly the same relation as the right part of the figure. There are questions as per magic square. The candidate has skills to find the certain rule to find the missing character. The candidate should know various basic mathematical operations, square, cube etc. and relate them accordingly.

Example 1:

2	4	3
3	5	7
4	6	8
81	225	?

Solution: $(2 + 3 + 4)^2 = 9^2 = 81$
$(4 + 5 + 6)^2 = 15^2 = 225$
$\therefore ? = (3 + 7 + 8)^2 = 18^2 = 324$

Example 2:

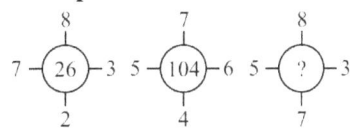

Solution: $(8 - 7)^2 + (3 + 2)^2 = 1 + 25 = 26$.
$(7 - 5)^2 + (6 + 4)^2 = 4 + 100 = 104$
$\therefore ? = (8 - 5)^2 + (3 + 7)^2$
$= 9 + 100 = 109$

Example 3:

6	12	15
7	6	6
8	4	16
42	36	?

Solution: $\dfrac{6 \times 7 \times 8}{8} = 42$; $\dfrac{12 \times 6 \times 4}{8} = 36$;

$\therefore ? = \dfrac{15 \times 6 \times 16}{8} = 180$

Example 4:
723 (180) 546   278 (136) 341   839 (?) 365

Solution:
$(7 + 2 + 3) \times (5 + 4 + 6) = 12 \times 15 = 180$
$(2 + 7 + 8) \times (3 + 4 + 1) = 17 \times 8 = 136$
$\therefore ? = (8 + 3 + 9) \times (3 + 6 + 5) = 20 \times 14 = 280$

Example 5:

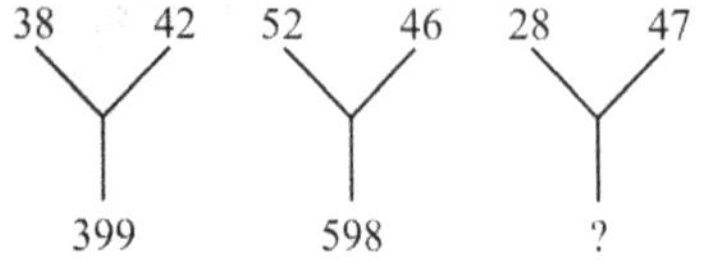

38 42   52 46   28 47
 Y   Y   Y
399   598   ?

Solution:

$\dfrac{38 \times 42}{4} = 399$; $\dfrac{52 \times 46}{4} = 598$;

$\therefore ? = \dfrac{28 \times 47}{4} = 329$

Example 6:

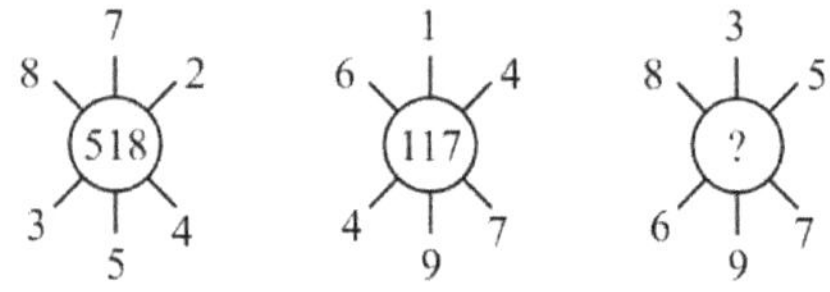

Solution: $872 - 354 = 518$; $614 - 497 = 117$;

$\therefore ? = 835 - 697 = 138$;

MULTIPLE CHOICE QUESTIONS

1.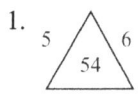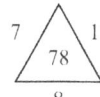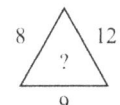
   (a) 85 (b) 86
   (c) 87 (d) 89

2.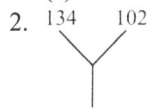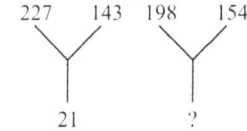
   (a) 11 (b) 12
   (c) 13 (d) 14

3.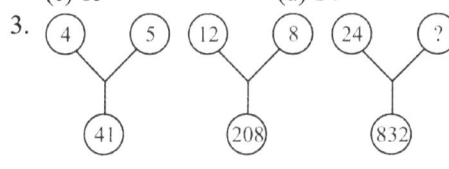
   (a) 14 (b) 16
   (c) 18 (d) 20

4.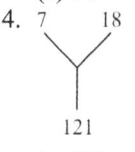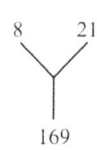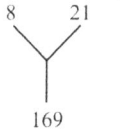
   (a) 121 (b) 144
   (c) 169 (d) 196

5.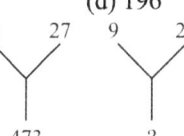
   (a) 446 (b) 448 (c) 456 (d) 458

6.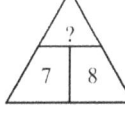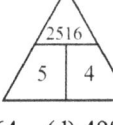
   (a) 4932 (b) 4916 (c) 4964 (d) 4981

7.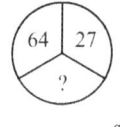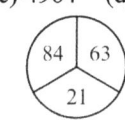
   (a) 11 (b) 12
   (c) 13 (d) 14

8.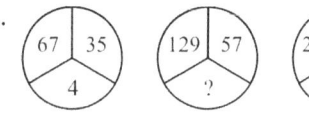
   (a) 8 (b) 9 (c) 10 (d) 12

9.
96	
16	12

162	
18	18

168	
?	24

   (a) 12 (b) 14 (c) 16 (d) 18

10.
112	
28	16

276	
48	23

304	
?	19

    (a) 64 (b) 14 (c) 84 (d) 68

11.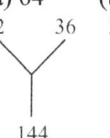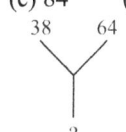
    (a) 392 (b) 394 (c) 302 (d) 304

12.
	8	
4	132	13
	7	

	5	
6	139	17
	9	

	6	
7	?	23
	6	

    (a) 270 (b) 172 (c) 180 (d) 190

13.
	11	
12	90	18
	9	

	13	
15	130	25
	13	

	17	
16	?	28
	13	

    (a) 238 (b) 248 (c) 268 (d) 278

14.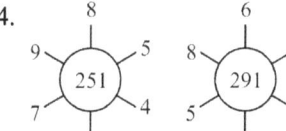
    (a) 266 (b) 256
    (c) 356 (d) None of these

15.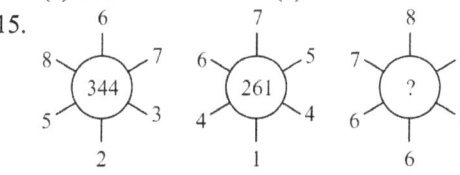
    (a) 142 (b) 132 (c) 122 (d) 112

Pattern

16. 83 (40) 27   96 (81) 84   79 (?) 68
    (a) 60   (b) 70   (c) 61   (d) 80

17.
5	7	8
2	1	3
3	6	4
38	86	?

(a) 98   (b) 89   (c) 69   (d) 79

18.
7	6	8
2	8	9
3	4	5
35	72	?

(a) 92   (b) 102   (c) 112   (d) 117

19.
8	6	9
5	2	3
9	7	8
27	28	?

(a) 96   (b) 48   (c) 45   (d) 68

20.
16	32	27
12	11	16
8	4	9
24	88	?

(a) 48   (b) 64   (c) 52   (d) 62

21. 83 (52) 74   68 (63) 35   92 (?) 27
    (a) 23   (b) 99
    (c) 45   (d) 32

22.
5	12	13
7	24	25
?	15	17

(a) 8   (b) 6
(c) 7   (d) 9

23.
6	7	18
5	6	13
4	5	3
60	105	?

(a) 117   (b) 351
(c) 234   (d) 78

24.
27	18	63
4	7	5
15	12	3
180	168	?

(a) 135   (b) 351
(c) 105   (d) 120

25.
5	8	9
1	6	3
7	?	5
35	144	135

(a) 3   (b) 4
(c) 5   (d) 6

26. 825 (304) 749, 659 (244) 598, 371 (?) 287
    (a) 332   (b) 336
    (c) 328   (d) 326

27. 27 – 5 – 52 – 9 – 38 – 7; 64, ?, 108; 19 – 3 – 37 – 4 – 29 – 5
    (a) 185   (b) 195
    (c) 215   (d) 175

28. 16 – 11 – 19 – 9 – 23 – 9; 1, 17, ?; 13 – 9 – 15 – 8 – 17 – 8
    (a) 21   (b) 31   (c) 41   (d) 51

29. 7, 11, 16; 5 – 13 – 5 – 9 – ? – 7 – 6 – 107 – 4; 6, 8, 13
    (a) 69   (b) 79   (c) 89   (d) 99

30. 4, 7, 12; 2 – 484 – 7 – 8 – ? – 5 – 6 – 1024 – 9; 9, 11, 5
    (a) 861   (b) 961   (c) 981   (d) 1031

Number Ranking   7

Learning Objectives : In this chapter, students will learn about:
- ✓ Solving questions related to number ranking

CHAPTER SUMMARY

As the name specifies, the problem based on number ranking consist of a set, group or series of numerals. We have to trace out the numerals following certain given conditions or lying at particular specified position according to a certain given pattern. We have to analyse the given series of numerals or number sequence and study the pattern to answer the appropriate option.

In the number sequence a number which comes after a given number is said to follow it while the number which comes before the given number precedes it. Sometimes a number is in between two odd numbers or two even numbers or a number is in between two of its factors.

In ranking test, the rank of a particular person from the top and from the bottom are mentioned, and the total number of people is asked. Sometimes the position of two people are inter changed and then we have to find their position from top or bottom.

Example 1: How many odd numbers are there in the series each of which is immediately followed by an even number?

7 2 5 6 8 7 3 2 5 9 6 7 5 3 2 1 4 6

(a) 3   (b) 4
(c) 5   (d) 6

Solution: (d)
7 2 5 6 8 7 3 2 5 9 6 7 5 3 2 1 4 6

Example 2: How many 8's are there in the sequence which is in between 5 and 7?

4 2 8 5 7 6 5 8 7 2 5 8 7 6 9 5 8 7 4

(a) 1   (b) 2
(c) 3   (d) 4

Solution: (c) 4 2 8 5 7 6 **5 8 7** 2 5 **8 7** 6 9 **5 8 7** 4

Example 3: What is the difference between sum of even digits and sum of odd digits in the number 6 8 5 3 4 3 2 5 8 9 ?

(a) 2   (b) 3
(c) 4   (d) 6

Solution: (b) Sum of even digits = 6 + 8 + 4 + 2 + 8 = 28
Sum of odd digits = 5 + 3 + 3 + 5 + 9 = 25
Difference = 28 – 25 = 3

Example 4: Rohan ranks 12th from the total and thirty-seventh from the bottom in a class. How many boys are there?

(a) 45   (b) 47
(c) 48   (d) 52

Solution: (c) Total number of boys
= 11 + 1 + 36 = 48

Example 5: Amit ranks 8th in a class of 70 students. What is his rank from last?

(a) 62   (b) 63
(c) 64   (d) 61

Solution: (b) Amit's rank from last
= (70 – 8) + 1 = 62 + 1 = 63

MULTIPLE CHOICE QUESTIONS

1. How many odd numbers are there in the sequence each of which is immediately followed by an odd number?

   5 1 4 7 3 9 8 5 7 2 6 3 1 5 8 6 3 8 5 2 2 4 3 4 9 6

   (a) 3 (b) 5 (c) 6 (d) 4

2. How many odd numbers are there in the sequence which are immediately preceded and also immediately followed by an even number in the sequence?

   5 1 4 7 3 2 5 6 8 9 6 7 3 2 1 5 6 4 3 2 7 4

   (a) 4 (b) 3 (c) 5 (d) 2

3. How many even numbers are there which are immediately followed by an odd number and also immediately preceded by an odd number in the sequence?

   8 4 7 6 5 3 2 5 1 6 4 3 2 6 7 9 8 5

   (a) 3 (b) 4 (c) 2 (d) 15

4. In the series

   2 5 3 4 8 7 4 2 6 7 1 5 8 3 7 4 5 3

   how many pair of successive numbers have a difference of 3?

   (a) 3 (b) 4 (c) 2 (d) 5

5. How many 5's are there in the sequence which are immediately preceded by 4 and immediately followed by 7?

   2 3 4 5 6 1 4 5 7 1 2 4 5 7 3 8 4 5 9 6 5 3

   (a) 1 (b) 2
   (c) 3 (d) 4

6. How many pair of successive numbers are there in the given series whose sum is 12?

   4 5 7 3 2 8 4 9 1 5 6 4 8 3 1 9 3 5 7

   (a) 2 (b) 3
   (c) 4 (d) 5

7. How many pair of successive numbers are there in the given series whose product is an even number?

   6 1 4 6 3 5 1 7 2 6 3 5 7 1 8 3 7 5

   (a) 6 (b) 7
   (c) 8 (d) 9

8. How many 8's are there in the series which are preceded by 5 but not followed by 7?

   4 3 8 6 5 8 2 3 5 8 4 7 5 8 7 4

   (a) 1 (b) 3
   (c) 2 (d) None of these

9. How many 9's are there in the series which are preceded by 7 but not followed by 8?

   4 2 9 6 7 9 2 4 7 9 8 4 7 9 3 6 8 9

   (a) 1 (b) 2 (c) 3 (d) 4

10. What is the product of sum of even digits and sum of odd digits in the number 8 6 7 4 3 5 2?

    (a) 180 (b) 250 (c) 280 (d) 300

11. What is the difference between the sum of even digits and sum of odd digits in the number 7 4 6 2 5 8 9 3?

    (a) 2 (b) 3 (c) 4 (d) 5

12. If the given series is written in the reverse order which number will be 5th to the right of the seventh number from the left?

    7, 3, 8, 7, 0, 3, 4, 6, 2, 5, 9, 6, 4, 7.

    (a) 4 (b) 5 (c) 7 (d) 3

13. In the given number sequence, how many even numbers are exactly divisible by its immediate preceding number but not exactly divisible by its immediate succeeding number?

    3 5 6 4 8 7 1 2 4 3 6 4 5 2 6 7

    (a) 2 (b) 3 (c) 4 (d) 5

14. From the given numbers

    823, 716, 539, 683, 937

    what will be the first digit of the second highest number after the position of only second and third digits within each number are interchanged?

    (a) 8 (b) 7 (c) 9 (d) 6

15. From the given numbers

    728, 593, 645, 296, 968

    what will be the first digit of the second highest number after the position of only first and third digits within each number are interchanged?

    (a) 5 (b) 6 (c) 7 (d) 8

16. Rohit is 14th from the right end in a row of 70 students. What is his position from left end?
    (a) 54th (b) 56th (c) 57th (d) 58th

17. Manak ranks 5th from the top and third-seventh from the bottom in a class, How many students are there in the class?
    (a) 28 (b) 40 (c) 41 (d) 42

18. Which is the 5th number to the left of the number which is exactly in the middle of the given sequence of numbers?
    6 1 3 5 2 1 7 6 8 4 3 2 1 3 8 9 7 6 8 2 6 9 8 3 4 5 6 7 2
    (a) 2 (b) 3 (c) 4 (d) 5

19. How many numbers from 50 to 150 are there each of which is exactly divisible by 4 and also has 4 as a digit?
    (a) 4 (b) 5 (c) 6 (d) 7

20. How many numbers from 1 to 100 are there which are exactly divisible by 7 but not by 3?
    (a) 7 (b) 8 (c) 9 (d) 10

21. Ranjit ranked fifteenth from the top and forty-sixth from the bottom in a class. How many students are there in the class?
    (a) 60 (b) 62
    (c) 63 (d) 64

22. Sunita ranks fifteenth in a class of 75 students. What is her rank from the last?
    (a) 59 (b) 60
    (c) 61 (d) 62

23. In a class of 45 students, Raju is 7th from the bottom, whereas Samir is placed 9th from the top. Peter is placed exactly in between these two. What is Raju's position from Peter?
    (a) 13 (b) 14 (c) 15 (d) 16

24. Kunal is 6th from the left end and Mohit is 14th from the right end in a row of boys. If there are 12 boys between Kunal and Mohit then how many boys are there in the row?
    (a) 30 (b) 31 (c) 32 (d) 33

25. In a row of boys, if Shankar who is 10th from the left and Mahesh who is 9th from the right interchange their positions, Shankar becomes 15th from the left. How many students are there in the row?
    (a) 23 (b) 24
    (c) 25 (d) 26

26. In a queue, Ankit is 9th from the back and Amrit is 8th from the front. Nitin is standing exactly between these two. What may be the minimum number of boys standing in the queue?
    (a) 8 (b) 9
    (c) 10 (d) 11

27. How many 6's are there in the given series each of which is immediately preceded by 2 or 5 and immediately followed by 3 or 9?
    2 6 3 8 4 3 6 7 5 6 9 1 3 2 6 3 4 7 9 2 6
    (a) 2 (b) 3
    (c) 4 (d) None of these

28. How many numbers are there from 1 to 200 which are exactly divisible by 21 but not by 7?
    (a) 7 (b) 8
    (c) 9 (d) None of these

29. W 1 R % 4 J E # 7 M T 2 I 9 B H 3 A $ 9 F Q 5 D G 6 U S P
    Which of the following is the seventh to the right of the eighteenth from the right end?
    (a) A (b) $
    (c) E (d) #

30. E & G B D M 4 N K H 2 A C Z S V 3 F 1 J L O Q 5 P R
    If every alternate letter/number is dropped (dropping start from E), then which letter/number will be the second to the left of the tenth letter/number from the left end?
    (a) V (b) B
    (c) Q (d) A

Number Ranking

Analytical Reasoning   8

Learning Objectives : In this chapter, students will learn about:
- ✓ Solving questions related to analytical reasoning

CHAPTER SUMMARY

In this chapter, the problems are related to the counting of geometrical figures in a given complex figure.

Example 1: What is the number of straight lines in the following figure?

(a) 10 (b) 12
(c) 13 (d) 17

Solution: (b)

Example 2: How many triangles are there in the following figure?

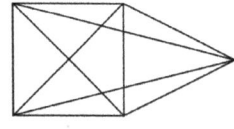

(a) 8 (b) 10
(c) 12 (d) 14

Solution: (c)

Example 3: How many triangles are there in the given figure?

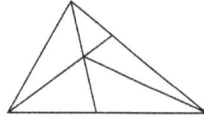

(a) 16 (b) 18
(c) 22 (d) 24.

Solution: (c)

Example 4: What is the number of parallelograms in the given figure?

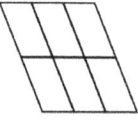

(a) 12 (b) 16
(c) 18 (d) 20

Solution: (c)

Example 5: Find the number of squares in the following figure.

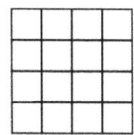

(a) 26 (b) 28
(c) 30 (d) 32

Solution: (c)

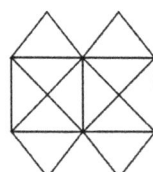

Example 6: In the given figure, what is the number of squares?

(a) 5 (b) 6
(c) 7 (d) 8

Solution: (c)

MULTIPLE CHOICE QUESTIONS

Direction (1 to 11): In each of the following problems, find the number of triangles in the given figure :

1.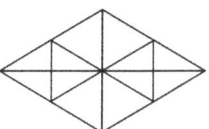

   (a) 22   (b) 24   (c) 28   (d) 32

2.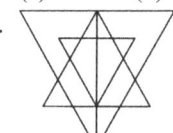

   (a) 22   (b) 23   (c) 25   (d) 27

3.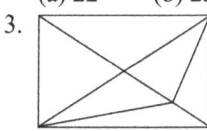

   (a) 14   (b) 15   (c) 16   (d) 17

4.

   (a) 16   (b) 17   (c) 18   (d) 22

5.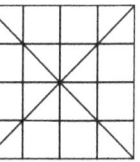

   (a) 48   (b) 46   (c) 52   (d) 56

6.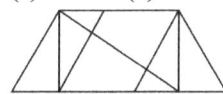

   (a) 12   (b) 14   (c) 16   (d) 18

7.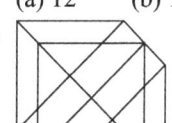

   (a) 22   (b) 24   (c) 26   (d) 28

8.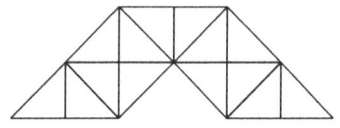

   (a) 27   (b) 29
   (c) 28   (d) 32

9.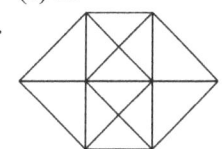

   (a) 19   (b) 21
   (c) 28   (d) 24

10.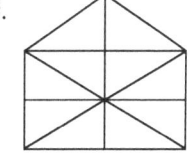

    (a) 21   (b) 19
    (c) 18   (d) 23

11.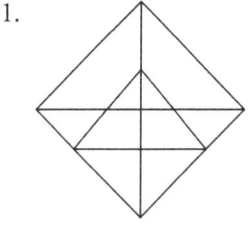

    (a) 17   (b) 18
    (c) 19   (d) 21

Direction (12 to 25): In the following problems, count the number of squares in each figure.

12.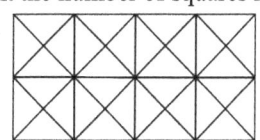

    (a) 24   (b) 27   (c) 26   (d) 28

13.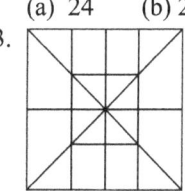

    (a) 14   (b) 16   (c) 18   (d) 20

Analytical Reasoning

14.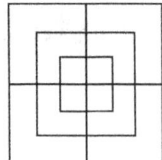
(a) 12 (b) 14 (c) 15 (d) 16

15.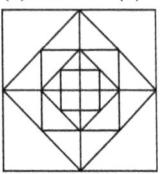
(a) 14 (b) 16 (c) 17 (d) 18

16.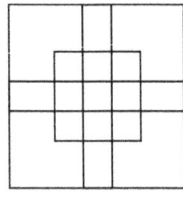
(a) 27 (b) 25 (c) 28 (d) 32

Direction (17 to 20): In the following problems, find the number of parallelograms in each of the following figures.

17.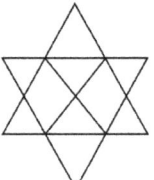
(a) 12 (b) 13 (c) 15 (d) 16

18.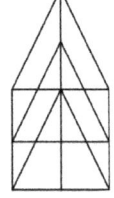
(a) 17 (b) 18 (c) 19 (d) 21

19.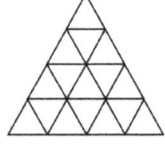
(a) 41 (b) 43 (c) 45 (d) 46

20.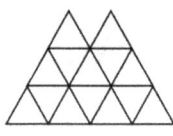
(a) 19 (b) 21 (c) 23 (d) 24

Direction (21 to 25): In the following questions, what is the minimum number of straight lines ?

21.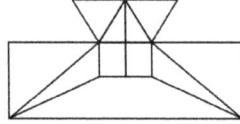
(a) 15 (b) 17 (c) 16 (d) 18

22.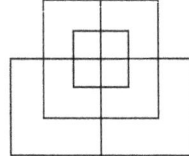
(a) 13 (b) 14 (c) 15 (d) 17

23.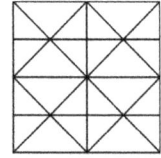
(a) 15 (b) 17 (c) 14 (d) 18

24.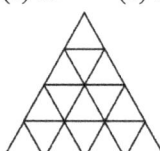
(a) 11 (b) 12 (c) 14 (d) 15

25.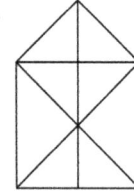
(a) 11 (b) 8
(c) 12 (d) 9

Direction (26 to 30): In each of the following questions, what is the number of triangles and squares in the given figure.

26.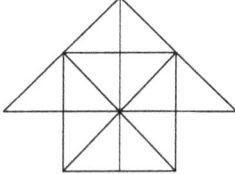

(a) 26 triangles, 6 squares
(b) 28 triangles, 6 squares
(c) 24 triangles, 8 squares
(d) 22 triangles, 8 squares

27.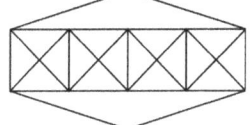

(a) 36 triangles, 8 squares
(b) 40 triangles, 7 squares
(c) 38 triangles, 6 squares
(d) 38 triangles, 8 squares

28.

(a) 28 triangles, 6 squares
(b) 26 triangles, 6 squares
(c) 28 triangles, 5 squares
(d) 26 triangles, 8 squares

29.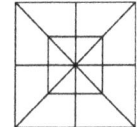

(a) 32 triangles, 8 squares
(b) 32 triangles, 10 squares
(c) 36 triangles, 8 squares
(d) 32 triangles, 12 squares

30.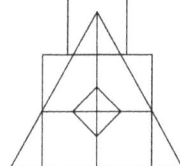

(a) 21 triangles, 7 squares
(b) 20 triangles, 12 squares
(c) 21 triangles, 9 squares
(d) 22 triangles, 10 squares

Analytical Reasoning

Venn Diagram

9

Learning Objectives : In this chapter, students will learn about:
- ✓ Solving questions related to Venn diagram

CHAPTER SUMMARY

In these problems we have to analyse the relation between certain given group of items and illustrate it diagrammatically. Each geometrical figure in the diagram represents a certain class.

Example 1:

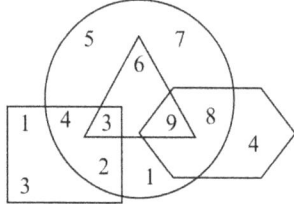

In the above figure, which number belong to all the figures?

    (a) 3   (b) 6
    (c) 9   (d) None of these

Solution: (d) There is no such number which belongs to all the given figures.

Example 2: What is the sum of the numbers which belong to one figure only?

    (a) 12   (b) 16
    (c) 21   (d) 18.

Solution: (c) In square, the numbers are 1, 3
In circle, the numbers are 1, 5, 7.
In hexagon, the number is 4.
Sum of the above numbers
$= 1 + 3 + 1 + 5 + 7 + 4 = 21$.

Direction (3 to 5): In the following diagram, the square represents girls, the circle represents singers, the triangle represents players and rectangle represents runners.

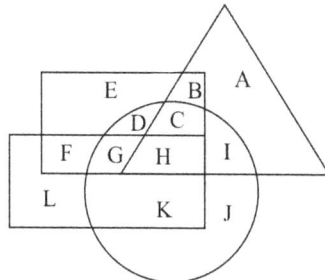

Example 3: Which letter represents girls who are runners, players but are not singers?

    (a) B   (b) F
    (c) E   (d) None of these

Solution: (d) H represents the girl who is runner and player, but it is a part of circle.

Example 4: Which letter represents singers who are runners but they are not players?

    (a) I   (b) K
    (c) J   (d) L

Solution: (b)

Example 5: Which letter represents girl singers who are runners but not player?

    (a) E   (b) F
    (c) G   (d) H

Solution: (c)

MULTIPLE CHOICE QUESTIONS

Direction (1 to 4): In the given figure, there are three intersecting circles, each representing certain section of people.

Different regions are marked p, d, r, s, t, u, v. Read the statement in the given question and choose the letter of the region which correctly represents the statement.

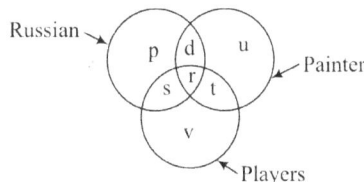

1. Russian who are painters but not players
   (a) d   (b) t
   (c) s   (d) v

2. Russian who are painters as well as players.
   (a) p   (b) d
   (c) r   (d) s

3. Russian who are players but not painters.
   (a) p   (b) d
   (c) r   (d) s

4. Painters who are neither Russian nor players.
   (a) d   (b) r
   (c) u   (d) t

Direction (5 to 8): In the following diagram, the circle represents teachers, the triangle stands for Accounts specialists and rectangle stands for musicians.

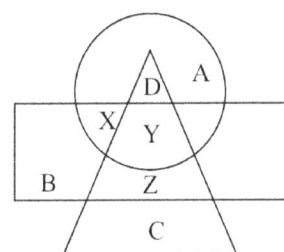

5. Teachers who are also Accounts specialist are represented by
   (a) A   (b) B
   (c) C   (d) D

6. Teachers who are also musicians are represented by
   (a) X   (b) Y
   (c) Z   (d) A

7. The Accounts specialists who are also musicians but not teacher are represented by
   (a) A   (b) B
   (c) Y   (d) Z

8. B represents
   (a) Teacher who are neither accounts specialist nor musician.
   (b) Teachers who are not accounts specialist.
   (c) Musician who are neither teachers nor accounts specialist.
   (d) Teachers who are not accounts specialist.

Direction (9 to 13): In the following figure, rectangle stands for wheat, square stands for gram, circle stands for maize and triangle represents linseed cultivation.

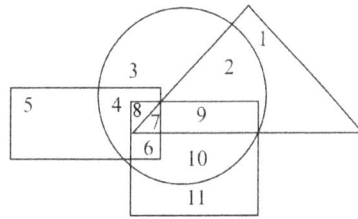

9. Which area is cultivated by all the four types of grain?
   (a) 7   (b) 9
   (c) 8   (d) 2

10. Which area is cultivated by linseed and maize and nothing else?
    (a) 2   (b) 7
    (c) 9   (d) 8

11. Which area is cultivated by linseed only
    (a) 1   (b) 2
    (c) 5   (d) 11

12. Which area is cultivated by wheat and maize only?
    (a) 5   (b) 4
    (c) 6   (d) 8

Venn Diagram

13. Which area is cultivated by maize only?
    (a) 10 (b) 3
    (c) 4 (d) 2

Direction (14 to 18): In the given diagram, the circle represents educated, triangle for urban, rectangle for honest people and square for hard working people. Different regions are numbered from 1 to 12. Choose the correct answer in the following questions.

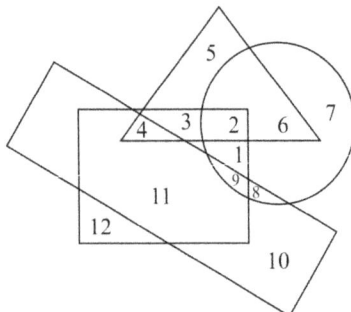

14. People who are educated hard working and honest but not urban are represented by
    (a) 8 (b) 9
    (c) 2 (d) 13

15. Urban people who are hard-working and educated but not honest are represented by
    (a) 4 (b) 3
    (c) 2 (d) 1

16. Hard working people who are uneducated dishonest and urban are represented by.
    (a) 3 (b) 4
    (c) 9 (d) 8

17. Non. Urban, educated people who are neither honest nor hard working are represented by
    (a) 7 (b) 10
    (c) 11 (d) 12

18. Urban educated people who are neither honest nor hard working are represented by
    (a) 6 (b) 9
    (c) 4 (d) 2

Direction (19 to 23): In the following diagram the triangle represents lawyers, the circle represents doctors and the rectangle represents writers.

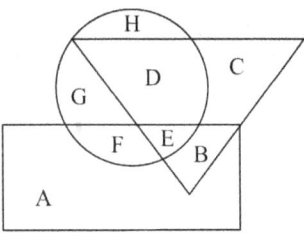

19. Which letter in the diagram represents lawyers who are also doctors and writers?
    (a) B (d) C
    (c) D (d) E

20. Which letters represent doctors who are neither writers nor lawyers?
    (a) A, B (b) C, D
    (c) F, G (d) G, H

21. Which letter represents writers who are neither doctors nor lawyers?
    (a) A (b) B
    (c) C (d) D

22. Which letter represents lawyers who are neither doctors nor writers?
    (a) B (b) C
    (c) D (d) E

23. Which letter represents writers who are also doctors?
    (a) D (b) F
    (c) G (d) H

Direction (24 to 29): In the given figure rectangle represents males, circle represents urban, square represents professor, triangle represents educated.

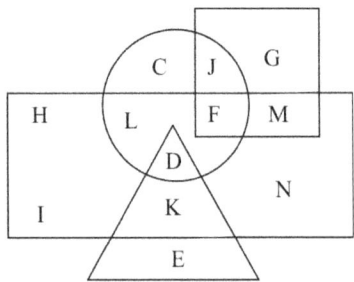

24. Who among the above is an educated male who is not an urban resident?
    (a) E (b) I (c) D (d) K

25. Who among the above is a female urban resident and also a professor?
    (a) F   (b) G
    (c) J   (d) M

26. Who among the above is an educated made who is from urban area?
    (a) D   (b) B
    (c) K   (d) L

27. Who among the following is uneducated and also an urban male?
    (a) B   (b) C
    (c) K   (d) L

28. Who among the above is only a professor but not a male nor urban oriented and uneducated?
    (a) G   (b) H
    (c) I   (d) N

29. Who among the above is a male, urban and also a professor but not educated?
    (a) M   (b) L
    (c) F   (d) J

30. Select a figure from the options that illustrates the relationship amongst "pigeons, birds, dogs".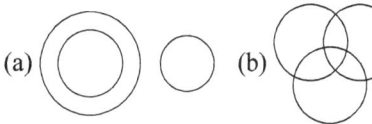

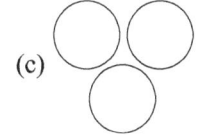 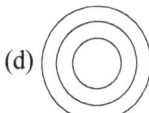

Venn Diagram

Embedded Figure   10

Learning Objectives : In this chapter, students will learn about:
- Solving questions related to embedded figures

CHAPTER SUMMARY

Embedded Figure : A figure (X) is said be embedded in a figure (Y), if figure (Y) contains figure (X) as its part.

In such types of problems, a fig. (X) is given, followed by four complex figures in such a way that fig. (X) is embedded in one and only one of them. The candidate has to select such figure in which fig. (X) is embedded.

Illustrative Examples

Direction: In each of the following questions, fig. (X) is embedded in any one of the four alternative figures (a), (b), (c) or (d). Find the alternative which contains fig. (X) as its part.

Example 1:

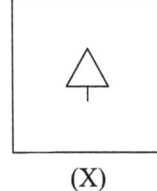   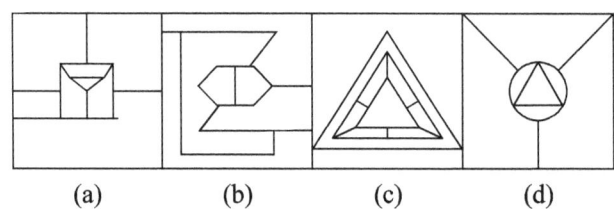

(X)   (a)   (b)   (c)   (d)

Solution: On close observation, we find that fig. (X) is embedded in fig. (c) as shown below:

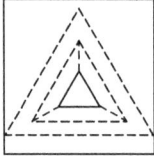

Hence, the answer is (c).

Example 2:

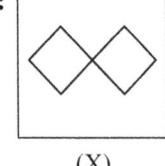   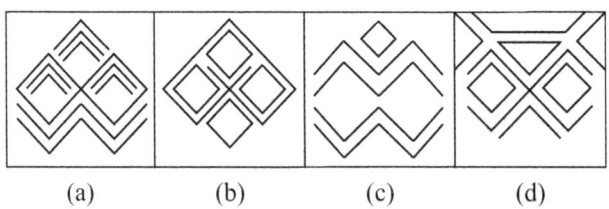

(X)   (a)   (b)   (c)   (d)

Solution: On close observation, we find that fig. (X) is embedded in fig. (a) as shown below :

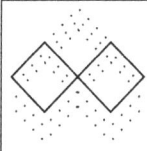

Hence, the answer is (*a*).

MULTIPLE CHOICE QUESTIONS

Direction: In each of the following questions, fig. (X) is embedded in one of the four alterative figures (a), (b), (c) or (d). Find the alternative which contains fig. (X) as its part.

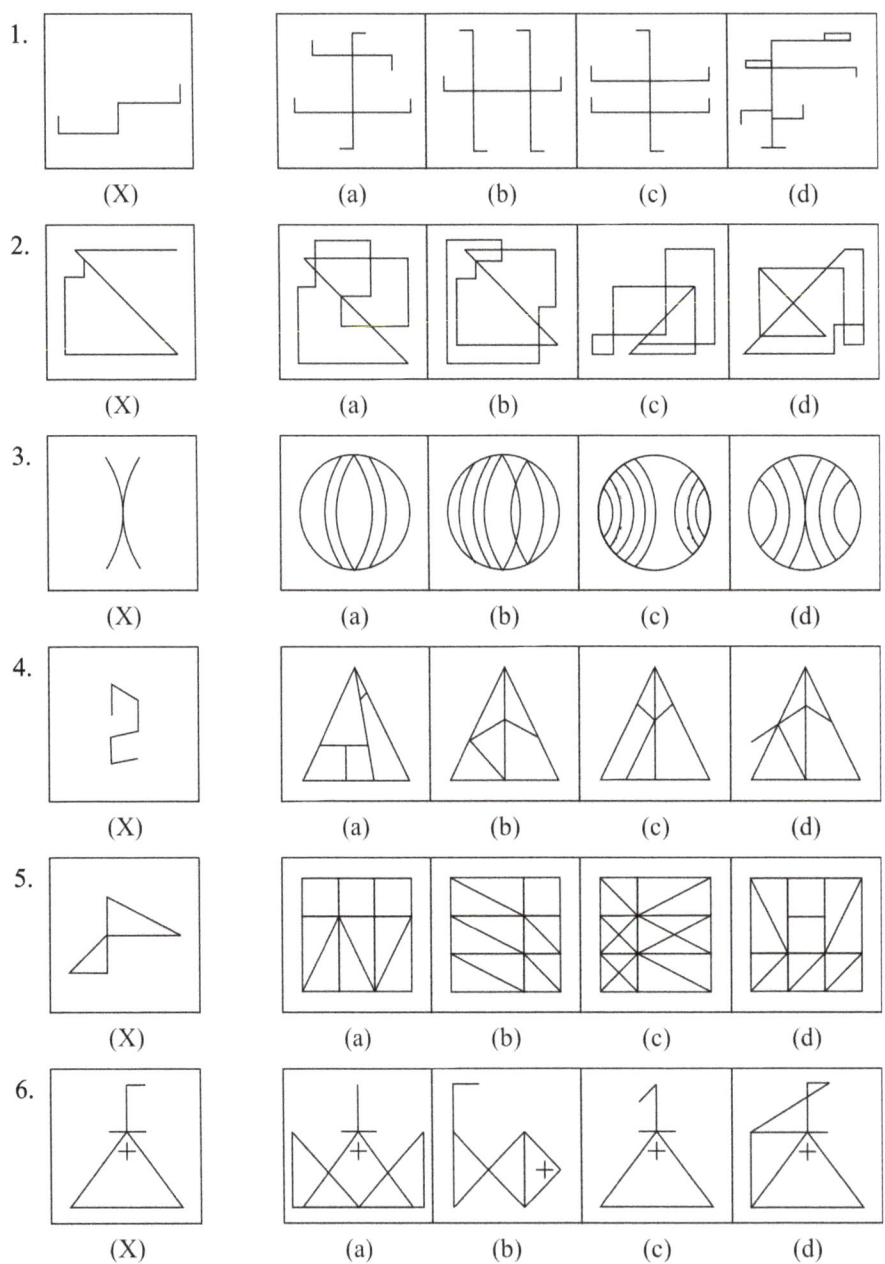

148 International Mathematics Olympiad – 8

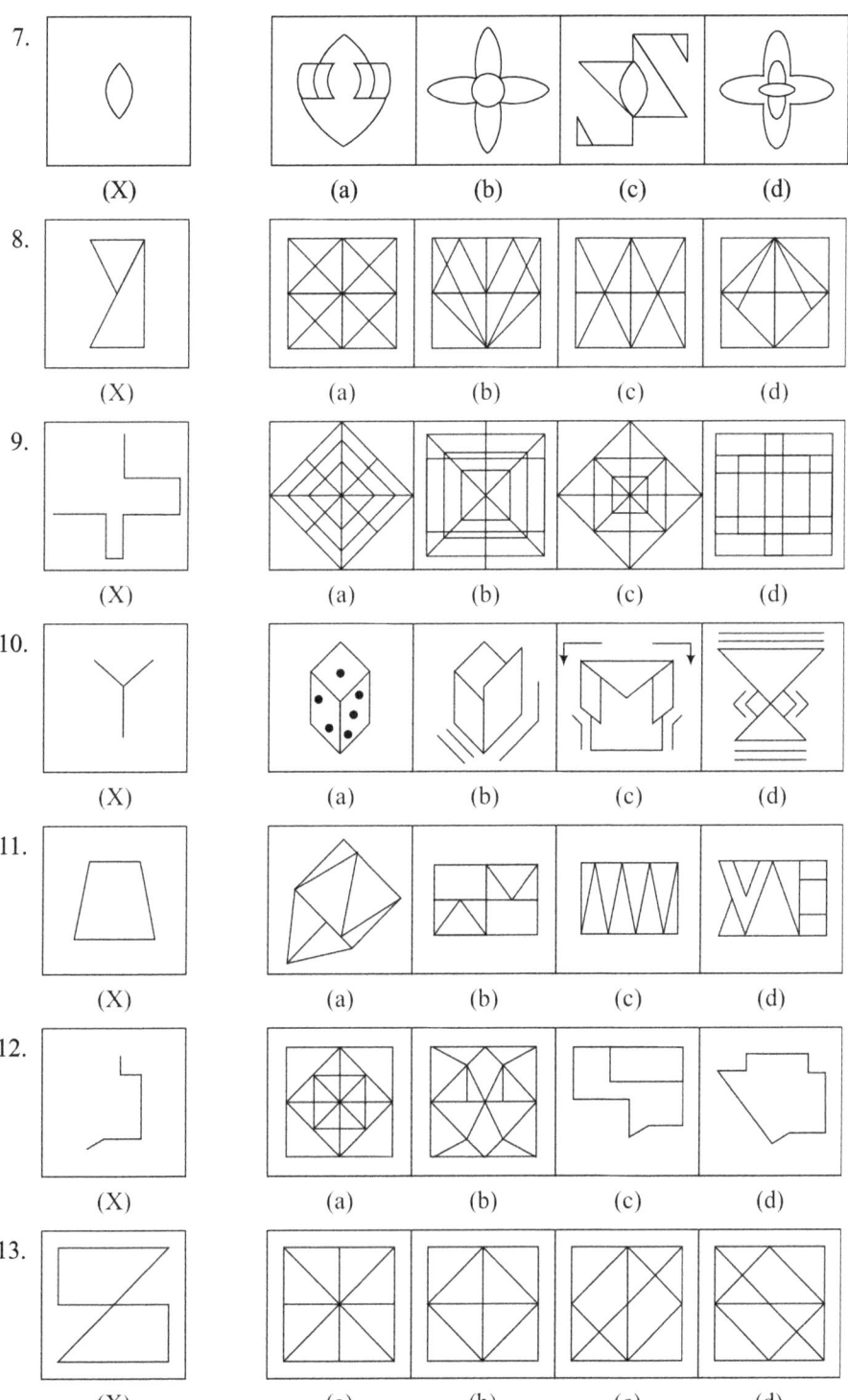

Embedded Figure

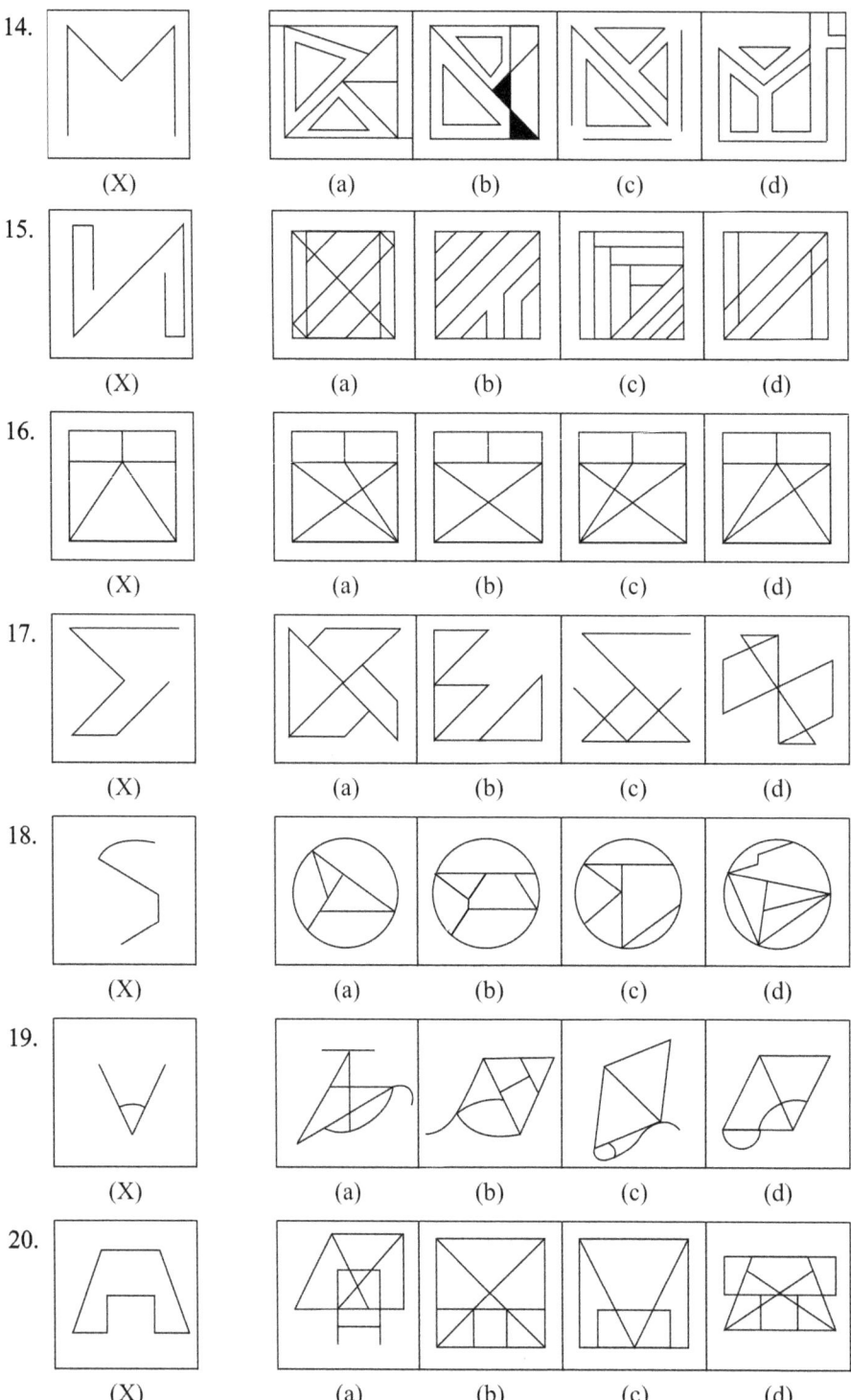

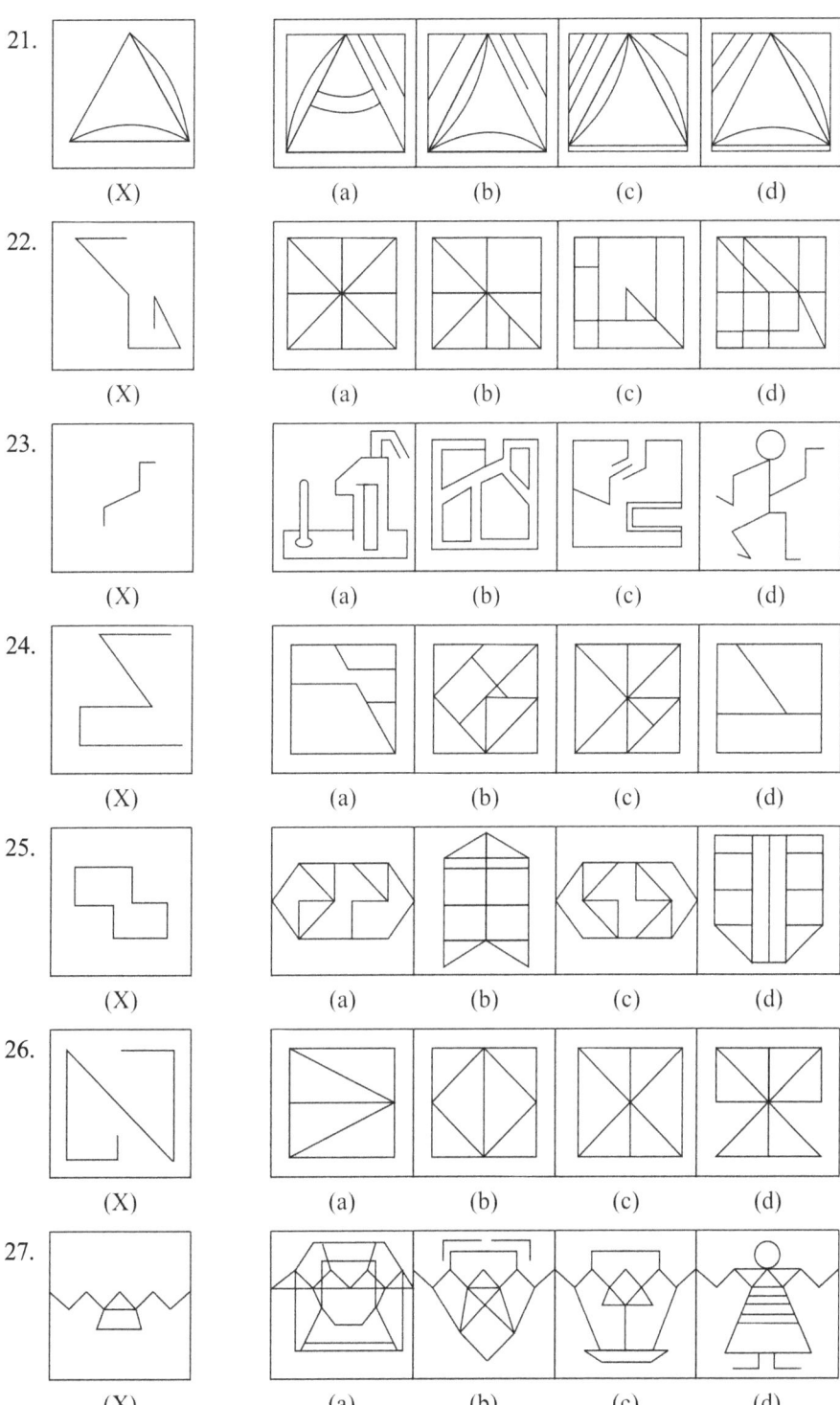

Embedded Figure

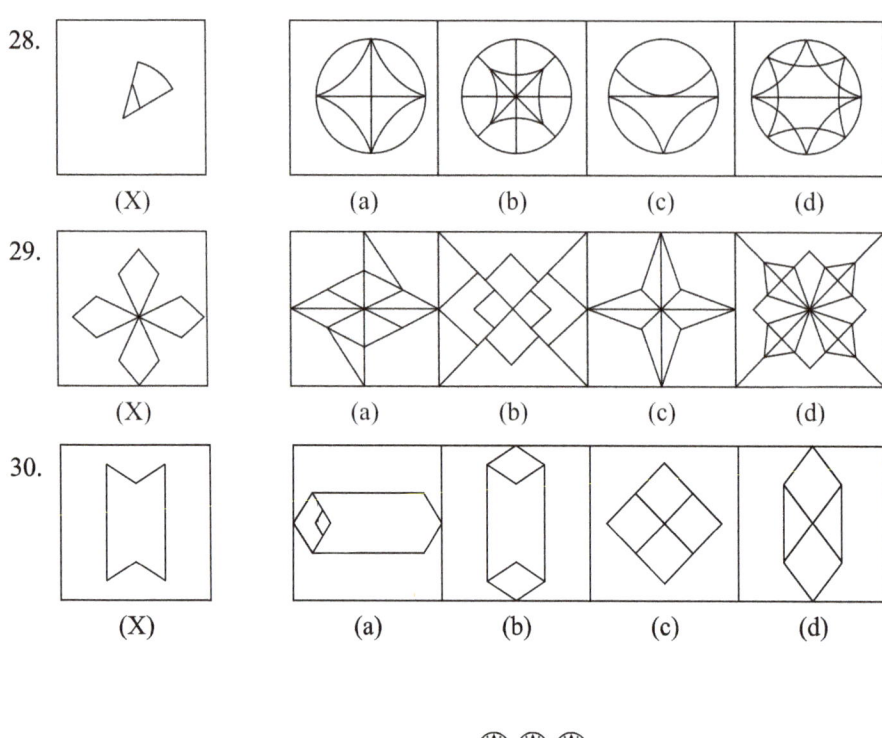

Completion of Incomplete Pattern 11

Learning Objectives : In this chapter, students will learn about:
- ✓ Solving questions related to completion of incomplete pattern

CHAPTER SUMMARY

In this type of problems, a figure or a matrix, containing a set of figures following a particular sequence or pattern is given, in which a part, generally a quarter, is left blank. This problem figure is followed by four alternative figures. The candidate is required to select the one which best fits into the blank space of problem figure so as to complete the original pattern.

Illustrative Examples

Example 1: Select a figure from amongst the four alternatives, which when placed in the blank space of fig. (X) would complete the pattern.

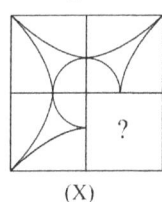 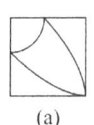   
(X) (a) (b) (c) (d)

Solution: Clearly, fig. (b) will complete the pattern when placed in the blank space of fig. (X) as shown below :

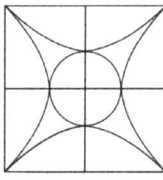

Hence, the answer is (b).

Example 2: Complete the pattern in fig. (X) by selecting one of the figures from the four alternatives.

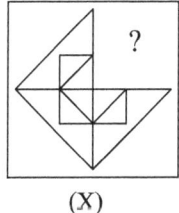 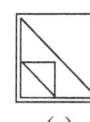 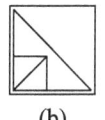  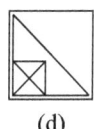
(X) (a) (b) (c) (d)

Solution: Clearly, fig. (a) will complete the pattern when placed in the blank space of fig. (X) as shown below :

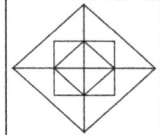

Hence, the answer is (a).

Example 3: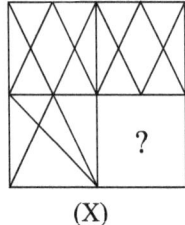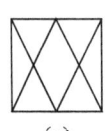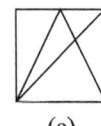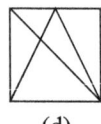

(X)   (a)   (b)   (c)   (d)

Solution: (d)

Example 4: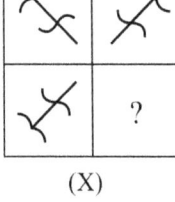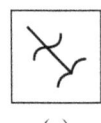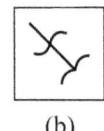

(X)   (a)   (b)   (c)   (d)

Solution: (b)

Example 5: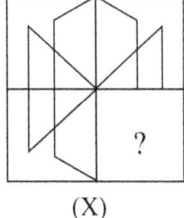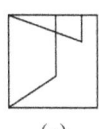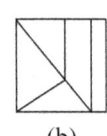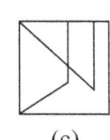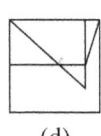

(X)   (a)   (b)   (c)   (d)

Solution: (a)

Example 6: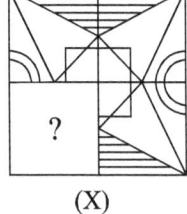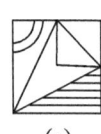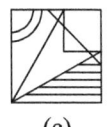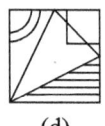

(X)   (a)   (b)   (c)   (d)

Solution: (b)

Example 7: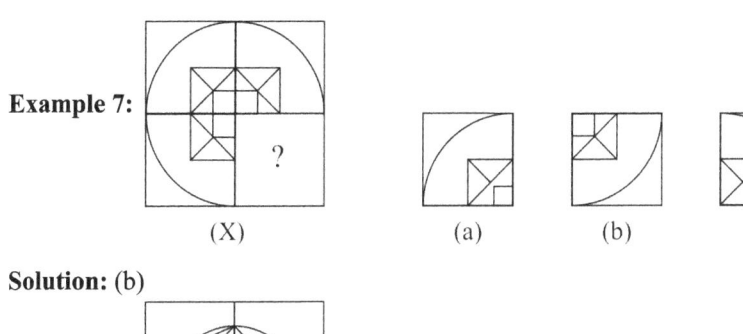

Solution: (b)

Example 8: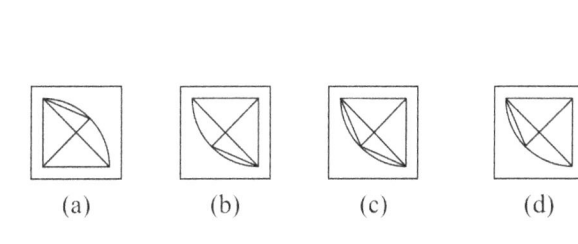

Solution: (d)

Completion of Incomplete Pattern

MULTIPLE CHOICE QUESTIONS

Direction (Q. 1-30): In the following problems, select a figure from amongst the four options which when placed in the blank space of figure (X) would complete the pattern.

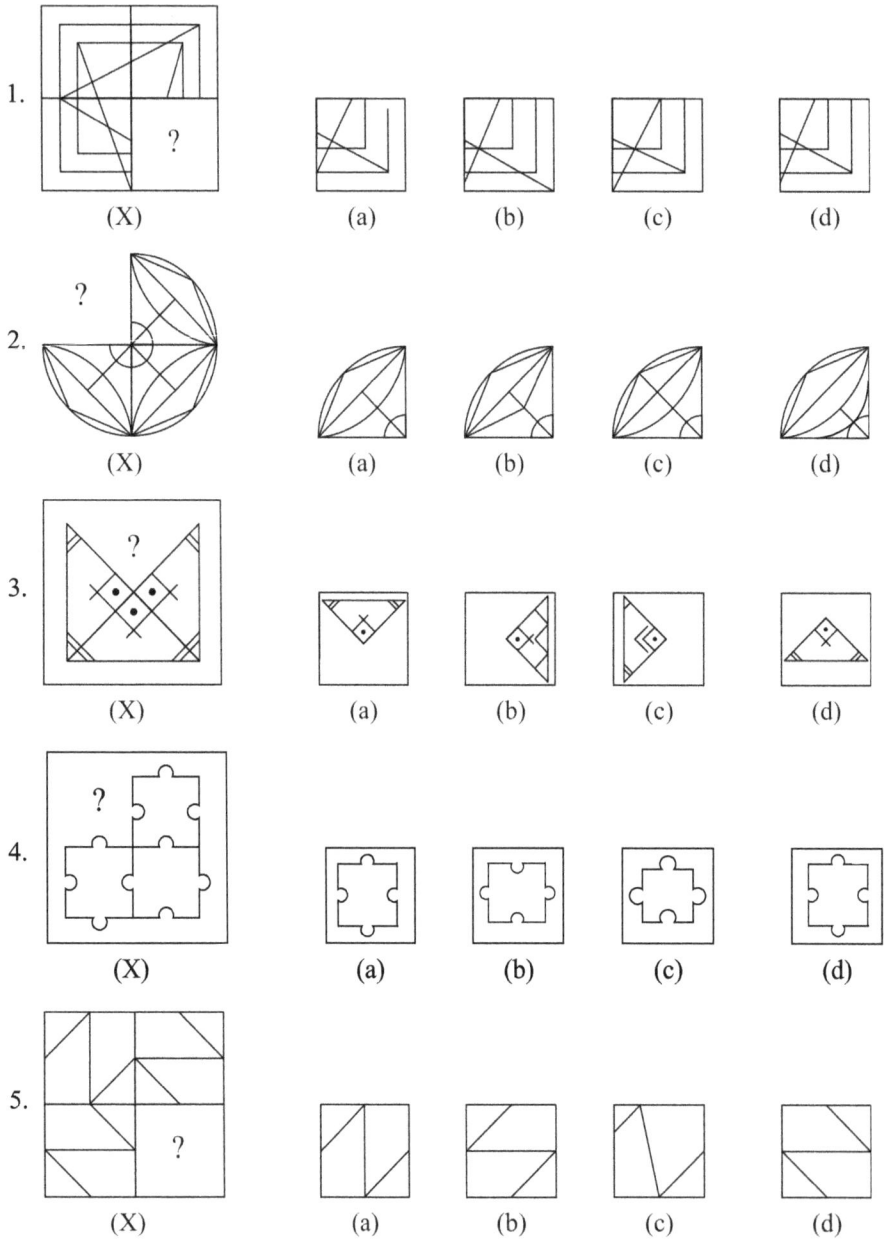

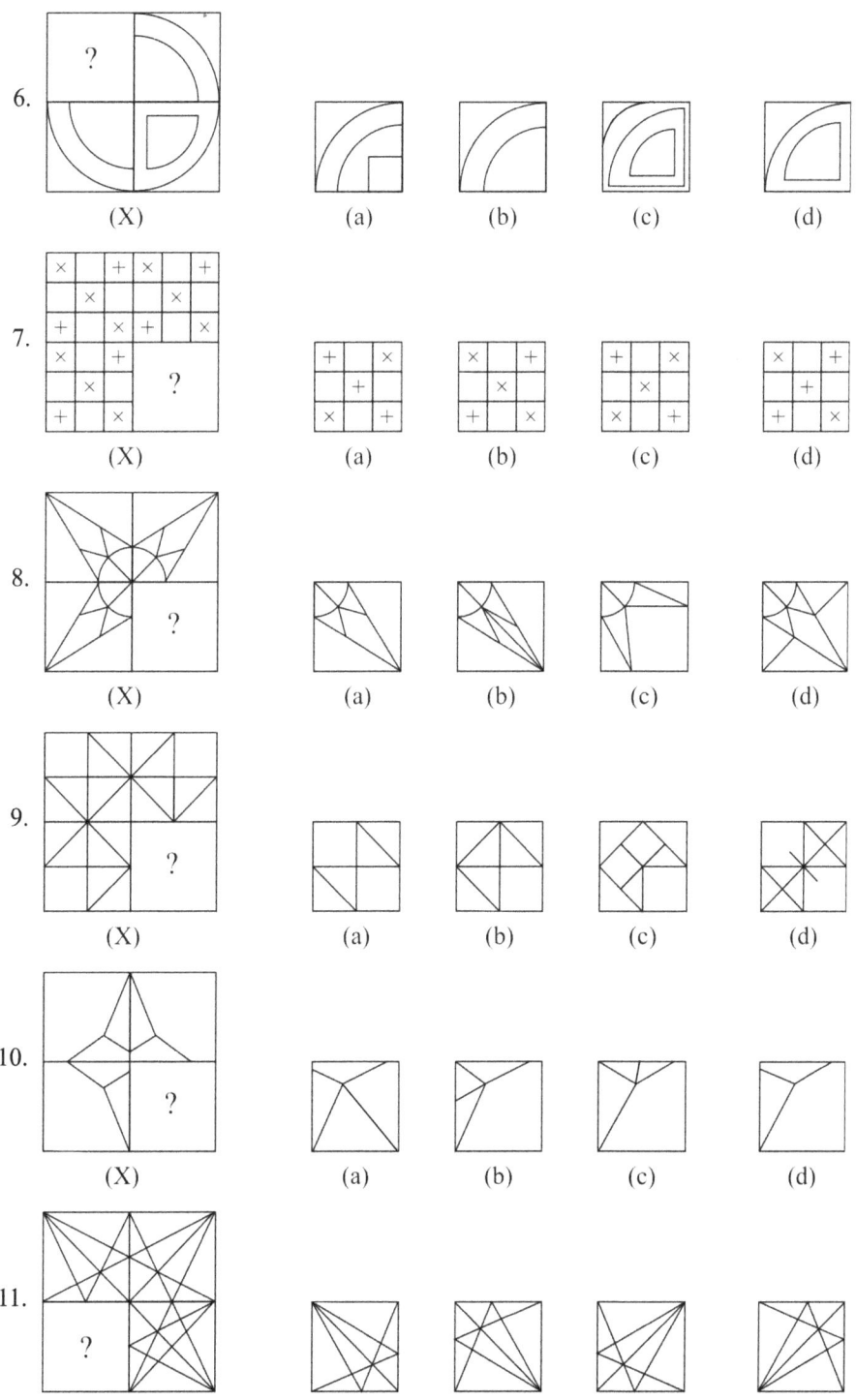

Completion of Incomplete Pattern

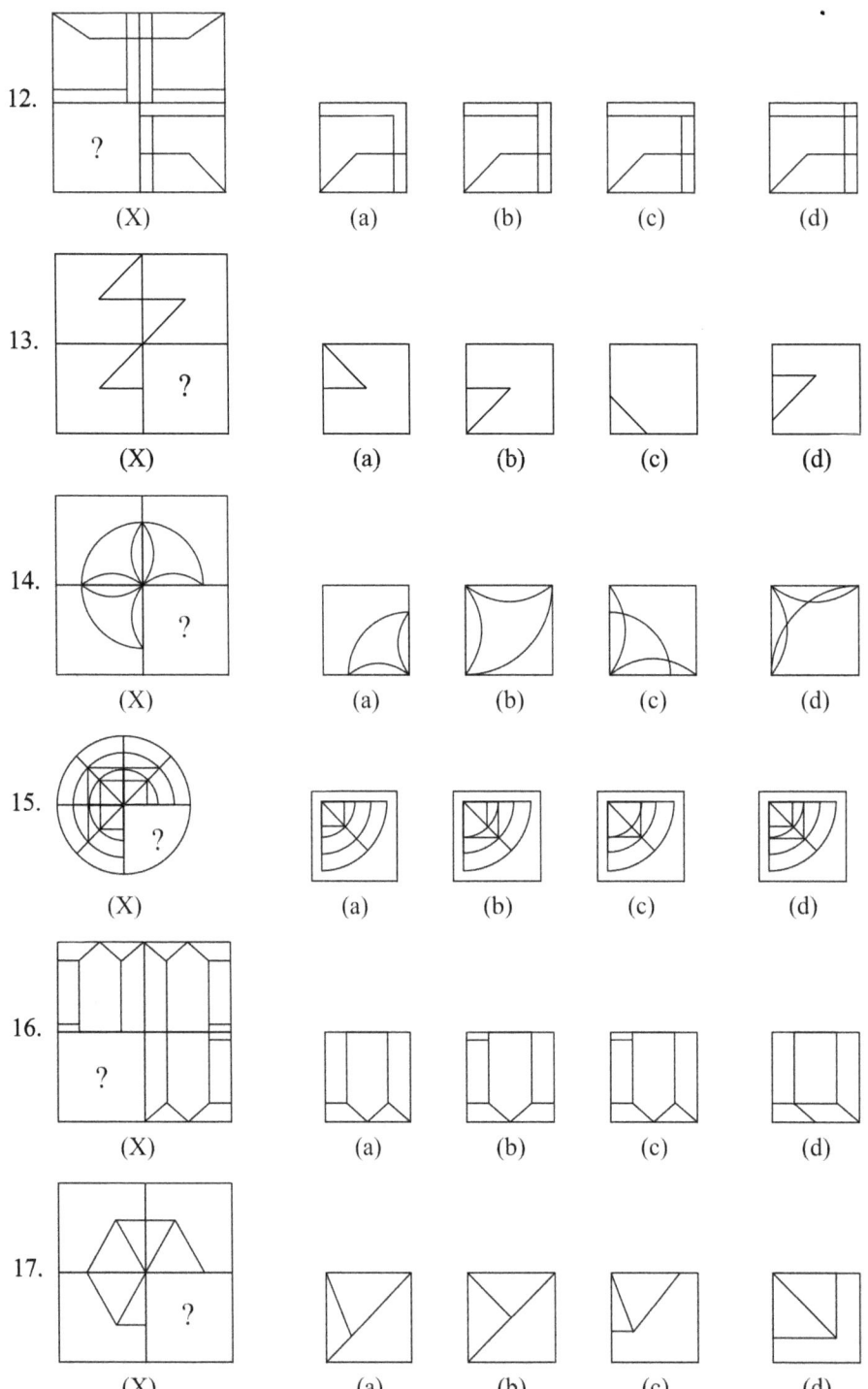

18.

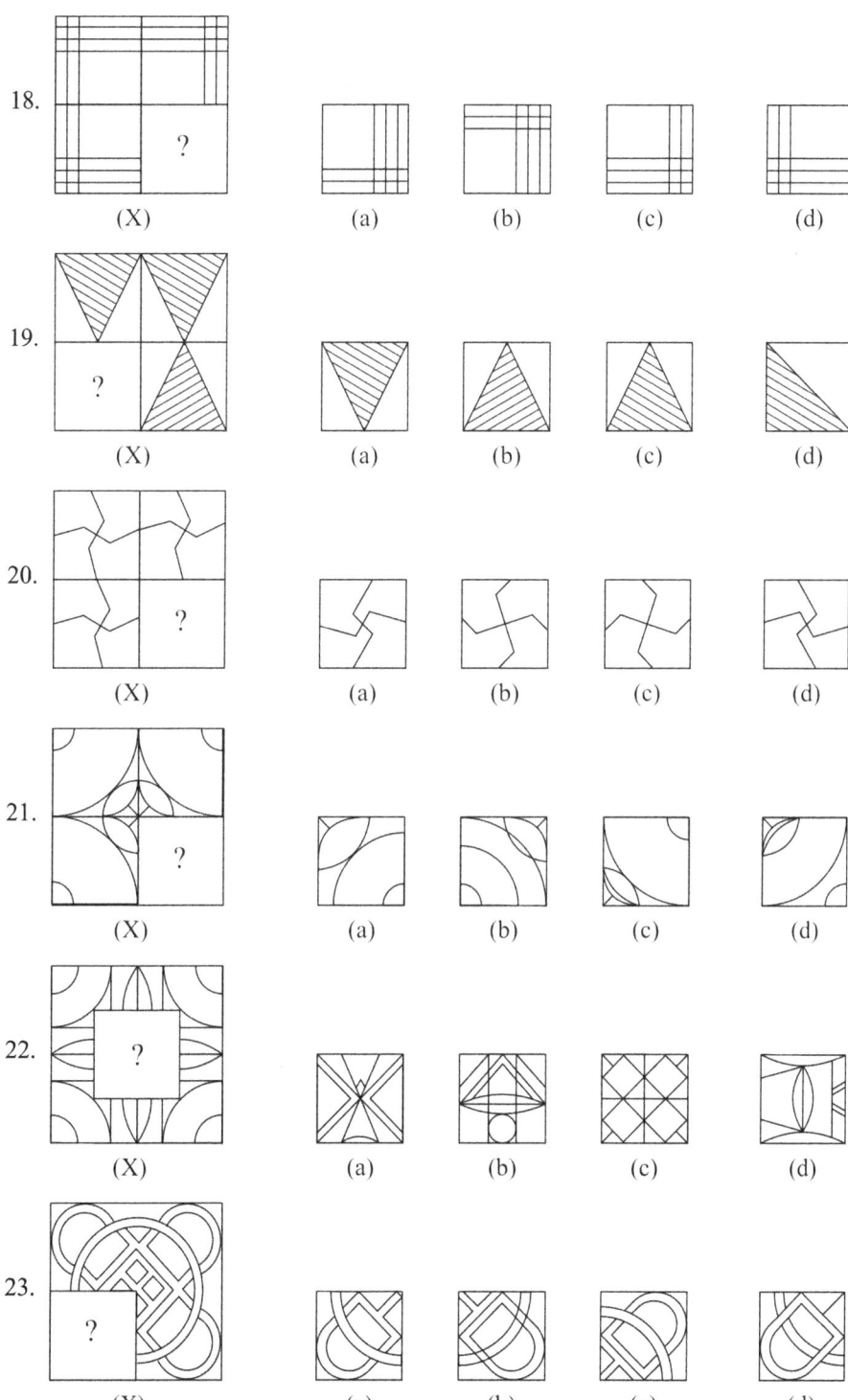

Completion of Incomplete Pattern

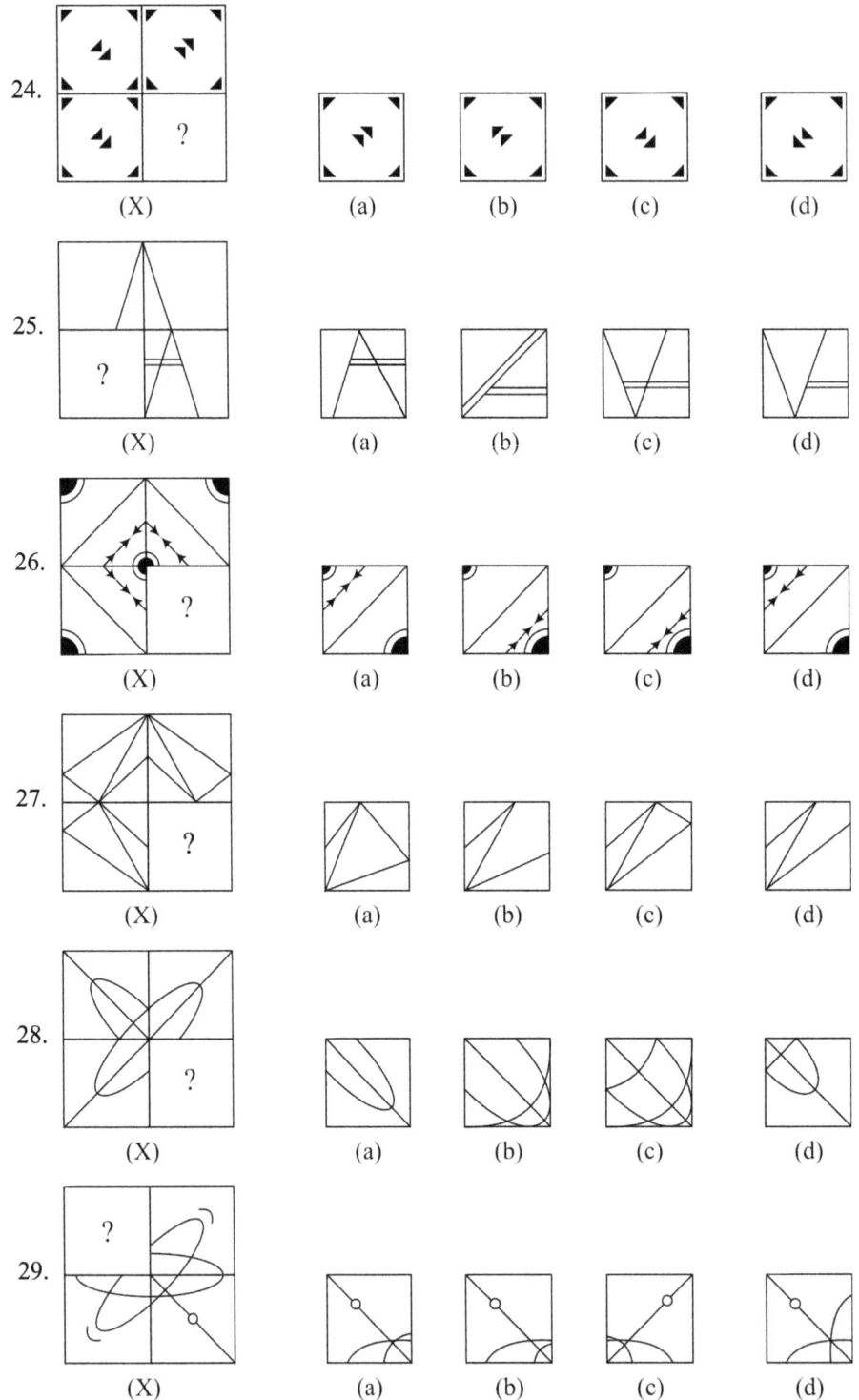

30.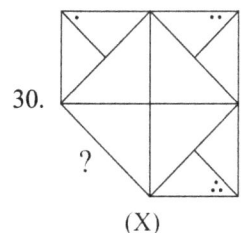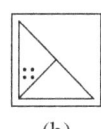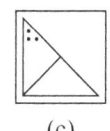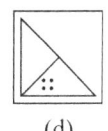

(X)   (a)   (b)   (c)   (d)

Completion of Incomplete Pattern

Water Images — 12

Learning Objectives : In this chapter, students will learn about:
- ✓ Water images of letters
- ✓ Water images of numbers

CHAPTER SUMMARY

Water Image
The reflection of an object, as seen in water, is called its water image. It is the inverted image obtained by turning the object upside down.

Water Images of Capital Letters

Letters	A	B	C	D	E	F	G	H	I
Water Images	∀	ꓭ	C	ꓷ	Ǝ	ꓞ	ꓨ	H	I
Letters	J	K	L	M	N	O	P	Q	R
Water Images	ſ	ꓘ	ꓶ	ꟽ	N	O	ꓑ	Ò	ꓤ
Letters	S	T	U	V	W	X	Y	Z	-
Water Images	S	ꓕ	ꓵ	ꓥ	ꟽ	X	⅄	Z	-

Remark 1. The letters whose water-images are identical to the letter itself are :

C, D, E, H, I, K, O, X,

Remark 2. Certain words which have water-images identical to the word itself are :

KICK, KID, CHIDE, HIKE, CODE, CHICK,

Water Images of Small Letters

Letters	a	b	c	d	e	f	g	h	i
Water Images	ɐ	q	ɔ	p	ə	ɟ	ᵷ	ɥ	¡
Letters	j	k	l	m	n	o	p	q	r
Water Images	ſ	ʞ	l	ɯ	u	o	d	b	ɹ
Letters	s	t	u	v	w	x	y	z	--
Water Images	s	ʇ	n	ʌ	ʍ	x	ʎ	z	--

Water-Images of Numbers

Numbers	0	1	2	3	4	5	6	7	8	9
Water Images	0	I	ᄅ	Ɛ	ㄣ	ꓢ	9	ㄥ	8	6

MULTIPLE CHOICE QUESTIONS

Direction (1 to 15): In each of the following questions, you are given a combination of alphabets and/or numbers followed by four alternatives (a), (b), (c) and (d). Choose the alternative which most closely resembles the water-image of the given combination.

1. DISC
   (a) CSID (b) ƆSID
   (c) DIƧC (d) DISC
2. FROG
   (a) ᖴᖇOG (b) GORF
   (c) ƆOᖴЯ (d) ᖴROG
3. RECRUIT
   (a) ᖇECЯUIT (b) ᖇECЯUIT
   (c) RECRUIT (d) TIUЯCEᖇ
4. ACOUSTIC
   (a) ACOUSTIC (b) ACOUSTIC
   (c) ACOUSTIC (d) ACOUSTIC
5. FAMILY
   (a) ᖴAMILY (b) ᖴAMILY
   (c) FAMILY (d) FAMILY
6. NUCLEAR
   (a) ᖇAELCUИ (b) ИUCLEAᖇ
   (c) ИUCLEAᖇ (d) ИUCLEAᖇ
7. QUARREL
   (a) ǪUAᖇᖇEL (b) QUAᖇᖇEL
   (c) QUAᖇᖇEL (d) ǪUAᖇᖇEL
8. U4P15B7
   (a) U4P15B7 (b) U4P15B7
   (c) U4P15B7 (d) U4P15B7
9. PQ8AF5BZ9
   (a) PQ8AF5BZ9 (b) PQ8AF5BZ9
   (c) PQ8AF5BZ9 (d) PQ8AF5BZ9
10. D6Z7F4
    (a) D9Z7F4 (b) D6Z7F4
    (c) D6Z7F4 (d) D6Z7F4
11. VAYU8436
    (a) VAYU8436 (b) VAYU8436
    (c) VAYU8436 (d) VAYU8436
12. BK50RP62
    (a) BK50RP62 (b) BK50RP62
    (c) BK50RP62 (d) BK50RP62
13. 96FSH52
    (a) 96FSH52 (b) 96FSH52
    (c) 96FSH52 (d) 96FSH22
14. RAJ589D8
    (a) RAJ58ᑫD8 (b) RAJ58ᑫD8
    (c) RAJ58ᑫD8 (d) RAJ589D8
15. GR98AP76ES
    (a) GR98AP76ES (b) GR98AP76ES
    (c) GR98AP76ES (d) GR98AP76ES

Direction (16 to 30): In the following questions, choose the correct water image of the figure (X) from the given four alternatives.

16.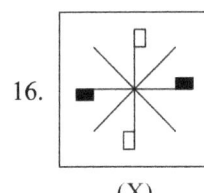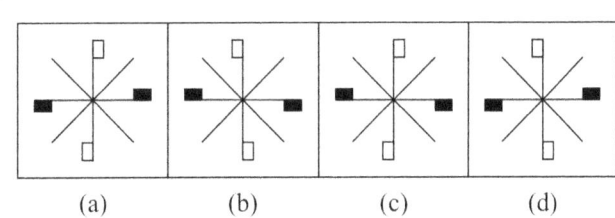
    (X)　　(a)　　(b)　　(c)　　(d)

Water Images

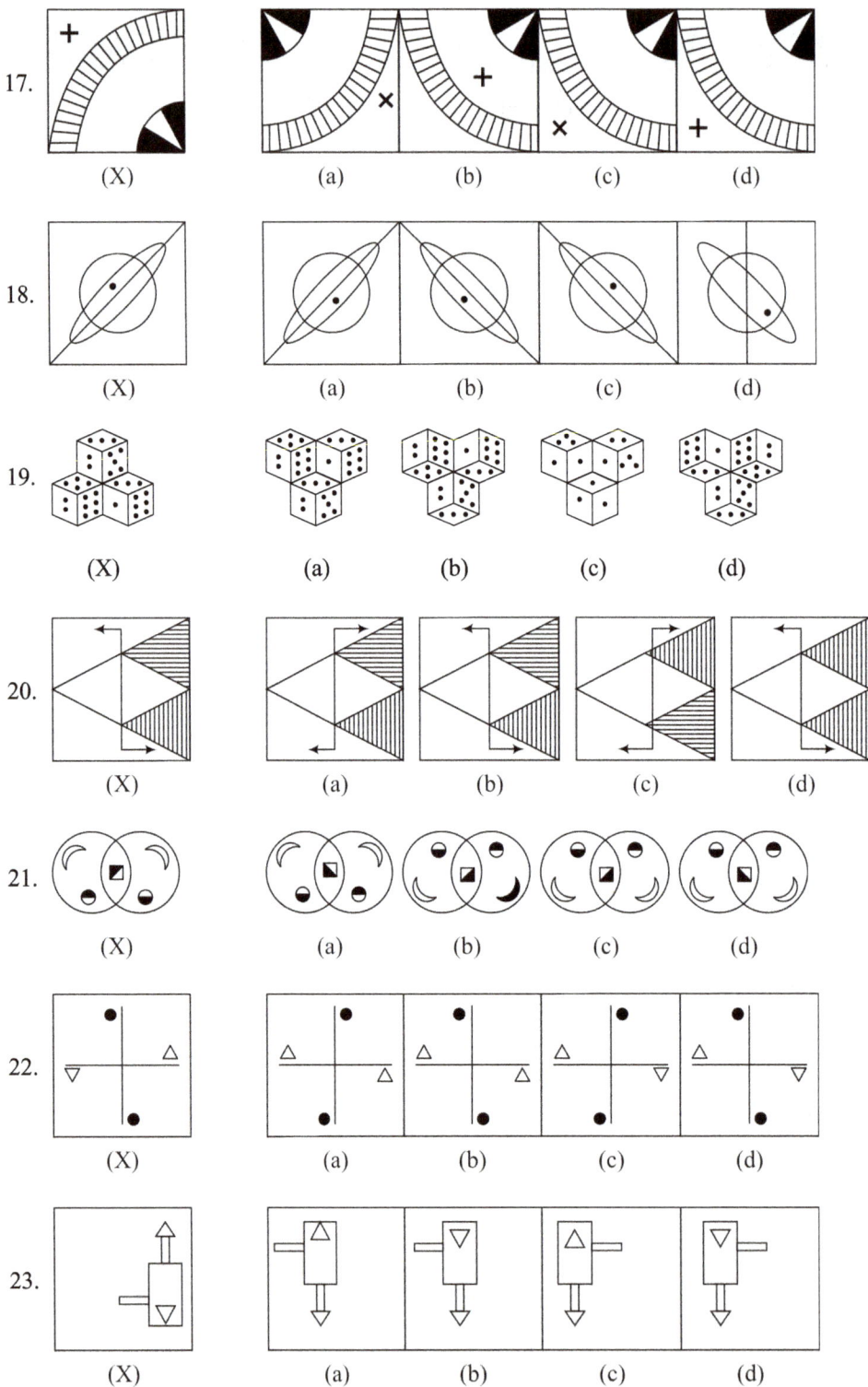

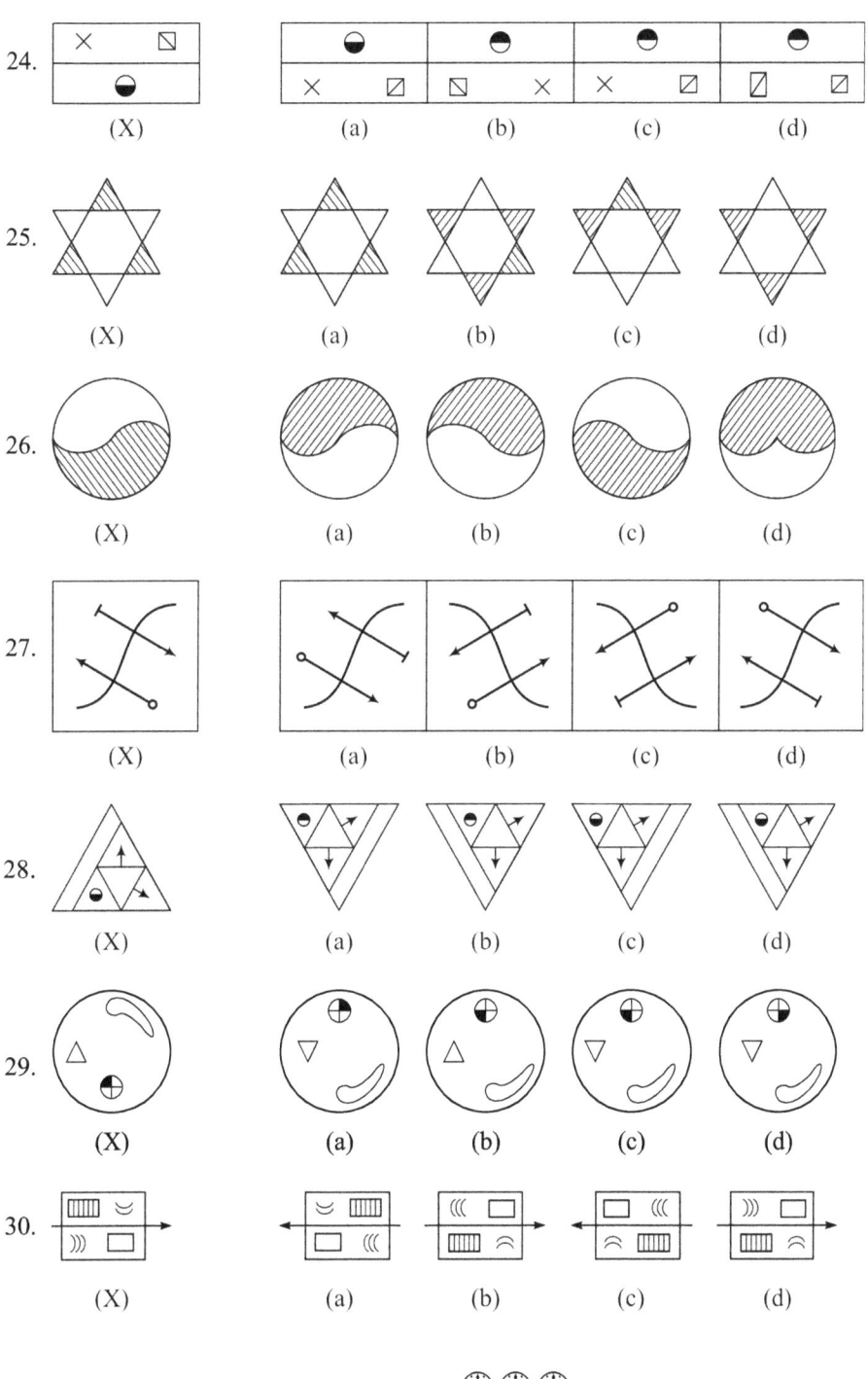

Figure Matrix   13

Learning Objectives : In this chapter, students will learn about:
- ✓ Solving questions related to figure matrix.

CHAPTER SUMMARY

In this type of problems, rows and columns are there. In each row and column, various figures are given. In these figures, the next figure is obtained by moving the left part or right part or lower part or upper part. Sometimes, the figures are getting laterally inverted in each step. In some figures, the next figure is obtained by rotating the first figure by 90° clockwise or anti clockwise. Sometimes the next figure is obtained by combining the two figures. In some figures, the next figure is obtained by reversing the direction. We have to study the pattern and fill the gap as per the following pattern. The examples are as given below.

Direction: In the following questions, study the given matrix and find the correct option for the question mark from the given four options.

Example 1:

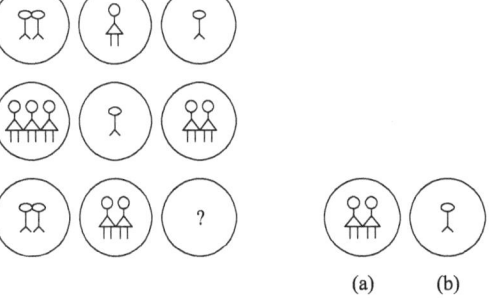

Answer: (c) In each row, the no. of elements in the 3rd figure is equal to the difference in the number of elements in the 1st and 2nd figures.

Example 2:

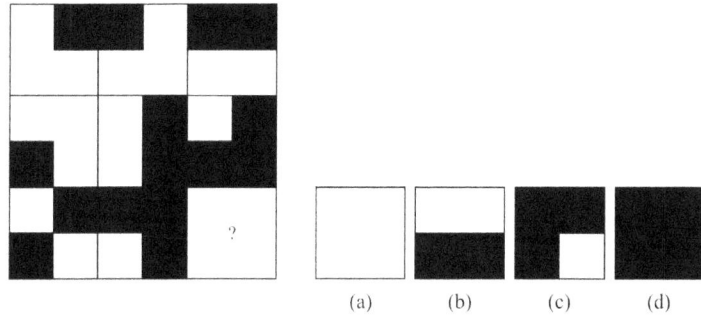

Answer: (d) In each row or column, the 3rd figure is the combination of elements of first and second figure.

Example 3:

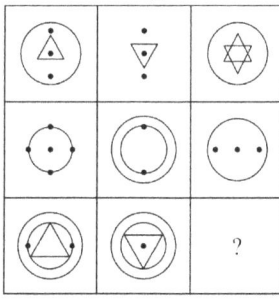

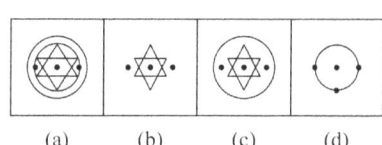

Answer: (b) Third figure in each row consists of parts which are not common to first two figures.

Example 4:

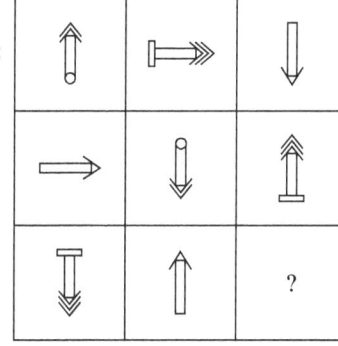

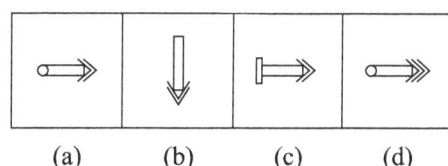

Answer: (a)

Direction: In the following questions, study the given matrix, and find the correct option for the question mark from the given four options.

Figure Matrix

MULTIPLE CHOICE QUESTIONS

1.

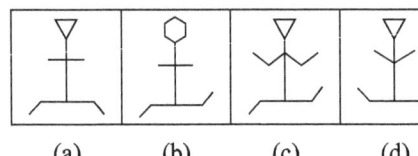

2.

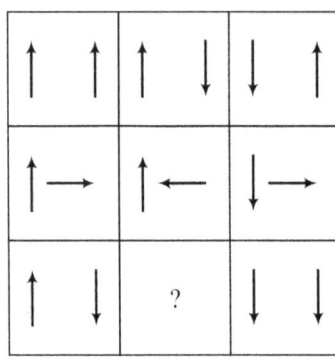

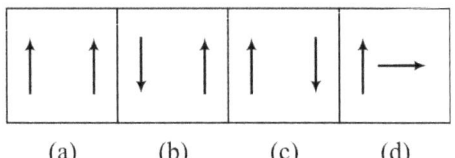

3.

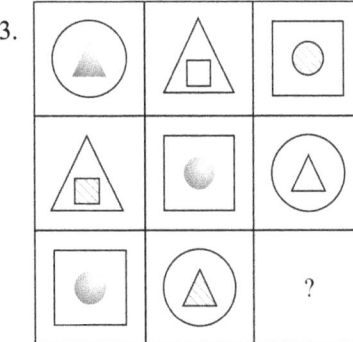

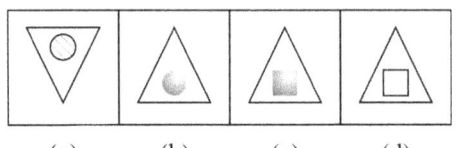

4.

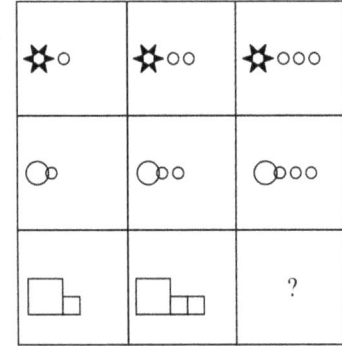

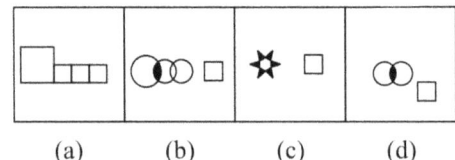

5.

6.

7.

8.

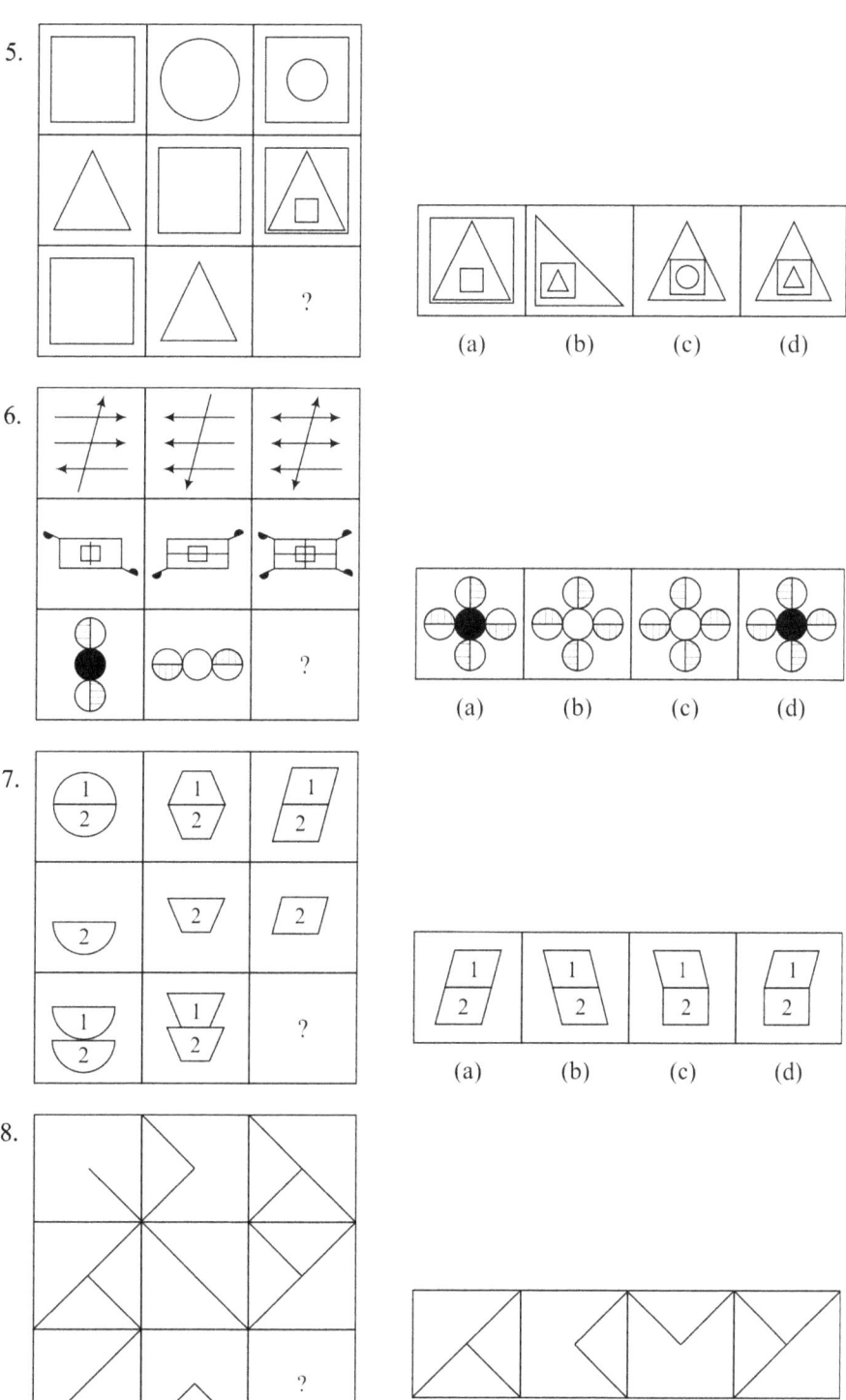

Figure Matrix

9.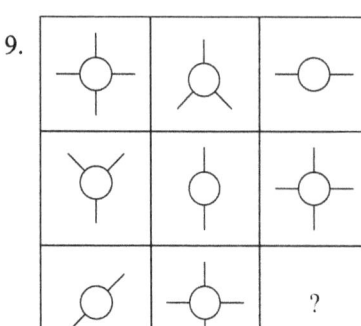
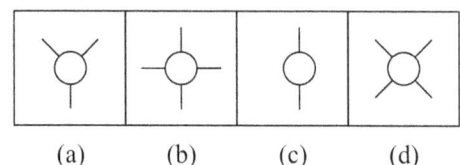

10.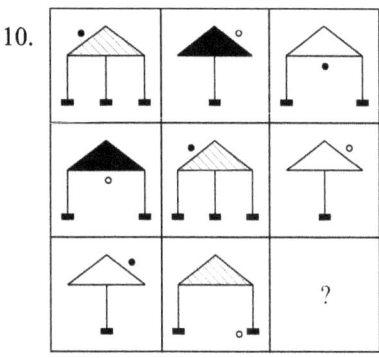
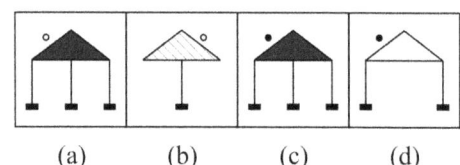

11.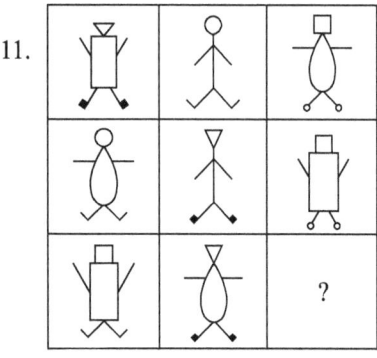
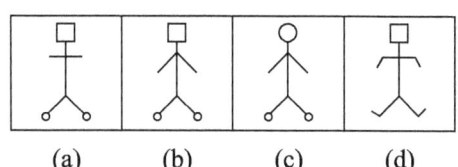

12.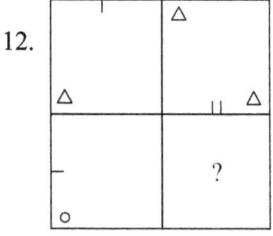
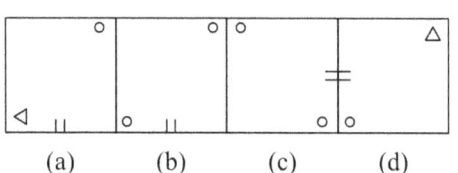

13.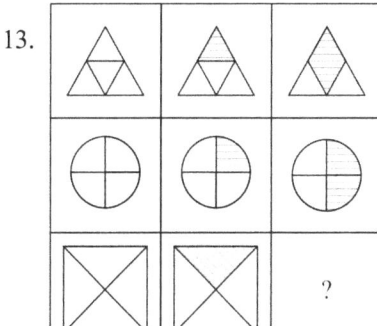

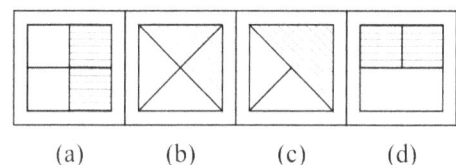

14.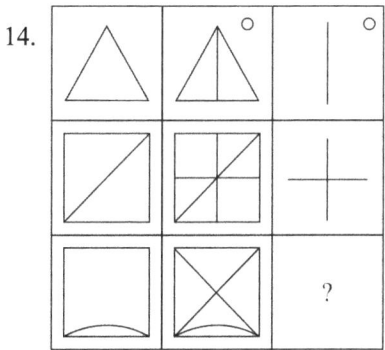

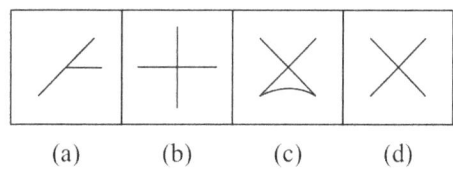

15.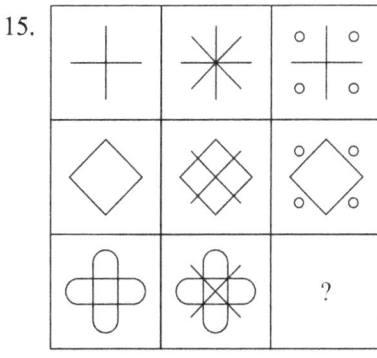

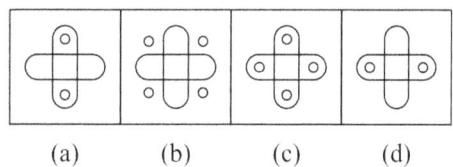

Figure Matrix

16.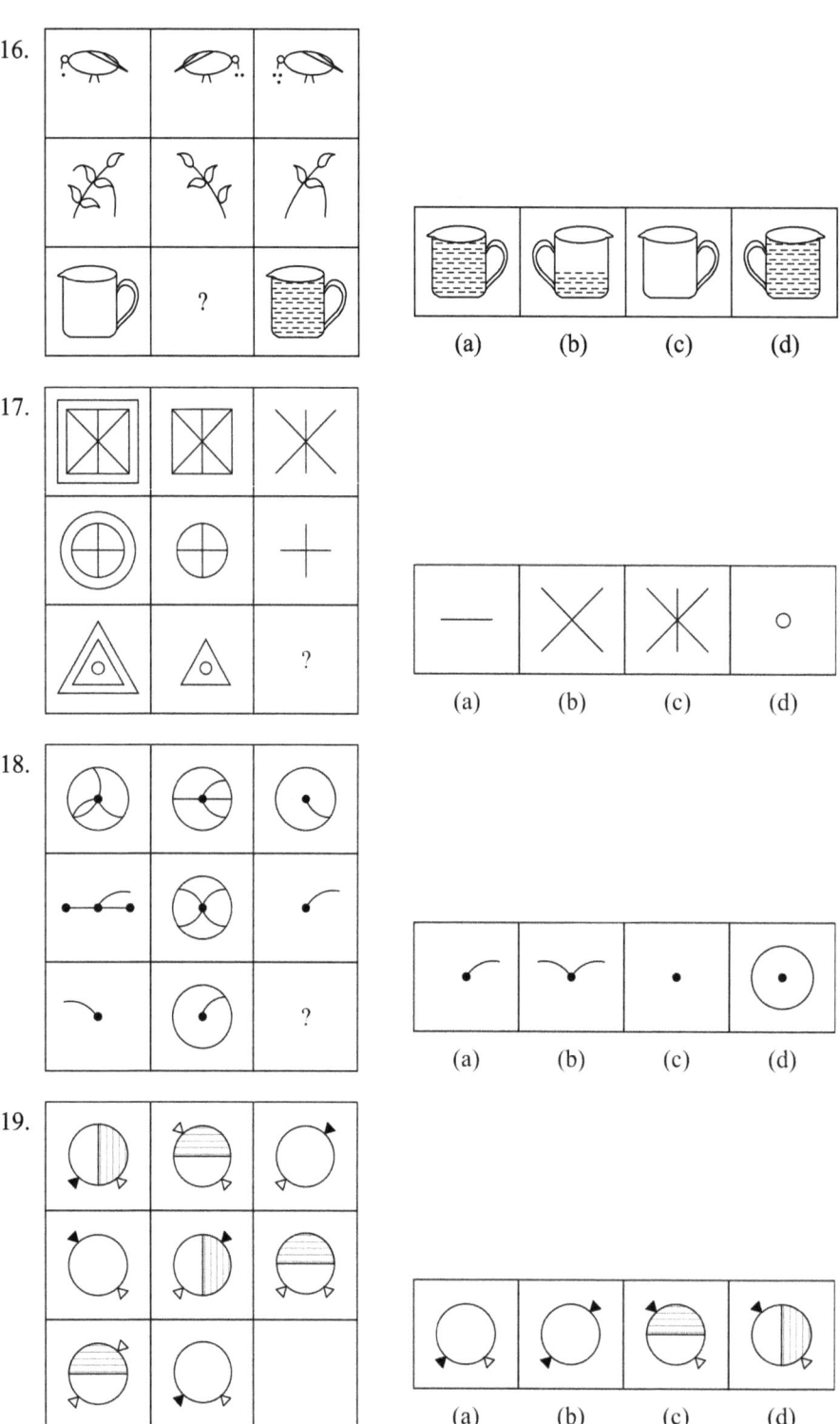

20.
21.
22.
23.

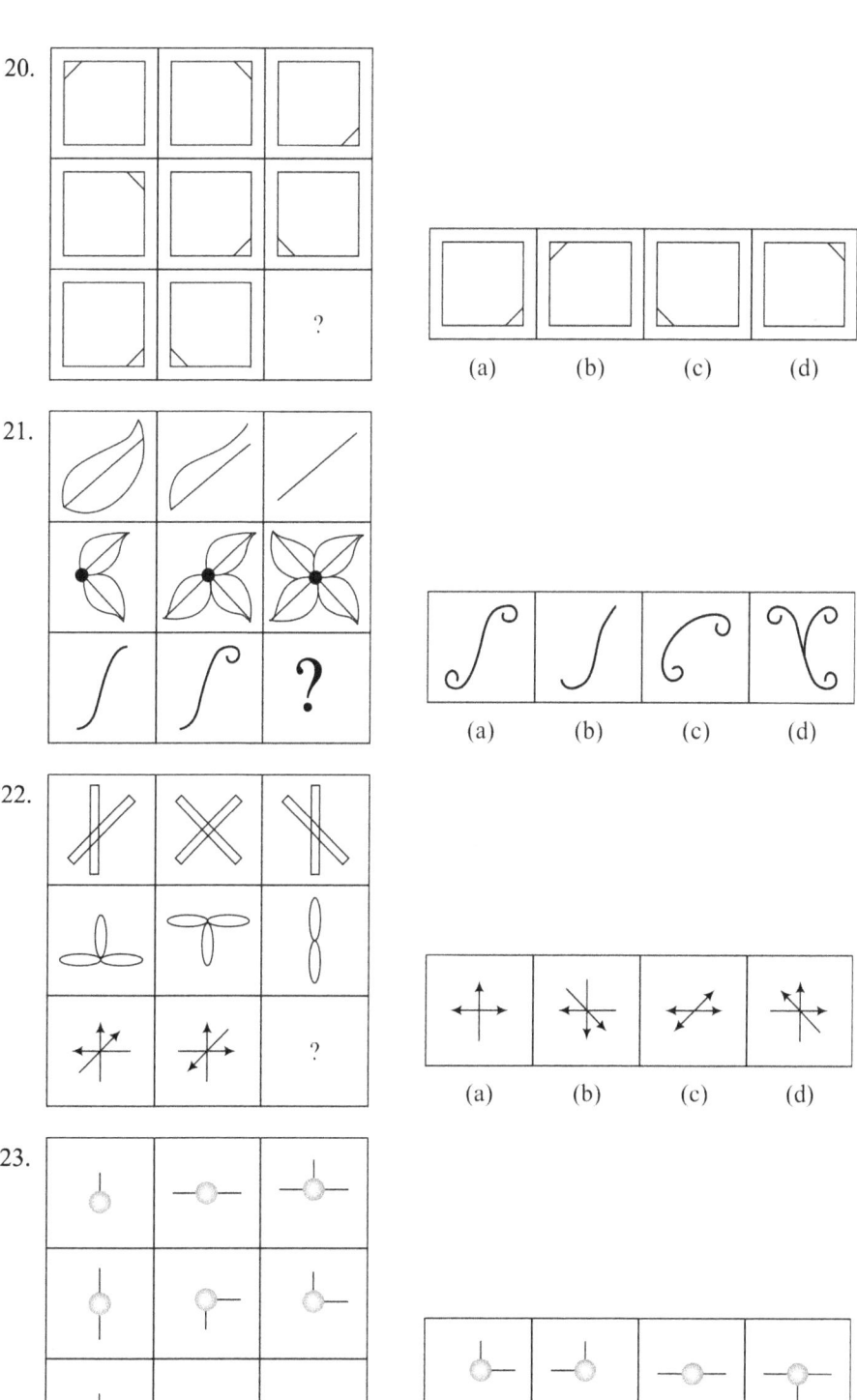

Figure Matrix

24.

25.

26.

27.

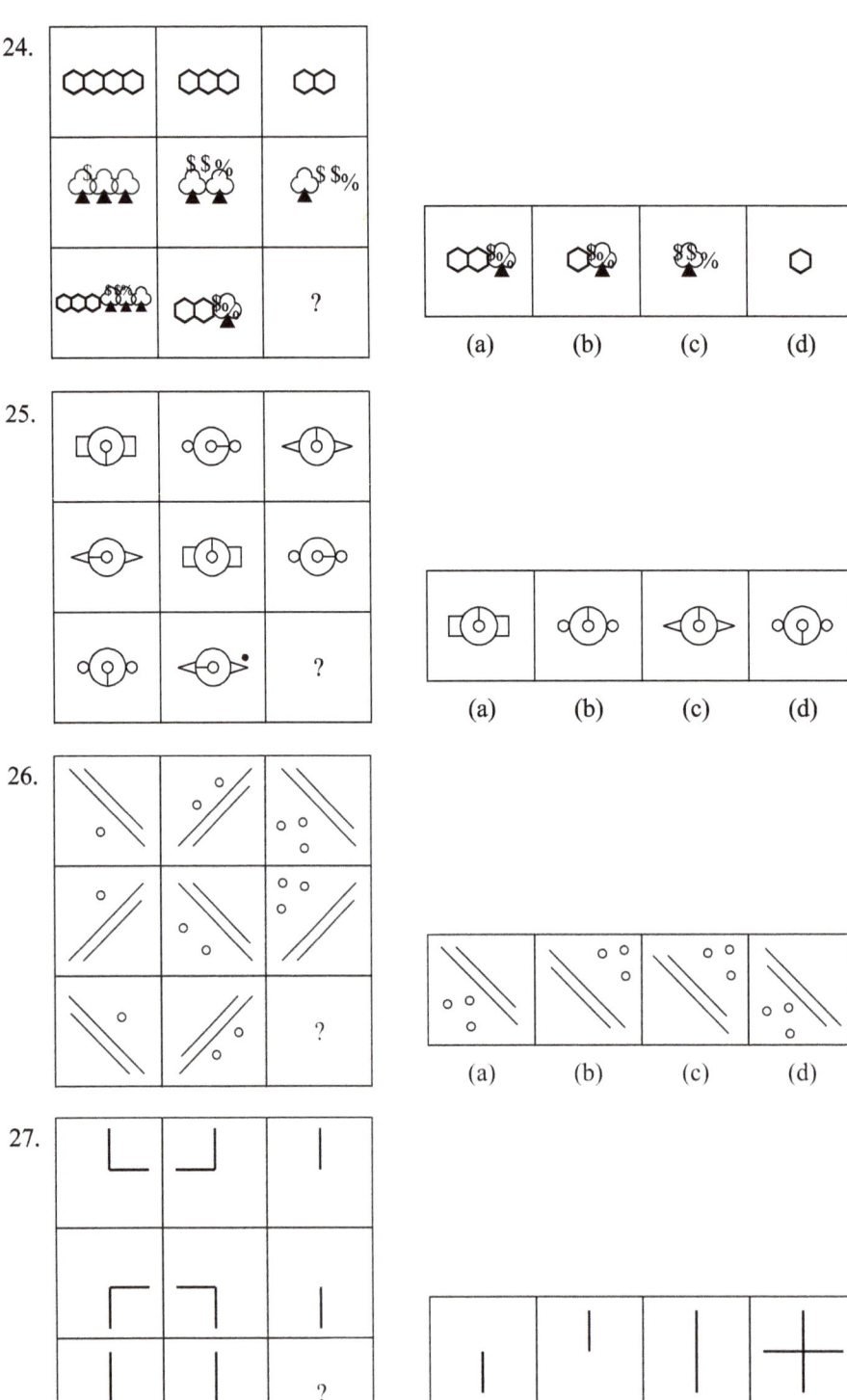

28.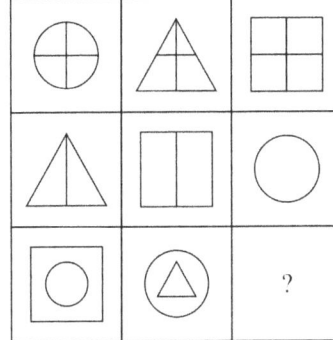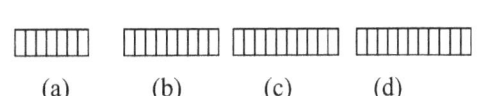

29.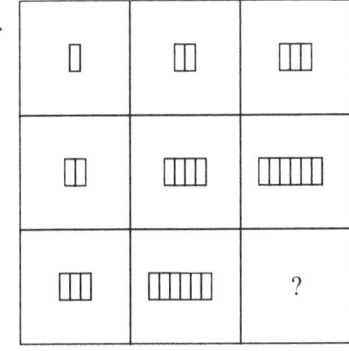

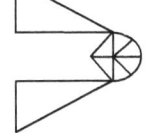 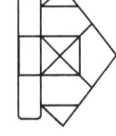
(a)   (b)   (c)   (d)

30. Select a figure from the options in which Fig. (X) is exactly embedded as one of its parts.

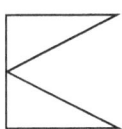

Fig. (X)

(a) 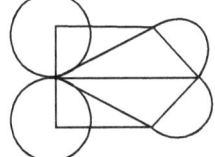 (b)

(c) (d)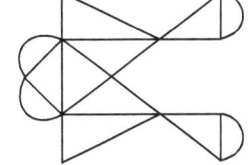

Figure Matrix

SECTION 3
ACHIEVERS' SECTION

Some Thoughtful Questions

1. Mention the commutativity, associative and distributive properties of rational numbers. Also, check $a \times b = b \times a$ and $a + b = b + a$ for $a = \dfrac{1}{2}$ and $b = \dfrac{3}{4}$

   Answer:
   Commutative property:
   For any two rational numbers a and b, $a + b = b + a$.
   For any two rational numbers a and b, $a \times b = b \times a$.
   Associative Property:
   For any three rational numbers a, b and c,
   $(a + b) + c = a + (b + c)$
   Distributive property states that for any three numbers x, y and z,
   $x \times (y + z) = (x \times y) + (x \times z)$
   $a*b = b*a$
   $a*b = \dfrac{1}{2} * \dfrac{3}{4} = \dfrac{3}{8}$
   $b*a = \dfrac{3}{4} * \dfrac{1}{2} = \dfrac{3}{8}$
   $a+b = \dfrac{3}{4} + \dfrac{1}{2} = \dfrac{5}{4}$
   $b+a = \dfrac{1}{2} + \dfrac{3}{4} = \dfrac{5}{4}$

2. Jane is 6 years older than her younger sister. After 10 years, the sum of their ages will be 50 years. Find their present ages.

   Answer:
   Let the age of Jane's younger sister is x.
   Age of Jane will be $x + 6$
   As per the question, after 10 years the sum of their ages will be 50.
   After 10 years,
   age of Jane = $x + 16$
   age of her younger sister = $x + 10$
   Therefore,
   $x + 16 + x + 10 = 50$
   $2x + 26 = 50$
   $2x = 24$
   $x = 12$
   Hence, the present age of Jane's younger sister is 12 years.
   And of Jane's is $12 + 6 = 18$ years.

3. A diagonal and a side of a rhombus are of equal length. Find the measure of the angles of the rhombus.

   Answer:
   Let ABCD be the rhombus.
   Thus, AB = BC = CD = DA

   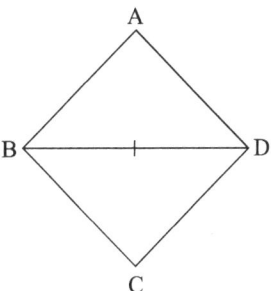

   Given that a side and diagonal are equal.
   AB = BD (say)
   Therefore, AB = BC = CD = DA = BD
   Now, all the sides of a triangle ABD are equal.
   Therefore, $\triangle$ABD is an equilateral triangle.
   Similarly,
   $\triangle$BCD is also an equilateral triangle.
   Thus, $\angle$A = $\angle$ABD = $\angle$ADB = $\angle$DBC = $\angle$C = $\angle$CDB = 60°
   $\angle$B = $\angle$ABD + $\angle$DBC = 60° + 60° = 120°
   And
   $\angle$D = $\angle$ADB + $\angle$CDB = 60° + 60° = 120°
   Hence, the angles of the rhombus are 60°, 120°, 60° and 120°.

4. Numbers 1 to 10 are written on ten separate slips (one number on one slip), kept in a box and mixed well. One slip is chosen from the box without looking into it. What is the probability of:
   (i) getting a number 6?
   (ii) getting a number less than 6?
   (iii) getting a number greater than 6?
   (iv) getting a 1-digit number?

   Answer:
   (i) The outcome of getting a number 6 from ten separate slips is one.
   Therefore, the probability of getting a number $6 = \dfrac{1}{10}$

   (ii) Numbers which are less than 6 are 1, 2, 3, 4 and 5. So total there are five numbers. Thus, there are 5 outcomes.
   Therefore, the probability of getting a number less than $6 = \dfrac{5}{10} = \dfrac{1}{2}$

   (iii) The number is greater than 6 out of ten that are 7, 8, 9, 10. So there are 4 possible outcomes.
   Therefore, the probability of getting a number greater than $6 = \dfrac{4}{10} = \dfrac{2}{5}$

   (iv) One digit numbers out of 1 to 10 are 1, 2, 3, 4, 5, 6, 7, 8, 9.
   Therefore, the probability of getting a 1-digit number $= \dfrac{9}{10}$

5. If $31z5$ is a multiple of 3, where z is a digit, what might be the values of z?

   Answer:
   Given, $31z5$ is a multiple of 3.
   Therefore according to the divisibility rule of 3, the sum of all the digits should be a multiple of 3.
   That is, $3 + 1 + z + 5 = 9 + z$
   Therefore, $9 + z$ is a multiple of 3.
   This is possible when the value of $9 + z$ is any of the values: 0, 3, 6, 9, 12, 15, and so on.
   At $z = 0$, $9 + z = 9 + 0 = 9$
   At $z = 3$, $9 + z = 9 + 3 = 12$
   At $z = 6$, $9 + z = 9 + 6 = 15$
   At $z = 9$, $9 + z = 9 + 9 = 18$
   The value of $9 + z$ can be 9 or 12 or 15 or 18.
   Hence 0, 3, 6 or 9 are four possible answers for z.

Model Test Paper 1

SECTION I: LOGICAL REASONING

1. Select a figure from the four options, which when placed in the blank space of figure (X) would complete the pattern.

   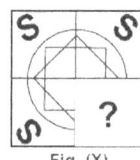
   Fig. (X)

   (a) 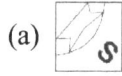   (b)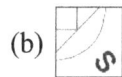

   (c) 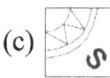   (d)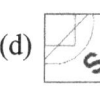

2. Which one of the following sets is best represented by the given diagrams?

   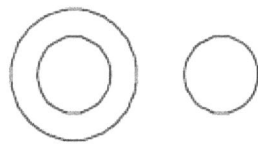

   (a) Animals, Insects, Cockroaches
   (b) Country, States, Districts
   (c) Sun, Planets, Earth
   (d) Classroom, Blackboard, School

3. In a certain code TELEPHONE is written as ENOHPELET. How is ALLIGATOR written in that code?
   (a) ROTAGILLA   (b) ROTAGAILL
   (c) ROTAGILLE   (d) OTAGILLAR

4. If '−' means 'x', 'x' means '+', '+' means '÷' and '÷' means '−', then
   8 x 5 − 8 + 40 ÷ 2 =?
   (a) 7   (b) 16
   (c) 44   (d) 4

5. Anusha remembers that her brother Kabir's birthday falls after 21st May but before 30th May, while Pia remembers that Kabir's birthday falls before 25th May but after 20th May. On what date Kabir's birthday falls?
   (a) 20th May   (b) 21st May
   (c) 22nd May   (d) 27th May

6. In the series 6 4 1 2 2 8 7 4 2 1 5 3 8 6 2 1 7 1 4 1 3 2 8, how many pairs of successive numbers have a difference of 1 each?
   (a) Four   (b) Five
   (c) Six   (d) Seven

7. The triangle, square, and circle shown here represent urban, hardworking and educated people respectively. Which one of the areas represents the urban educated people who are not hard-working?

   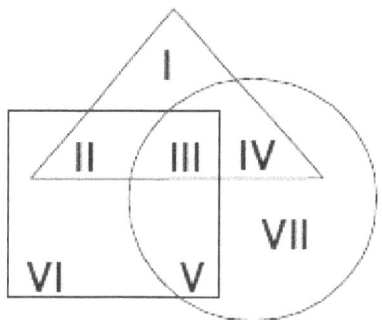

   (a) IV   (b) II
   (c) V   (d) VII

8. Find amongst the four options the figure which most nearly contains the Fig. (X).

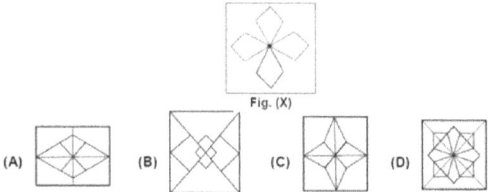

9. Letters of the word given below have been jumbled up. The letters have been numbered and followed by four options. Choose the option which gives the correct order of the letters to form a meaningful word.

I	N	L	A	S	G
1	2	3	4	5	6

(a) 2, 4, 3, 6, 1, 5
(b) 3, 4, 6, 1, 2, 5
(c) 5, 1, 6, 2, 4, 3
(d) 6, 1, 3, 5, 4, 2

10. Find the odd one out.
(a) UTSR   (b) IHGE
(c) NMLK   (d) ZYXW

11. How many triangles are there in the given figure?

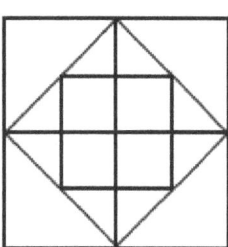

(a) 20   (b) 26
(c) 23   (d) 24

12. Which number would replace the blank place in the given series?
3, 15, _, 63, 99, 143
(a) 27   (b) 35
(c) 45   (d) 56

13. Shreya saw the restaurant sign shown below.

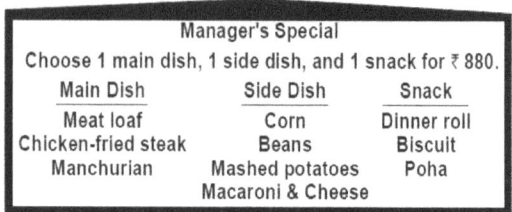

How many different combinations are possible if Shreya buys the Manager's special?
(a) 8   (b) 16
(c) 24   (d) 36

14. Find the mirror image of the Figure (X) if mirror is placed along M_1M_2.

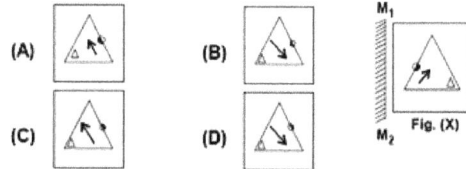

15. The given question consists of four figures 1, 2, 3 and 4 called the Problem Set. There is a definite relationship between the figures 1 and 2. Establish a similar relationship between the figures 3 and 4 by selecting a suitable figure from the options that would replace the question mark (?) in the figure (4)?

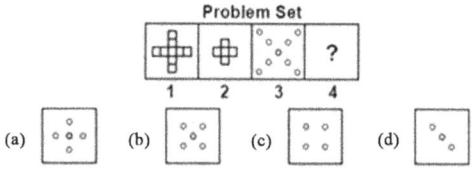

16. Pointing towards a person, a man said to a woman, "His mother is the only daughter of your father". How is the woman related to that person?
(a) Daughter   (b) Sister
(c) Mother   (d) Sister-in-law

17. If 'eraser' is 'box', 'box' is 'pencil', 'pencil' is 'sharpener', and 'sharpener' is 'bag', what will a child write with?
    (a) Eraser   (b) Box
    (c) Pencil   (d) Sharpener

18. If you cut out and fold the pattern shown below to make a cube, which letter will be on the face of the cube opposite the face labelled 2?

    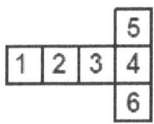

    (a) 4   (b) 1
    (c) 5   (d) 6

19. Which of the following figures comes next in the given pattern?

    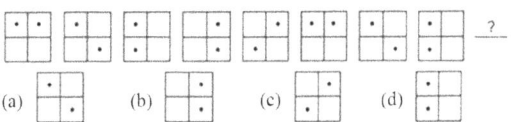

20. Find the missing character from among the given options.

    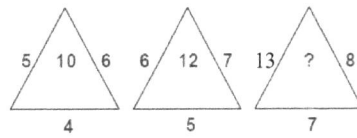

    (a) 4   (b) 6
    (c) 12   (d) 3

SECTION II: MATHEMATICAL REASONING

21. Father's age is equal to the sum of the ages of his five children. After 15 years, his age will be only half of the sum of the children's ages. How old is the father?
    (a) 42 years   (b) 43 years
    (c) 44 years   (d) 45 years

22. What is the value of $x^3 + y^3 + z^3 - 3xyz$, when $x = 2, y = 1$ and $z = -3$?
    (a) 6   (b) 0
    (c) 2   (d) −4

23. Find the value of:
    $$\frac{\sqrt[6]{0.001}\sqrt[6]{x^{1296}}}{\sqrt{10}}$$
    (a) $10x$ (b) $\frac{x^6}{10^3}$
    (c) $\frac{x^{36}}{10}$ (d) $\left(\frac{10x}{x^5}\right)^{1/6}$

24. What is the value of x in the given equation?
    $(3x - 8)(3x + 2) - (4x - 11)(2x + 1) = (x - 3)(x + 7)$
    (a) 2   (b) 4
    (c) 3   (d) 5

25. Last year Mr. Nitin earned Rs. 19600 from the corn he grew on his farm. This year he expects a 7% increase in the income from corn. How much does he expect to earn from corn this year?
    (a) Rs. 13720   (b) Rs. 30972
    (c) Rs. 10972   (d) Rs. 20972

26. Evaluate:
    $$\sqrt{10 + \sqrt{25 + \sqrt{108 + \sqrt{154 + \sqrt{225}}}}}$$
    (a) 4   (b) 6
    (c) 8   (d) 10

Model Test Paper

27. What is the measure of x in the given figure?

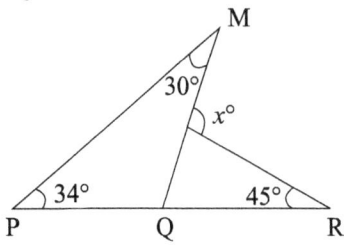

(a) 112° (b) 110°
(c) 109° (d) 107°

28. Write $(3^{-7} \div 3^{-10}) \times 3^{-5}$ in simplest form.
(a) 1/3   (b) 3^2
(c) 3^{-2} (d) 3^4

29. A 2 cm long grasshopper can jump 160 cm. If a 6-metre tall animal had the same height and jump ratio, how far could he jump?
(a) 48 m   (b) 480 m
(c) 180 m   (d) 8000 m

30. John made the given grid to show some locations in his garden.

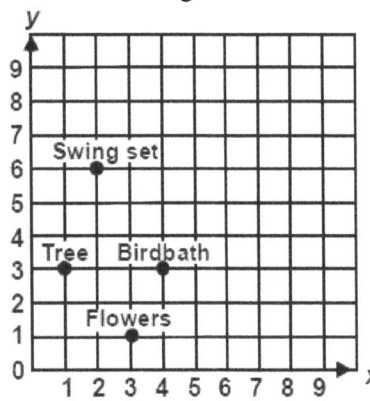

Which ordered pair best represents the point on the grid labelled "Birdbath"?
(a) (2, 6)   (b) (3, 4)
(c) (1, 3)   (d) (4, 3)

31. Students at a local college were asked how many hours they slept the previous night. The given chart shows the data. The probability of the students who slept for 6 hours is _____.

Hours of Sleep	No. of Students
6	14
7	26
8	28
9	15
More than 10	6

(a) 15/89   (b) 6/89
(c) 14/28   (d) 14/89

32. What is the average of the sixth even number, and fifth and eighth odd number after 200?
(a) 210   (b) 211
(c) 212   (d) 213

33. Addition of rational numbers does not satisfy which of the following property ?
(a) Commutative   (b) Associative
(c) Closure   (d) None of these

34. How many cubic metres of earth must be dug out to make a well 22.5 m deep and of diameter 7 m.
(a) 866.25 m³   (b) 495 m³
(c) 77.82 m³   (d) 748 m³

35. When a number is divided by 125, the remainder is 82, then when the same number is divided by 25, the remainder will be _____.
(a) 8   (b) 9
(c) 6   (d) 7

36. Between which two consecutive whole numbers does $\sqrt{2000}$ lie?
(a) 41 and 42   (b) 44 and 45
(c) 43 and 44   (d) 45 and 46

37. Which two quadrilaterals have exactly four lines of symmetry ?

(1)   (2)   (3)   (4)   (5)

(a) (1) and (5)   (b) (3) and (2)
(c) (3) and (4)   (d) (2) and (5)

38. In the given figure, if $\angle A = (2x + 10)°$, $\angle B = (x + 20)°$, $\angle C = (y - 50)°$ and $\angle D = (y - 10)°$, the values of x and y are ____.
  (a) x = 30°, y = 20°
  (b) x = 60°, y = 40°
  (c) x = 50°, y = 120°
  (d) x = 70°, y = 90°

39. The compound interest on a certain sum for 2 years at 10% per annum is Rs.525. The simple interest on the same sum for double the time at half the rate percent per annum is _____.
  (a) Rs. 400   (b) Rs. 500
  (c) Rs. 600   (d) Rs. 800

40. Factorise : $3 - 12(a - b)^2$
  (a) $3(1 + 2a + 2b)(1 - 2a + 2b)$
  (b) $3(1 - 2a - 2b)(1 + 2a - 2b)$
  (c) $3(1 + 2a - 2b)(1 - 2a + 2b)$
  (d) $3(1 - 2a - 2b)(1 - 2a - 2b)$

SECTION III: EVERYDAY MATHEMATICS

41. A trader marks his goods 40% above the cost price and gives a discount of 20% on the marked price. Find his gain percent.
  (a) 10%   (b) 12%
  (c) 14%   (d) 15%

42. A man sold 10 eggs for Rs.5 and gained 20%. How many eggs did he buy for Rs. 5?
  (a) 12   (b) 25/12
  (c) 25   (d) None of these

43. 729 ml of a mixture contains milk and water in the ratio 7 : 2. How much more water is to be added to get a new mixture containing milk and water in the ratio 6: 3 ?
  (a) 60 ml   (b) 71ml
  (c) 52 ml   (d) 81 ml

44. Mrs. Nysa needs to take a taxi to the doctor's clinic. The taxi ride costs Rs. 15 for the first km and Rs. 8 for each additional km and part thereof. How much does Mrs. Nysa pay for a 3.8 km taxi ride?
  (a) Rs. 35   (b) Rs. 28
  (c) Rs. 32   (d) Rs. 38

45. Anusha and three of her friends worked together to make a quilt. The given table lists the fractional part of the quilt that each of the girls made. Which list shows the girls in the order from the one who sewed the least to the one who sewed the most?

Girl	Parts Sewn
Anusha	$\frac{5}{9}$
Kirti	$\frac{1}{5}$
Sara	$\frac{3}{5}$
Rehana	$\frac{11}{13}$

  (a) Rehana, Anusha, Sara, Kirti
  (b) Sara, Anusha, Kirti, Rehana
  (c) Rehana, Kirti, Anusha, Sara
  (d) Kirti, Sara, Anusha, Rehana

46. Two flower beds in a park are similar rectangles of same width. The longest side of the large flower bed is 48 cm long, and the longest side of the small flower bed is 16 cm. If L is the area of the large flower bed and S is the area of the small flower bed, which equation is true?
    (a) S = L – 16
    (b) S = L + 16
    (c) S = (1/9) L
    (d) S = (1/3) L

47. The Wright brothers had their first successful flight near Kitty Hawk, North Carolina. Mr. Mohit finds it easy to remember the year in which the flight occurred because the number is the square root of his telephone number 3629025. In which year did the flight occur?
    (a) 1925
    (b) 1935
    (c) 1945
    (d) 1905

48. Dhruv plans to leave his home in Delhi at 8:00 A.M. He will drive at an average speed of 40 km per hour and plans to arrive at his destination just before 12:00 P.M. If he makes no stops along the way, which of the four places is his destination?

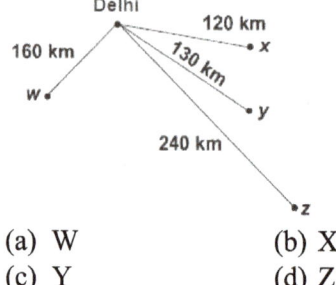

(a) W
(b) X
(c) Y
(d) Z

49. Kareena is on the fifth floor of a building. Her car is in the parking garage which is three levels below the ground floor. She gets in the elevator and travels from the fifth floor above ground level to the third floor below ground level. How many floors did she travel?
    (a) 7
    (b) 6
    (c) 4
    (d) 8

50. Jiah is building birdhouses. It takes her 5.5 hours to build 4 birdhouses. Which of the following is an equivalent rate?
    (a) 14 hours to build 18 birdhouses
    (b) 28 hours to build 35 birdhouses
    (c) 11 hours to build 8 birdhouses
    (d) 22 hours to build 28 birdhouses

Model Test Paper 2

SECTION I: LOGICAL REASONING

1. If in a certain code, 'when' means 'x', 'you' means '÷','come' means '–' and 'will' means '+', then what will be the value of "8 when 12 will 16 you 2 come 10" ?
   (a) 45 (b) 94
   (c) 96 (d) 112

2. How many numbers from 11 to 50 are there, which are exactly divisible by 7 but not by 3?
   (a) Two (b) Four
   (c) Five (d) Six

3. The given table shows the ticket prices of an amusement park. Mohit sells tickets to 7 adults, 15 youth and 10 children. How much does he earn?

   Ticket Prices

Type of Tickets	Price
Child	₹ 20
Youth	₹ 15
Adult	₹ 20

   (a) ₹ 565 (b) ₹ 470
   (c) ₹ 500 (d) ₹ 865

4. Rahul bought 4 packets of notebook papers for school last year. Each packet contained 50 notebook papers. He used about 20 notebook papers every week. Find the number of notebook papers Rahul was left with after 7 weeks?
   (a) 67 (b) 17
   (c) 70 (d) 60

5. Priyanka is shorter than Shikha and longer than Sneha. If Sneha is longer than Yukti, who is the shortest among them?
   (a) Priyanka (b) Shikha
   (c) Sneha (d) Yukti

6. If 'paper' is called 'wood', 'wood' is called 'straw', 'straw' is called 'grass', 'grass' is called 'rubber' and 'rubber' is called 'cloth', what is furniture made up of ?
   (a) Paper (b) Wood
   (c) Straw (d) Grass

7. Ranbir is sixth from the left end and Vikram is tenth from the right end in a row of boys. If there are eight boys between Ranbir and Vikram, how many boys are there in that row?
   (a) 23 (b) 25
   (c) 24 (d) 26

8. How many squares are there in the given figure?

   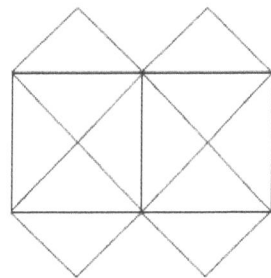

   (a) 6 (b) 7
   (c) 8 (d) 9

9. Which pair of eagle pictures shows reflection?

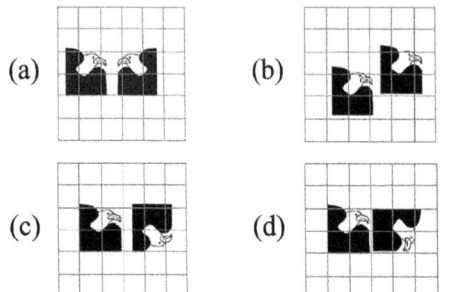

10. A parent group is planning an awards dinner for students, teachers and parents. The parent group plans to seat the guests around a circular table that has seating for 30. The guests will be seated in the order of student, teacher and parent in a repeating pattern. Who will be the 23rd guest?
    (a) Student
    (b) Teacher
    (c) Parent
    (d) Cannot be determined

11. A community swimming pool is open on different days depending on the air temperature. The given table shows the air temperature on different days. The dates listed in the table show that the pool was closed on July 1, August 1 and October 1. If the pool was open on all the other dates listed, which of the following statements best describes the air temperature when the pool is open?

Swimming Pool

Date	Air Temperature
May 1	68° F
June 1	73° F
July 1	82° F
August 1	87° F
September 1	80° F
October 1	95° F

(a) The air temperature must be between 74° F and 90° F
(b) The air temperature must be lower than 91° F
(c) The air temperature must be higher than 75° F
(d) The air temperature must be between 67° F and 81° F

12. Choose the correct mirror image of Figure (X), when the mirror is placed along PQ.

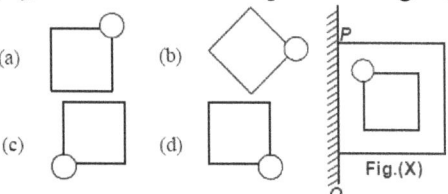

13. Which one of the following diagrams best illustrates the three classes : "Sailor, Ship, Ocean" ?

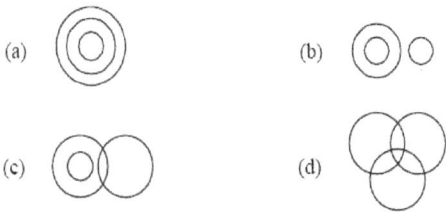

14. If 1st and 26th, 2nd and 25th, 3rd and 24th, and so on, the letters of the English alphabet are paired, which of the following pairs is correct?
    (a) GR   (b) CW
    (c) IP   (d) EV

15. Rohan plans to make a display by stacking cans. The top 3 rows are shown here. The display will be a total of 9 rows. How many cans in all will Rohan need to make the display?

(a) 49 (b) 45
(c) 47 (d) 42

16. A zoo had 17 tigers. All but eight died. How many were left with the zoo?
    (a) Nil (b) 8
    (c) 9 (d) 17

17. Read the graph and answer the given question. On which day did Samir receive exactly 45 text messages?

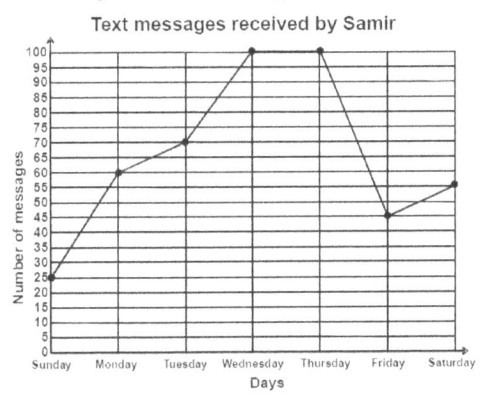

    (a) Monday (b) Thursday
    (c) Friday (d) Sunday

18. Armaan walks 30 metres towards south. Then, turning to right, he walks 30 metres. Then, turning to his left, he walks 20 metres. Again, he turns to his left and walks 30 metres. How far is he from his initial position?
    (a) 20 metres (b) 50 metres
    (c) 60 metres (d) 80 metres

19. How many lines of symmetry does the figure have?

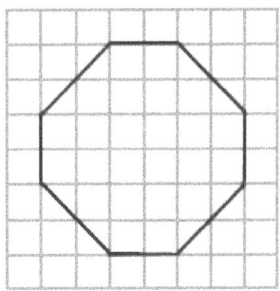

    (a) 1 (b) 2
    (c) 3 (d) 4

20. Find the odd one out.
    (a) 176 – 168 (b) 214 – 206
    (c) 577 – 568 (d) 319 – 311

SECTION II: MATHEMATICAL REASONING

21. A mistake was made in simplifying the expression given below.

    Simplify: $5 + 2(6 + 4)^2 - 2^3$,

    Step 1: $5 + 2(10) - 2^3$,

    Step 2: $5 + 20 - 8$,

    Step 3: $25 - 8$,

    Step 4: 17.

    In which step did the first mistake appear?
    (a) Step 1 (b) Step 2
    (c) Step 3 (d) Step 4

22. What percentage of the figures are circles?

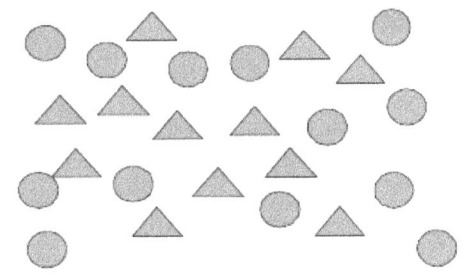

    (a) 48% (b) 50%
    (c) 52% (d) 54%

23. Find the value of the expression given below?

$$\left(\frac{3a^2 + 2a \times 5 - 4}{4}\right) + 5a - 2, \text{ when } a = 4$$

(a) 24 (b) 39
(c) 27 (d) 36

24. Which of the following figures has 10 vertices?

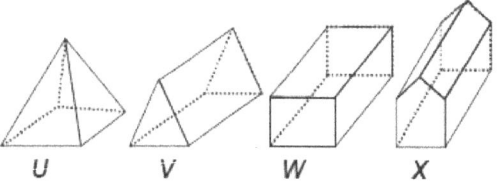

(a) Figure U (b) Figure V
(c) Figure W (d) Figure X

25. Which list of integers is in order from greatest to least ?
(a) - 42, –39, – 4, 40, 41
(b) - 42, 41, 40, – 39, – 4
(c) - 4, – 39, 40, 41, 42
(d) 41, 40, – 4, – 39, – 42

26. Which model best represents the expression $\frac{1}{2} \times \frac{1}{3}$?

(A) 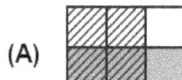 (B)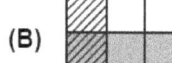

(C)  (D)

27. Mr. Sameer was trying to find a tablecloth for his rectangular dining table. He knew the area and perimeter of the tabletop.

Area = 40 square metres, Perimeter = 28 metres

Which of the following best represents the width and length of the tabletop?

(a) Length = 10 m, Width = 4 m
(b) Width = 2 m, Length = 20 m
(c) Width = 5 m, Length = 8 m
(d) Width = 4 m, Length = 12 m

28. If 2 unit cubes, one on each are placed on the unit cubes marked 'X', which solid will be obtained?

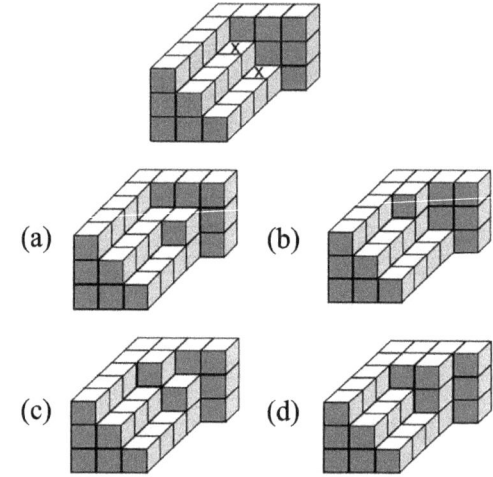

29. Fill in the blank of the statement given below.

70 has _____ factors.
(a) 2 (b) 4
(c) 6 (d) 8

30. Which of the following is true for the two given congruent figures?

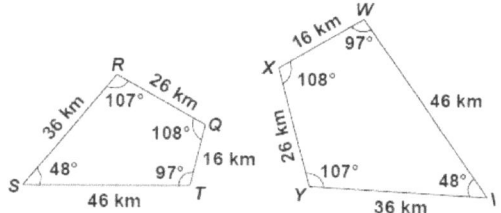

(A) $\overline{TQ} \cong \overline{XY}$
(B) $\overline{ST} \cong \overline{XY}$
(C) $\overline{TQ} \cong \overline{WX}$
(D) $\angle Q \cong \angle Y$

31. The total cost of 5 teddy bears is the same as the total cost of 9 clowns. Find the cost of a teddy bear.

(a) Rs. 27   (b) Rs. 28
(c) Rs. 30   (d) Rs. 32

32. The perimeter of the given figure is ____.

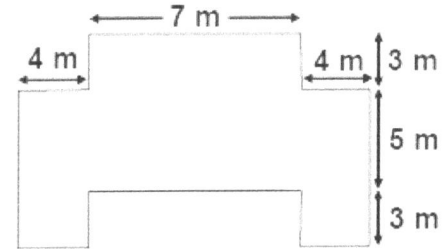

(a) 68 m   (b) 48 m
(c) 58 m   (d) 50 m

33. Which of the following digits makes the given statement true?

The number 606__19 is divisible by 9.
(a) 3   (b) 6
(c) 5   (d) 8

34. Given that,

If each 😟 stands for $\frac{1}{4}$, what does each 😊 stand for ?
(a) 3/4   (b) 3/2
(c) 3/8   (d) 3/5

35. Asha looked at different flower arrangements before purchasing one. The arrangements varied in price from Rs.15.62 to Rs. 37.50. Which measure of data can be used to describe the variation between maximum and minimum price?
(a) Mean   (b) Mode
(c) Range   (d) Median

36. Which of the following figures are acute isosceles triangles ?

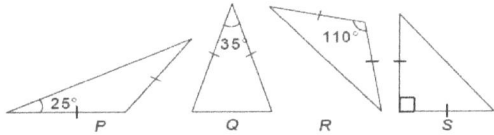

(a) P only   (b) Q only
(c) R only   (d) R and S only

37. Evaluate:

$$\frac{3}{4} + 5\frac{1}{2} - 1\frac{1}{3} - \frac{1}{2} \times \frac{9}{10}$$

(a) 4.48   (b) –4.46
(c) –4.82   (d) 4.46

38. Ashwin used the rule listed below to rewrite the expression $10^2 \times 10^5 = 10^7$.
$10^m \times 10^n = 10^{m+n}$
Based on this rule, which of the following is equivalent to the expression $8^{-8} \times 8^6$?
(a) 8^{-10}, because $8^{-4} \times 8^6 = 8^{-4-6}$
(b) 8^{-12}, because $8^{-4} \times 8^{-8} = 8^{-4-8}$
(c) 8^{-2}, because $8^{-8} \times 8^6 = 8^{-8+6}$
(d) 8^2, because $8^{-4} \times 8^6 = 8^{-4+6}$

39. A building is 24 m long. The bottom of the ladder is 10 m away from the foot of the building. Find the length of the ladder?
(a) 12 m   (b) 24 m
(c) 26 m   (d) 8 m

40. Amit counted the number of people in line for tickets at the movie theatre. Every time he saw 7 people, he added a tick mark on his counting sheet, as shown below.

Amit saw 6 more people after he added his last tick mark. Which expression can be used to find u, the total number of people he saw?
(a) $16 \div 6 + 7 = u$
(b) $16 \times 6 \times 7 = u$
(c) $16 \times 7 + 6 = u$
(d) $16 + 7 - 6 = u$

SECTION III: EVERYDAY MATHEMATICS

41. It took Abhilasha 20 minutes to apply a coat of paint to a piece of pottery. After each coat she waited for 1 hour 30 minutes for the paint to dry. Which is a reasonable amount of time it could have taken for Abhilasha to have applied 5 coats of paint and for the pottery to be completely dry ?
    (a) 505 minutes (b) 8 hours
    (c) 195 minutes (d) 9 hours

42. The average of three numbers is $9m + 8$. Two of the three numbers are $2m + 3$ and $4m + 5$. Express the third number in terms of m in the simplest form.
    (a) $9m + 8$ (b) $27m + 24$
    (c) $21m + 16$ (d) $21m + 32$

43. Hrishant packs boxes for an appliance company. He can pack a large box in 10 minutes and a small box in 4 minutes. He needs to pack 10 large boxes and 20 small boxes. If he starts his work 3.5 hours before closing time, will Hrishant have time to finish the work before closing time if he works without stopping?
    (a) Yes, Hrishant will finish the work in 3 hours.
    (b) No, it will take Hrishant 4 hours to finish.
    (c) Yes, Hrishant will finish the work in 2.5 hours.
    (d) No, it will take Hrishant 6 hours to finish.

44. The total length of all songs on a CD, Anshuman bought is about 74 minutes. Each song is between 4 to 6 minutes long. Which is a reasonable number of songs that could be on the CD?
    (a) 10 (b) 40
    (c) 74 (d) 16

45. Ishika and Sasha raced their toy cars. The given diagram shows the distance travelled by the cars during the race. How far did Ishika's car travel than Sasha's car?

    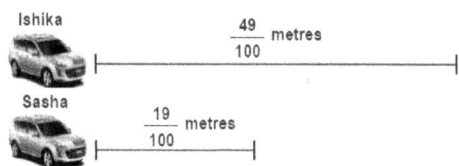

    (a) 3/10 m (b) 4/10 m
    (c) 32/10 m (d) 68/100 m

46. Tameena has 4 old coins : P, Q, R and S. Coin R is worth Rs. 2.5. Coin S is worth 2 times the value of coin R. Coin Q is worth 3 times the value of coin R. The four coins are worth Rs. 40 altogether. What is the value of coin P?
    (a) Rs. 14 (b) Rs. 18
    (c) Rs. 25 (d) Rs. 15

47. Ankit can run 100 metres in 12.5 seconds. If he competes in the 400 metres race, about how many seconds will he take to run the race?
    (a) 50 seconds (b) 40 seconds
    (c) 80 seconds (d) 20 seconds

48. Misha answered 56% of the 150 problems on her history homework correctly. How many problems on her homework did she answer correctly?
    (a) 56 (b) 65
    (c) 84 (d) 92

49. There are 338 cows and goats on a farm. $\frac{2}{3}$ of the cows are equal to $\frac{1}{5}$ of the goats on the farm. How many cows are there on the farm?
    (a) 78   (b) 260
    (c) 72   (d) 270

50. Which of the following statements represents the greatest percent of change?
    (a) A tree grew from 6 feet to 12 feet in 1 year.
    (b) An aquarium that was originally priced at Rs. 90 is now priced at Rs.140.
    (c) A person whose salary was Rs. 1000 per week is now earning Rs. 1500 per week.
    (d) A baby who weighed 5 pounds at birth now weighs 20 pounds.

Answer Keys

Scan the QR Code to see the Hints and Solutions

Access Content Online on Dropbox: https://www.dropbox.com/scl/fi/1ytekiwscpktjdl0dbu9o/IMO-5-Math-Olympiad-Hints-Solution-Dropbox.pdf?rlkey=qnw9lcelb5g1yg523pl02tthz&dl=0

SECTION 1: MATHEMATICAL REASONING

1. PLAYING WITH NUMBERS

Answer Key

1. (b)	2. (c)	3. (d)	4. (a)	5. (b)	6. (c)	7. (b)	8. (a)	9. (b)	10. (c)
11. (b)	12. (b)	13. (b)	14. (a)	15. (b)	16. (a)	17. (c)	18. (b)	19. (d)	20. (a)
21. (d)	22. (b)	23. (a)	24. (c)	25. (d)	26. (c)	27. (d)	28. (b)	29. (a)	30. (b)
32. (a)	32. (b)	33. (c)	34. (c)	35. (c)	36. (a)	37. (c)	38. (a)	39. (b)	40. (d)
41. (a)	42. (c)	43. (b)	44. (a)	45. (b)	46. (a)	47. (c)	48. (a)	49. (d)	50. (b)

HOTS

1. (a)	2. (b)	3. (b)	4. (b)	5. (a)

2. RATIONAL NUMBERS

Answer Key

1. (c)	2. (b)	3. (a)	4. (b)	5. (a)	6. (b)	7. (a)	8. (a)	9. (a)	10. (b)
11. (c)	12. (b)	13. (d)	14. (b)	15. (a)	16. (c)	17. (c)	18. (b)	19. (a)	20. (b)
21. (d)	22. (a)	23. (a)	24. (d)	25. (d)	26. (b)	27. (c)	28. (a)	29. (d)	30. (b)

HOTS

1. (a)	2. (a)	3. (c)	4. (d)	5. (a)

3. SQUARES AND SQUARE ROOTS

Answer Key

1. (d)	2. (b)	3. (c)	4. (d)	5. (b)	6. (a)	7. (c)	8. (a)	9. (d)	10. (d)
11. (d)	12. (d)	13. (a)	14. (b)	15. (c)	16. (c)	17. (c)	18. (c)	19. (c)	20. (b)
21. (a)	22. (d)	23. (d)	24. (b)	25. (d)					

	HOTS			
1. (a)	2. (b)	3. (b)	4. (b)	5. (b)

4. CUBES AND CUBE ROOTS

Answer Key

1. (c)	2. (a)	3. (b)	4. (c)	5. (a)	6. (b)	7. (c)	8. (c)	9. (c)	10. (b)
11. (a)	12. (b)	13. (a)	14. (c)	15. (d)	16. (b)	17. (c)	18. (c)	19. (a)	20. (c)
21. (d)	22. (b)	23. (d)	24. (c)	25. (b)	26. (a)	27. (c)	28. (c)	29. (b)	30. (b)

	HOTS			
1. (b)	2. (a)	3. (a)	4. (a)	5. (d)

5. EXPONENTS AND POWERS

Answer Key

1. (c)	2. (d)	3. (c)	4. (b)	5. (b)	6. (b)	7. (c)	8. (b)	9. (c)	10. (b)
11. (d)	12. (d)	13. (d)	14. (a)	15. (a)	16. (c)	17. (b)	18. (c)	19. (a)	20. (d)
21. (b)	22. (c)	23. (d)	24. (c)	25. (b)	26. (c)	27. (a)	28. (c)	29. (d)	30. (d)

	HOTS			
1. (a)	2. (a)	3. (c)	4. (a)	5. (a)

6. PROFIT AND LOSS

Answer Key

1. (a)	2. (b)	3. (a)	4. (b)	5. (b)	6. (a)	7. (a)	8. (b)	9. (a)	10. (a)
11. (b)	12. (c)	13. (b)	14. (a)	15. (b)	16. (a)	17. (a)	18. (d)	19. (b)	20. (b)
21. (b)	22. (b)	23. (c)	24. (c)	25. (d)	26. (a)	27. (b)	28. (c)	29. (a)	30. (a)

	HOTS			
1. (c)	2. (a)	3. (b)	4. (c)	5. (d)

Answer Keys

7. ALGEBRAIC EXPRESSIONS AND THEIR IDENTITIES

Answer Key

1. (a)	2. (b)	3. (b)	4. (b)	5. (c)	6. (a)	7. (b)	8. (c)	9. (b)	10. (a)
11. (a)	12. (a)	13. (b)	14. (a)	15. (b)	16. (b)	17. (c)	18. (b)	19. (b)	20. (b)
21. (d)	22. (a)	23. (b)	24. (a)	25. (a)	26. (d)	27. (a)	28. (b)	29. (c)	30. (a)

HOTS

1. (d)	2. (a)	3. (a)	4. (a)	5. (c)

8. LINEAR EQUATIONS IN ONE VARIABLE

Answer Key

1. (a)	2. (b)	3. (a)	4. (b)	5. (c)	6. (c)	7. (a)	8. (a)	9. (a)	10. (d)
11. (b)	12. (a)	13. (a)	14. (d)	15. (c)	16. (c)	17. (a)	18. (a)	19. (a)	20. (d)

HOTS

1. (d)	2. (c)	3. (c)	4. (b)	5. (c)

9. QUADRILATERALS

Answer Key

1. (d)	2. (b)	3. (c)	4. (a)	5. (b)	6. (d)	7. (b)	8. (b)	9. (b)	10. (a)
11. (b)	12. (a)	13. (c)	14. (d)	15. (c)	16. (d)	17. (a)	18. (a)	19. (c)	20. (b)
21. (a)	22. (b)	23. (c)	24. (c)	25. (a)	26. (a)	27. (c)	28. (d)	29. (d)	30. (d)

HOTS

1. (c)	2. (b)	3. (b)	4. (a)	5. (c)

10. MENSURATION

Answer Key

1. (a)	2. (a)	3. (b)	4. (c)	5. (c)	6. (c)	7. (b)	8. (a)	9. (c)	10. (a)
11. (c)	12. (d)	13. (a)	14. (b)	15. (a)	16. (b)	17. (b)	18. (b)	19. (c)	20. (b)
21. (c)	22. (c)	23. (a)	24. (b)	25. (a)	26. (b)	27. (a)	28. (a)	29. (b)	30. (c)

HOTS

| 1. (a) | 2. (d) | 3. (a) | 4. (a) | 5. (d) |

11. VISUALISING SOLID SHAPES

Answer Key

1. (a)	2. (b)	3. (a)	4. (d)	5. (d)	6. (c)	7. (a)	8. (b)	9. (b)	10. (b)
11. (c)	12. (a)	13. (b)	14. (d)	15. (c)	16. (b)	17. (d)	18. (a)	19. (b)	20. (d)
21. (b)	22. (a)	23. (b)	24. (c)	25. (c)	26. (b)	27. (b)	28. (d)	29. (b)	30. (c)

HOTS

| 1. (b) | 2. (d) | 3. (a) | 4. (d) | 5. (a) |

12. DATA HANDLING

Answer Key

| 1. (c) | 2. (a) | 3. (b) | 4. (d) | 5. (c) | 6. (b) | 7. (b) | 8. (a) | 9. (c) | 10. (c) |
| 11. (d) | 12. (a) | 13. (d) | 14. (b) | 15. (c) | 16. (b) | 17. (b) | 18. (a) | 19. (a) | 20. (b) |

HOTS

| 1. (b) | 2. (d) | 3. (c) | 4. (d) | 5. (c) |

13. DIRECT AND INVERSE VARIATIONS

Answer Key

1. (a)	2. (b)	3. (b)	4. (c)	5. (a)	6. (d)	7. (c)	8. (c)	9. (c)	10. (b)
11. (c)	12. (d)	13. (d)	14. (a)	15. (c)	16. (c)	17. (b)	18. (b)	19. (d)	20. (c)
21. (b)	22. (c)	23. (b)	24. (d)	25. (c)					

HOTS

| 1. (a) | 2. (c) | 3. (b) | 4. (d) | 5. (b) |

14. FACTORISATION

Answer Key

| 1. (b) | 2. (a) | 3. (d) | 4. (b) | 5. (a) | 6. (b) | 7. (c) | 8. (d) | 9. (a) | 10. (b) |
| 11. (b) | 12. (d) | 13. (a) | 14. (d) | 15. (a) | 16. (a) | 17. (c) | 18. (b) | 19. (d) | 20. (d) |

Answer Keys

		HOTS		
1. (c)	2. (d)	3. (a)	4. (c)	5. (b)

15. INTRODUCTION TO GRAPHS

				Answer Key					
1. (c)	2. (d)	3. (a)	4. (c)	5. (b)	6. (a)	7. (d)	8. (b)	9. (a)	10. (c)
11. (d)	12. (c)	13. (c)	14. (b)	15. (a)	16. (b)	17. (a)	18. (d)	19. (a)	20. (c)

		HOTS		
1. (c)	2. (b)	3. (b)	4. (a)	5. (b)

SECTION 2: LOGICAL REASONING

1. ALPHABET TEST

				Answer Key					
1. (c)	2. (d)	3. (c)	4. (b)	5. (a)	6. (a)	7. (b)	8. (a)	9. (a)	10. (c)
11. (c)	12. (a)	13. (a)	14. (a)	15. (a)	16. (d)	17. (a)	18. (d)	19. (c)	20. (c)
21. (b)	22. (d)	23. (c)	24. (b)	25. (c)	26. (b)	27. (b)	28. (c)	29. (b)	30. (b)

2. ODD ONE OUT

				Answer Key					
1. (a)	2. (d)	3. (b)	4. (a)	5. (b)	6. (a)	7. (c)	8. (d)	9. (b)	10. (a)
11. (b)	12. (b)	13. (b)	14. (d)	15. (c)	16. (b)	17. (c)	18. (d)	19. (c)	20. (c)
21. (d)	22. (d)	23. (c)	24. (d)	25. (c)	26. (b)	27. (a)	28. (c)	29. (c)	30. (b)

3. CODING DECODING

				Answer Key					
1. (a)	2. (b)	3. (b)	4. (b)	5. (a)	6. (b)	7. (c)	8. (a)	9. (a)	10. (a)
11. (a)	12. (a)	13. (b)	14. (c)	15. (a)	16. (a)	17. (b)	18. (b)	19. (a)	20. (c)
21. (b)	22. (b)	23. (a)	24. (c)	25. (b)	26. (a)	27. (b)	28. (a)	29. (a)	30. (b)

4. DIRECTION SENSE TEST

Answer Key

1. (b)	2. (c)	3. (a)	4. (b)	5. (a)	6. (d)	7. (b)	8. (b)	9. (c)	10. (c)
11. (c)	12. (d)	13. (d)	14. (b)	15. (b)	16. (d)	17. (b)	18. (b)	19. (c)	20. (a)
21. (a)	22. (d)	23. (a)	24. (a)	25. (b)					

5. SERIES COMPLETION

Answer Key

1. (a)	2. (c)	3. (b)	4. (c)	5. (b)	6. (b)	7. (d)	8. (a)	9. (a)	10. (d)
11. (c)	12. (a)	13. (c)	14. (c)	15. (c)	16. (a)	17. (c)	18. (d)	19. (d)	20. (c)
21. (c)	22. (a)	23. (c)	24. (c)	25. (a)					

6. PATTERN

Answer Key

1. (c)	2. (a)	3. (b)	4. (b)	5. (b)	6. (c)	7. (c)	8. (b)	9. (b)	10. (a)
11. (d)	12. (c)	13. (c)	14. (b)	15. (c)	16. (a)	17. (b)	18. (c)	19. (b)	20. (a)
21. (d)	22. (a)	23. (b)	24. (c)	25. (a)	26. (b)	27. (b)	28. (b)	29. (c)	30. (b)

7. NUMBER RANKING

Answer Key

1. (c)	2. (a)	3. (a)	4. (b)	5. (b)	6. (d)	7. (d)	8. (c)	9. (b)	10. (d)
11. (c)	12. (d)	13. (d)	14. (a)	15. (d)	16. (c)	17. (c)	18. (c)	19. (d)	20. (d)
21. (a)	22. (c)	23. (c)	24. (c)	25. (a)	26. (c)	27. (b)	28. (d)	29. (b)	30. (a)

8. ANALYTICAL REASONING

Answer Key

1. (c)	2. (d)	3. (b)	4. (c)	5. (a)	6. (b)	7. (b)	8. (b)	9. (c)	10. (a)
11. (d)	12. (a)	13. (b)	14. (c)	15. (c)	16. (a)	17. (c)	18. (a)	19. (c)	20. (c)
21. (b)	22. (a)	23. (c)	24. (a)	25. (d)	26. (a)	27. (b)	28. (c)	29. (b)	30. (a)

9. VENN DIAGRAM

Answer Key

1. (a)	2. (c)	3. (d)	4. (c)	5. (d)	6. (a)	7. (d)	8. (c)	9. (a)	10. (a)
11. (a)	12. (b)	13. (b)	14. (b)	15. (c)	16. (a)	17. (a)	18. (a)	19. (d)	20. (d)
21. (a)	22. (b)	23. (b)	24. (d)	25. (c)	26. (a)	27. (d)	28. (a)	29. (c)	30. (a)

10. EMBEDDED FIGURE

Answer Key

1. (c)	2. (a)	3. (d)	4. (a)	5. (c)	6. (d)	7. (c)	8. (c)	9. (d)	10. (a)
11. (c)	12. (d)	13. (a)	14. (d)	15. (d)	16. (d)	17. (c)	18. (b)	19. (d)	20. (d)
21. (d)	22. (d)	23. (d)	24. (d)	25. (c)	26. (c)	27. (d)	28. (b)	29. (d)	30. (b)

11. COMPLETION OF INCOMPLETE PATTERN

Answer Key

1. (d)	2. (a)	3. (a)	4. (b)	5. (a)	6. (d)	7. (b)	8. (a)	9. (b)	10. (d)
11. (d)	12. (b)	13. (b)	14. (b)	15. (d)	16. (c)	17. (c)	18. (c)	19. (b)	20. (d)
21. (a)	22. (c)	23. (a)	24. (a)	25. (a)	26. (d)	27. (c)	28. (d)	29. (a)	30. (d)

12. WATER IMAGES

Answer Key

1. (c)	2. (a)	3. (b)	4. (b)	5. (b)	6. (d)	7. (a)	8. (c)	9. (d)	10. (c)
11. (b)	12. (b)	13. (c)	14. (a)	15. (c)	16. (b)	17. (d)	18. (b)	19. (b)	20. (a)
21. (d)	22. (c)	23. (a)	24. (c)	25. (d)	26. (b)	27. (c)	28. (b)	29. (c)	30. (d)

13. FIGURE MATRIX

Answer Key

1. (d)	2. (a)	3. (d)	4. (a)	5. (d)	6. (d)	7. (b)	8. (b)	9. (b)	10. (c)
11. (b)	12. (c)	13. (b)	14. (d)	15. (b)	16. (b)	17. (d)	18. (c)	19. (d)	20. (b)
21. (a)	22. (c)	23. (b)	24. (b)	25. (a)	26. (b)	27. (c)	28. (c)	29. (b)	30. (c)

MODEL PAPER – 1

Answer Key

1. (d)	2. (c)	3. (a)	4. (a)	5. (c)	6. (b)	7. (a)	8. (d)	9. (c)	10. (b)
11. (d)	12. (b)	13. (d)	14. (a)	15. (b)	16. (c)	17. (d)	18. (a)	19. (b)	20. (a)
21. (d)	22. (b)	23. (c)	24. (b)	25. (d)	26. (a)	27. (c)	28. (c)	29. (b)	30. (d)
31. (d)	32. (c)	33. (d)	34 (a)	35. (d)	36. (b)	37. (c)	38. (c)	39. (b)	40. (c)
41. (b)	42. (a)	43. (d)	44. (d)	45. (c)	46. (d)	47. (d)	48. (a)	49. (d)	50. (c)

MODEL PAPER – 2

Answer Key

1. (b)	2. (b)	3. (a)	4. (d)	5. (d)	6. (c)	7. (c)	8. (b)	9. (a)	10. (b)
11. (d)	12. (a)	13. (a)	14. (d)	15. (b)	16. (b)	17. (c)	18. (b)	19. (d)	20. (c)
21. (a)	22. (c)	23. (b)	24. (d)	25. (d)	26. (b)	27. (a)	28. (c)	29. (d)	30. (c)
31. (a)	32. (c)	33. (c)	34 (c)	35. (c)	36. (b)	37. (d)	38. (c)	39. (c)	40. (c)
41. (d)	42. (c)	43. (a)	44. (d)	45. (a)	46. (c)	47. (a)	48. (c)	49. (a)	50. (d)

Appendix

There are different organizations that conduct these examinations and covering all of them is not needed as the focus should be to understand the main type of exams conducted. They are similar for these organizations with the difference being the change in name of the exam.

SCIENCE OLYMPIAD FOUNDATION (SOF)		
S. No.	Name of Exam	Grade
1.	National Science Olympiad (NSO)	Class 1-10
2.	National Cyber Olympiad (NCO)	Class 1-10
3.	International Mathematics Olympiad (IMO)	Class 1-10
4.	International English Olympiad (IEO)	Class 1-10
5.	International Commerce Olympiad (ICO)	Class 1-10
6.	International General Knowledge Olympiad (IGKO)	Class 1-10
7.	International Social Studies Olympiad (ISSO)	Class 1-10
INDIAN TALENT OLYMPIAD (ITO)		
S. No.	Name of Exam	Grade
1.	International Science Olympiad (ISO)	Class 1-12
2.	International Math Olympiad (IMO)	Class 1-12
3.	English International Olympiad (EIO)	Class 1-12
4.	General Knowledge International Olympiad (GKIO)	Class 1-12
5.	International Computer Olympiad (ICO)	Class 1-12
6.	International Drawing Olympiad (IDO)	Class 1-12
7.	National Essay Olympiad (NESO)	Class 1-12
8.	National Social Studies Olympiad (NSSO)	Class 1-12
EDUHEAL FOUNDATION		
S. No.	Name of Exam	Grade
1.	Eduheal International Cyber Olympiad (ICO)	Class 1-12
2.	Eduheal International English Olympiad (IEO)	Class 1-12
3.	National Interactive Math Olympiad (NIMO)	Class 1-12
4.	National Interactive Science Olympiad (NISO)	Class 1-12
5.	International General Knowledge Olympiad (IGO)	Class 1-12
6.	National Space Science Olympiad (NSSO)	Class 1-12

HUMMING BIRD EDUCATION

S. No.	Name of Exam	Grade
1.	Humming Bird Commerce Competency Olympiad (HCC)	Class 1-12
2.	Humming Bird Cyber Olympiad (HCO)	Class 1-12
3.	Humming Bird English Olympiad (HEO)	Class 1-12
4.	Humming Bird General Knowledge Olympiad (HGO)	Class 1-12
5.	Humming Bird Hindi Olympiad (HHO)	Class 1-12
6.	Humming Bird Mathematics Olympiad (HMO)	Class 1-12
7.	Humming Bird Science Olympiad (HSO)	Class 1-12
8.	Humming Bird Aptitude and Reasoning Olympiad (ARO)	Class 1-12
9.	Humming Bird Spelling Competition (Spell BEE)	Class 1-12
10.	Humming Bird Language Olympiad	Class 1-12

INTERNATIONAL ASSESSMENTS FOR INDIAN SCHOOLS (IAIS) (MACMILLAN AND EEA COLLABORATION)

S. No.	Name of Exam	Grade
1.	IAIS Maths Olympiad	Class 3-12
2.	IAIS ScienceOlympiad	Class 3-12
3.	IAIS English Olympiad	Class 3-12
4.	IAIS Digital Technologies Olympiad	Class 3-12

SILVERZONE FOUNDATION

S. No.	Name of Exam	Grade
1.	International Informatics Olympiad	Class 1-12
2.	International Olympiad of Mathematics	Class 1-12
3.	International Olympiad of Science	Class 1-12

UNIFIED COUNCIL

S. No.	Name of Exam	Grade
1.	Unified Council Cyber Exam	Class 1-12
2.	Unified International English Olympiad.	Class 1-12
3.	Unified International Mathematics Olympiad (UIMO)	Class 1-12

UNICUS

S. No.	Name of Exam	Grade
1.	Unicus Non-Routine Mathematics Olympiad (UNRMO)	Class 1-11
2.	Unicus Mathematics Olympiad (UMO)	Class 1-11

S. No.	Name of Exam	Grade
3.	Unicus Science Olympiad (USO)	Class 1-11
4.	Unicus English Olympiad (UEO)	Class 1-11
5.	Unicus Cyber Olympiad (UCO)	Class 1-11
6.	Unicus General knowledge Olympiad (UGKO)	Class 1-11
7.	Unicus Critical Thinking Olympiad (UCTO)	Class 1-11

CREST (ONLINE MODE)

S. No.	Name of Exam	Grade
1.	Mathematics (CMO)	Classes KG-10
2.	Science (CSO)	Classes KG-10
3.	English (CEO)	Classes KG-10
4.	Computer (CCO)	Classes 1-10
5.	Reasoning (CRO)	Classes 1-10
6.	Spell Bee Summer (CSB)	Classes 1-8
7.	Spell Bee Winter (CSBW)	Classes 1-8
8.	Mental Maths (MMO)	Classes 1-12
9.	Green Warrior Olympiad (GWO)	Classes 1-12

HOW TO APPLY?

Anyone willing to participate in the Olympiad exam can follow these steps to apply for the exam:

- Log in to the official website of the conducting organization.
- Find the Registration Option to register
- Fill up the details such as Student Name, Parent Name, School Name, Class, Postal Address, E-mail Address, Password, etc.
- Select the subjects you want to apply for. Pay the necessary registration fees and you are done.
- You will receive necessary details on your email id.

There are no minimum marks required by the Olympiad conducting organizations to apply for the exam.

AWARDS

Based on the organization rules, students as well as schools participating in these exams are awarded with several recognitions based on the marks they score.

www.ingramcontent.com/pod-product-compliance
Lightning Source LLC
Chambersburg PA
CBHW062129160426
43191CB00013B/2244